THE PIG WAR

THE PIG WAR

Standoff at Griffin Bay

Mike Vouri

Basalt Books
PO Box 645910
Pullman, Washington 99164-5910
Phone: 800-354-7360
Email: basalt.books@wsu.edu
Website: basaltbooks.wsu.edu

Previous editions of this title were published by Griffin Bay Bookstore in 1999 and 2006 and by Discover Your Northwest in 2013 and 2016.

First Basalt Books printing 2022

Library of Congress Cataloging-in-Publication Data

Names: Vouri, Mike, 1947- author.
Title: The Pig War : standoff at Griffin Bay / Mike Vouri.
Description: [Third edition] | Pullman, Washington : Basalt Books, [2022] |
    "Previous editions of this title were published by Griffin Bay
    Bookstore in 1999 and 2006 and by Discover Your Northwest in 2013 and
    2016." | Includes bibliographical references and index.
Identifiers: LCCN 2022007579 | ISBN 9781638640028 (paperback)
Subjects: LCSH: Pig War, Wash., 1859. | San Juan Islands
    (Wash.)--History--19th century. | Northwest boundary of the United
    States.
Classification: LCC F897.S2 V68 2022 | DDC 979.7/74--dc23/eng/20220216
LC record available at https://lccn.loc.gov/2022007579

Basalt Books is an imprint of Washington State University Press.

Cover and interior design by Ben Nechanicky
Cover photo: Soldiers of the 3rd Artillery pose with a Napoleon gun.
Back cover photo: Looking forward, toward the bow of HMS *Satellite*.

The Washington State University Pullman campus is located on the homelands of the Niimíipuu (Nez Perce) Tribe and the Palus people. We acknowledge their presence here since time immemorial and recognize their continuing connection to the land, to the water, and to their ancestors. WSU Press is committed to publishing works that foster a deeper understanding of the Pacific Northwest and the contributions of its Native peoples.

For Julia

CONTENTS

PREFACE

On Jan. 11, 1969 my pilot, Capt. Frank Birchak, was killed when the O-1 Bird Dog he was flying was shot down over the Mekong Delta in the old Republic of Vietnam. As his crew chief, I had launched him early that morning. Hardly a day goes by that I don't think of him in some way, most especially how he was taken from his wife and family in the prime of life.

Wars have indelible effects on those who must fight in them, which underscores why what happened on San Juan Island in 1859 was so exceptional: peace was chosen over war. I believe in this story. I believe that individuals and nations *can* sometimes resolve their differences peacefully without resorting to violence. I have to.

Since the first edition of this book was published in 1999, the United States has been involved in seemingly endless wars far from our shores. The reasons for these conflicts are complex, and often far beyond the comprehension of the participants. So it was with the San Juan Boundary Dispute. Yet, despite the fact that the San Juan Island group was separated by a six-week journey from the closest seat of government in Washington, DC, the military and naval officers of both sides, as well as the diplomats in the respective capitals, resisted the usual popular enthusiasm for war.

To be fair, there were compelling reasons for Great Britain and the United States not to fight, including the mutually beneficial trade legislation passed by the respective governments in 1846 and enormous British capital investment in the growing U.S. industrial infrastructure. But as has been proven countless times in history—most tragically in 1914 involving one of these same nations—prosperous economic relationships do not make war obsolete. That is what makes this story so special.

As park historian and chief of interpretation at San Juan Island National Historical Park, I am continually refreshing the park's archives. I have had occasion to continue researching the topic over the years in archives in Canada, the United States, and Great Britain. I also have had the good fortune to meet and develop strong working relationships with other scholars of the period. Some of the information and images from these sources are included in this second edition. While working in the various archives and private collections I was repeatedly struck by the tone of language in correspondence exchanged by both sides, particularly the euphemisms employed in allusion to fighting.

For example, after what he describes as "mature reflection," Gov. James Douglas of the crown colonies of Vancouver Island and British Columbia wrote Royal Navy Capt. Geoffrey Phipps Hornby: "I place the fullest reliance on your firmness of temper and discretion and I trust that Captain Pickett will be reasonable and mitigate as much as possible the *evils* that must necessarily arise out of conflicting jurisdiction of a joint occupation, I hope they will not seek to force a quarrel upon us..." Three more times in separate correspondences the same word *evil(s)* is used to describe the outbreak of war. Was this a mere Victorian convention? Or was war truly viewed as *evil* among these men?

I hope for the benefit of our children and our children's children, that war is someday universally recognized as such, and will go the way of chattel slavery.

— San Juan Island, January 2, 2013

ACKNOWLEDGMENTS

I wish to acknowledge and thank the following mentors, colleagues, friends, and family for their friendship, guidance and support leading to this project over the years: Robert E. Scott, Bill Gleason, Maureen Briggs, Dr. Julie K. Stein, Kelly Cahill, Ron Garner, Doug Halsey, David Kennedy, Jerry McElyea, Ken Arzarian, Darlene Wahl, Jerald Weaver, Sean O'Meara, Bud and Mary Dale, Jim Adams, Ben Nechanicky, Diane Ludeman, Gordon and Elly Smith, Jim Meredith, Diane Timm, Janet Oakley, Detlef and Kathy Wieck, Chris DeStaffany, Michael Cohen, Oren and Peggy Combs, Doreen Beard, Richard Selcer, Candace Wellman, Kevin Loftus, Michael and Susan Upton, Susan Eyerly, Frank and Erin Eyerly, Boyd and Lovel Pratt, Cal and Mary Karen Ryan, Martha Scott, Consuelo Larrabee, James Patterson, Laura Norris and Ken Crawbuck, George Thomas, John Olbrantz, Mark and Lynn Morrow, John Stark, Bruce Brown, Lane Morgan, Randy Fisher, Bill Distler, Thomas Burford, Keith Murray, Larry DeLorme, Carl Schuler, Dick and Joan Beardsley, Carolyn Dale, Dennis Lee Lackey, Bob Sims, Pete Steffens, Ann and Alan Grodin, Jeff Clausen, Judy Woods, Jerry Hedlund, Joe Baker, Marty and Kathy Mata, Pat Cimino, Lynn Hyde, Don and Ameta Macaluso, Everett C. Brown, Russ Greenberg, Gene Miller, Jerry Hare, Frank Birchak, Dave Potter, John Queen, Nolan Campbell, John Palmieri, Ron Olson, Marge Silva, Keith Weidkamp, Larry Christman, Ron and Joan Redding, Ron and Fran Toburen, Terry Hart, Tim and Denise Binderup, Francis and Rebecca Smith, Rick and Chris Homme, Joe Coffey, Janette Coffey, Bob Bentley, Dave Bentley, my sister Denise Vouri, my parents John and Norine Vouri, my wife Julia Coffey Vouri, and my son Alex Vouri.

INTRODUCTION

This book is about the San Juan Boundary Dispute, the political machinations that led to it, and the crisis that nearly plunged Great Britain and the United States into war. It is the best-known period in island history and the primary reason for the creation of San Juan Island National Historical Park. The park commemorates the peaceful resolution of the dispute, and it preserves and protects more than 2,000 acres of an increasingly fragile ecosystem.

The rich and diverse environment of the island cannot be separated from the thousands of years of human history that, over the long pull—and depending on your perspective—reduce the Pig War to a brief chapter. Well before English and American camps were established—and continuing to this day—the island has sheltered a medley of thriving cultures attracted by its temperate climate, rich soil, abundant timber, and marine resources.

Lying at the crossroads of three great waterways, San Juan Island has long been a magnet for human habitation. People have wanted to come here, whether to stake a life or find rest and relaxation amid an abundant food source.

Ancestors of today's Northern Straits Coast Salish people first began to appear in the wake of the receding continental ice sheet. Archaeological evidence suggests that this island supported hun-ting and gathering between 6,000 and 8,000 years ago. The rich marine culture encountered by the early European explorers developed about 2,500 years ago, and traces of its once thriving villages remain in shell middens found along shorelines throughout the San Juan Islands.

By early historic times, the indigenous people of the San Juan Islands and nearby mainland areas were primarily members of six tribes who spoke the Northern Straits and the closely related Klallum (Clallum) languages. In addition to sharing related languages, the tribes shared a culture and way of life through which they used a wide range of marine, riverine, and terrestrial resources. They followed patterns of seasonal movement between islands and the mainland, moving from large winter villages to smaller resource collection camps in the warmer seasons.

European diseases reduced the population to a scattering of villages long before 1791, when the *Isla y Archipelago de San Juan* was first named by Francisco Eliza, one of several explorers charged with retrenching the Spanish presence in the Pacific Northwest.

It was the quest for natural resources, in conjunction with the China trade, that lured Spain, Great Britain, and the United States to the region. Each explored, charted, and named the islands while staking overlapping claims to the Oregon Country—the states of Washington, Oregon, Idaho, portions of Wyoming and Montana, and the province of British Columbia.

Spain had abandoned its claims by the time an Anglo-American agreement in 1818 provided for joint occupation of the region. Although lucrative trade agreements and capital investments existed between the two nations, primarily on the Eastern seaboard, tensions mounted among those living in the Oregon Country. Americans considered the British presence an affront to their "manifest destiny." The British believed they had a legal right to lands guaranteed by earlier treaties, explorations and the commercial activities of the Hudson's Bay Company (HBC).

Nevertheless, in June 1846 the Treaty of Oregon was signed in London, setting the boundary on the 49th parallel, from the Rocky Mountains "to the middle of the channel which separates the continent from Vancouver's Island" then south through the channel to the Strait of Juan de Fuca and west to the Pacific Ocean.

Difficulty arose over language. The "channel" described in the treaty was actually two channels: Haro Strait, nearest Vancouver Island, and Rosario Strait, nearer the mainland. The San Juan Island group lay between, and both sides claimed them.

As early as 1845 the HBC, based at Fort Victoria, claimed San Juan Island, only seven miles across the Haro Strait. By 1851 the company established salmon-curing stations along the island's western shoreline, salting and barreling fish purchased from Indians who had fished the same grounds for more than 2,000 years. By 1853, the islands were claimed as U.S. possessions in the newly created Washington Territory. In response, the HBC in December 1853 established Belle Vue Sheep Farm on San Juan Island's southern shore. While this move was politically motivated, again, the island's natural attributes made the farm a lucrative concern. In a mere six years the flock expanded from 1,369 to more than 4,500 scattered in sheep stations throughout the island.

Reports of the island's good soil and bountiful resources by joint-Northwest Boundary Survey naturalists quickly circulated among American settlers on the mainland. By spring 1859, 18 Yankees had settled on claims staked on HBC prime sheep grazing lands. They expected the U.S. Government to recognize these as valid. The British considered the claims illegal and the claimants little more than "squatters" or trespassers. Incidents mounted and tempers grew shorter by the day.

The crisis came on June 15, 1859, when Lyman Cutlar, an American, shot and killed a company pig he'd caught rooting in his garden. The problem was he had chased the animal to the edge of the woods and committed the deed far from his cabin. When British authorities threatened to arrest Cutlar and evict all his countrymen from the island as trespassers—a clear violation of joint occupation agreement— a delegation of Amerians sought military protection from the commander of the Department of Oregon— U.S. Army Brig. Gen. William S. Harney, a confirmed Anglophobe.

Harney responded by ordering Company D, 9th U.S. Infantry under Capt. George E. Pickett (of later Civil War fame) to San Juan. Pickett's 64-man unit landed on July 27 and encamped near the HBC wharf on Griffin Bay, just north of Belle Vue Sheep Farm. When HBC chief factor and provincial governor James Douglas learned of the landing he immediately dispatched Royal Navy warships and the "difficulty" (as it was termed in the British press) was underway. It is this crisis and the joint occupation that followed that provides both the climax and anti-climax of this story. For in the end, no one died save the pig.

As I point out in *Outpost of Empire: The Royal Marines and the Joint Occupation of San Juan Island*, peace among the growing civil population from both nations was maintained because the commanders of both military camps strictly enforced it. Following the Pig War crisis, the last thing either nation wanted was another international dispute over an island 16½ miles long and six miles wide—especially while the United States was engaged in civil war and power politics continued to be played in Europe.

This peaceful climate also served to grow the community, which developed into a cooperative of British subjects, Native Hawaiians, U.S. citizens, and Indians. The latter continued to seasonally fish and farm in traditional ways, and in many cases, saw their daughters married to Euro-American and Hawaiian settlers. Many of the soldiers and marines, especially Americans, took their discharges on the island and staked claims once the boundary was resolved and the joint occupation concluded. It was not easy pioneering on a small island located far from the comforts of civilization, but it created a generous community spirit and a love of place that remains as vital today as it was in 1860s.

DRAMATIS PERSONAE

Capt. Alfred Pleasonton—Harney's acting adjutant

2nd Lt. Henry M. Robert—Corps of Engineers sapper team commander

Lt. Gen. Winfield Scott—U.S. Army commander

Isaac I. Stevens—Governor, Washington Territory (1854)

Henry Webber—Deputy Collector of Customs (1854)

The British

Rear Adm. R. Lambert Baynes—Pacific Station commander

Capt. George Bazalgette—English Camp commander (1860–1867)

Alexander Grant Dallas—Governor, Hudson's Bay Company (1859)

John de Courcy—British Civil Magistrate

Capt. Michael de Courcy—HMS *Pylades* commander, Acting Pacific Station commander (1859)

James Douglas—Governor, Crown Colonies of Vancouver Island and British Columbia

William A. Delacombe—English Camp commander (1867–1872)

Charles J. Griffin—Hudson's Bay Company agent at Belle Vue Sheep Farm

Capt. Geoffrey Phipps Hornby—HMS *Tribune* commander

Richard Bickerton Pemell Lyons—2nd Viscount (Lord) Lyons—British envoy in Washington City

Capt. James Prevost—HMS *Satellite* commander and British water boundary commissioner

Capt. George Richards—HMS *Plumper* commander

Lord John Russell—British Foreign Secretary

James Sangster—British customs inspector

George Simpson—Governor, Hudson's Bay Company

Chapter I

PICKETT HAS LANDED

Charles Griffin probably heard it long before he saw it. There was no mistaking that sound at mid-19th century. Steamers could be detected from miles away, the great cylinders panting over the flat, blue inland seas with the steady thump of bass drums. As he later noted in his journal it was between 8 and 9 p.m., Tuesday, July 26, 1859. It had been a beautiful evening, typical of San Juan Island in midsummer. A southwest breeze made the prairie grasses shimmer above the silver waters of the Strait of Juan de Fuca below the headlands a quarter mile from his cabin porch. Looking south across the strait, the snow-capped Olympic mountains rose from a bank of clouds, effacing a sky turning pink. Directly west, Victoria was locked in a haze of wood smoke from slash being burned to make room for the rapidly growing British colony.

It had been nearly six years since Vancouver Island Gov. James Douglas had dispatched Griffin to San Juan Island to establish a sheep farm and agricultural station. The governor, also chief factor of the Hudson's Bay post at Victoria, hoped the farm would entrench Great Britain's claim to the island. An ambiguity in the language of the Oregon Treaty of 1846, which set the international boundary between the United States and Great Britain at the 49th Parallel, had placed the San Juan Islands in limbo. Both nations claimed them and 13 years later the dispute remained unresolved.

In this, his first management opportunity with the Company, Griffin had done well by any standard. His flocks had grown from 1,369 to nearly 4,500 sheep, and he could take satisfaction in the 80 acres of fenced truck gardens, cleared roads, and the eight tidy cabins that composed the farm establishment on the home prairie. It had not always been easy. He'd had to be vigilant about rapidly changing weather, marauding Indians, and most especially, rapacious Yankees from the mainland. In their haste to solidify claim to the islands, the Americans threatened his business. First it had been customs collectors from Port Townsend, then tax collectors from Whatcom County, and now his prairies were being overrun by squatters, one of whom the month before had shot one of his prize boars and threatened to shoot Griffin himself if he again "trespassed" on the American's "property." Griffin expected a magistrate to arrive soon from Victoria aboard HMS *Satellite*, a 21-gun steam corvette, to deal with that fellow and the other squatters who had grown increasingly belligerent. That was probably the steamer he heard. It would be long dark before it docked, so he went to bed.

The next morning Griffin awoke to thunder and lightning and the news—probably from one of his herdsmen—that the ship was not *Satellite*. It was an American warship—the U.S. Propeller *Massachusetts*. Griffin left his cabin and rode his horse up the rough track over the ridge and down to the bay named for him by British boundary survey officers. He took care to steer clear of several other American squatter cabins. From the crest of the ridge the bay formed a broad crescent, defining the southern end of the island from Cattle Point to Bald Mountain, giving on to Lopez Island to the east across San Juan Channel. To the north were the rugged fingers of Orcas Island. Rain squalls hid the white cone of Mount Baker rising from the North Cascades, 50 miles distant on the mainland. The *Massachusetts* was anchored a few hundred yards off his dock. The black-hulled auxiliary steamer was used by the U.S. Army to ferry troops and provisions about Puget Sound and the northern straits region. Anchored a few hundred yards away from her was the *Shubrick*, a U.S.

lighthouse tender that also had arrived the day before, presumably seeking anchorage for the evening.

Griffin had been seeing U.S. government vessels with increasing regularity, but they usually were smaller wind-powered revenue cutters bearing customs agents or, on two occasions, small detachments of soldiers in pursuit of Indian raiders. Clunker though she was—she could only make three knots wide open and was in constant need of repair—the *Massachusetts* still mounted eight 32-pound naval guns on her decks and could carry a company or more of soldiers. Griffin had not been aware of any recent raids, either by local Indians or the bands generally labeled as "Northerners" from Queen Charlotte Islands or Russian America. What he did know was that on the American Independence Day three weeks before the Yankee squatters had erected a flagpole in the yard of the so-called U.S. customs house and run up the stars and stripes. Griffin, in turn, raised the Union flag from the Company pole. He hadn't worried then. Patriotic posturing was usually harmless. But the American flag was still flying five days later, attracting the attention of Brig. Gen. William Selby Harney, commander of the U.S. Army's Department of Oregon, headquartered at Vancouver Barracks. The general had been aboard this same *Massachusetts* earlier that month on his return from a visit with Governor Douglas in Victoria. His curiosity piqued (the governor hadn't breathed a word of the pig incident), Harney had stepped ashore, huddled with the American deputy customs collector, Paul K. Hubbs, Jr., and several others, and then walked to the very ridge where Griffin now stood and observed the HBC farm. But that had apparently been the end of it. After a stay of barely 20 minutes, Harney left for Fort Steilacoom.

Now here was the *Massachusetts* again, and Griffin could see long boats from both vessels approaching the shore bearing men in blue, lumber, tents, and what appeared to be field guns. Cannon! Griffin cautiously made his way down the hill and watched from his wharf as the soldiers spilled out of the boats and began stacking their cargo on the beach. Choosing not to make contact until he had more information, he turned for home.

Unbeknownst to Griffin, Hubbs had been roused the night before by a sharp rap on his cabin door. He opened it to find a U.S. Army sergeant in full regalia: blue frock coat with dazzling brass buttons and shoulder scales, dark-blue trousers with a sky-blue stripe running down each leg, a sword slung from a shoulder strap and a black slouch hat with the brim turned up on one side, garnished by a black ostrich plume. This was 1ˢᵗ. Sgt. William Smith of Company D, Ninth Infantry, late of Fort Bellingham, the unit commanded by Hubbs's Indian war comrade, Capt. George E. Pickett.

Smith told Hubbs that the company was scheduled to land the next morning to establish a camp for the purpose of protecting American settlers from the British. The captain was already ashore. Would Hubbs come along and help them locate a camp site? Hubbs hurriedly dressed and followed the sergeant along the gravel beach. The black silhouette of the *Massachusetts* rose from the bay, while ahead in the twilight Hubbs saw a clutch of men near a long boat. One of them left the group and approached. It was 1ˢᵗ Lt. John Howard, "a fiery Southerner," who immediately offered a flask of brandy and escorted Hubbs to his commanding officer.

Thirty-four years-old, slight of build with curly brown hair that extended to his shoulders beneath his regulation kepi, Pickett was well-known as a Mexican War hero and raconteur among the officer caste. Enlisted men were not so enchanted. But Hubbs, a civilian and son of a prominent Tennessee attorney and diplomat, had shared campfires with the Virginian in 1856 during the Indian campaigns along the White River. Only weeks before, Hubbs had rowed to Fort Bellingham to complain to his old friend about the treatment American settlers on San Juan were receiving at the hands of the Hudson's Bay Company. Presumably, Pickett had told

General Harney and now here was the result. The men smoked and drank while the Virginian laid out his plans for Hubbs. At last, justice would come to San Juan Island.

One man in the area who was not surprised by the *Massachusetts'* arrival was U.S. Boundary Commissioner Archibald Campbell aboard *Shubrick*. He had received a dispatch a few days earlier from Harney's acting adjutant, Capt. Alfred Pleasonton, advising him that Pickett was coming to San Juan to head off Indian attacks. Campbell had been given no hint (he later claimed) that the soldiers' stay was to be permanent. Having spent more than a year arguing with his British counterpart, Capt. James Prevost, over the ownership of the islands, Campbell had come to San Juan to see for himself why the British were so insistent on keeping them. He had spent a pleasant Tuesday afternoon hiking along the bay and taking shots at the small black-tailed deer that emerged from the woods in surprising numbers to nibble the prairie grasses. He thought nothing of the *Massachusetts'* arrival, even after visiting Pickett aboard the ship that evening, until he saw the mounds of stores being shuttled to the beach the following morning. Had the dispute been settled without his knowledge? And if so, how had he been left out of the loop? Worse, if the dispute had not been settled, he could well imagine the British reaction to what could only be construed as a provocative act.

There would be hell to pay, and it had been a long time coming.

Chapter 2

THE QUEST FOR WEALTH: SOURCES OF TROUBLE

For more than 50 years, the United States and Great Britain contended over the international boundary in the Oregon Country, a more than half million square-mile area comprising the present states of Washington, Oregon and Idaho, portions of Montana and Wyoming and the province of British Columbia.

Complicating matters were the tremendous distances between West Coast outposts and the home governments in Washington City, and London, which resulted in serious breakdowns in communications. Local officials groped through murky foreign policy, interpreting and enforcing treaties and attendant provisos according to instructions that changed with each new government. With the transcontinental telegraph still several years away, steamships often crossed paths bearing dispatches containing conflicting information. Policies enforced had to be undone. Confrontations escalated—or vice versa—before reports reached their readers.

Through it all, the governments of Great Britain and the United States never stopped talking. The "disastrous difficulty" that Royal Navy Capt. Geoffrey Phipps Hornby portended on San Juan in 1859 never came about. Perhaps it was due to a spirit of Christian brotherhood and a sincere desire to avoid bloodshed. Perhaps it was because the two nations, more than 75 years removed from the Revolutionary War, remained closely tied through language and institutions. No doubt, the hard reality of economic interest, despite a lot of pontificating over questions of "honor," was probably the greatest motivator. Great Britain, in the first half of the 19th century, was more concerned with the free flow of commerce than she was in paying the high price of empire.

The competition between Great Britain and the United States over the Oregon Country—"that pine swamp," as the British Lord Aberdeen termed it—began with the race to the West Coast in the wake of the Alexander MacKenzie and Lewis and Clark expeditions. But the contest was Pan-European 300 years before the American merchant captain Robert Gray established the first serious American claim to the region in 1792.

Then as in Gray's time the end game was the China trade, a prize that spurred Spanish and Portuguese voyages seeking a direct ocean route to the Indies. Not two years after Columbus's first voyage in 1492, the Spanish and Portuguese, with help from a Spanish pope, divided the New World into spheres of influence with the Spanish laying claim to all newly discovered lands 370 leagues west of the Cape Verde Islands or approximately 46° 37 longitude. Vasco Nunez Balboa's 1513 discovery of the Pacific—which he named the *Mar del Sur* (South Sea)—added further weight to the Spanish claim, which was solidified when in 1529 the two nations agreed to a pole-to-pole demarcation that gave Spain everything east of the Moluccas in the Pacific basin.[1]

But the Spanish had little to do with the northern Pacific beyond Cabrillo's coastal expeditions (1542-43) that may have reached southern Oregon, and, after 1565, the regular transit of the Manila galleons. Each July a *Nao de la China* (Ship of China), laden with silks, spices, porcelains and other high-demand items, would leave the Philippines and sail north to Japan, where it picked up winds and currents that would in four months bring the vessel to Cape Mendocino in northern California. Barring shipwreck or scurvy, the ship pushed south to Acapulco, where these treasures were added to gold and silver from South America and portaged across Mexico to Vera Cruz. The cargos were then shipped to Cuba to become part of the annual treasure convoy from Spain.

The prospect of treasure ships approaching the lightly defended shores of New Spain—as opposed to risking Spanish warships in the Caribbean—attracted English privateer Francis Drake whose nation did not recognize the exclusivity of Spain in the Western Hemisphere. Drake, by March 1579, rounded Cape Horn and captured the gold ship *Cacafuego*, outbound from Peru with 1,700 tons of gold and silver off the coast of New Spain. What he did next had a direct bearing on boundary disputes between Britain and Spain, and then Britain and the United States into the late 19th century. Moreover it still generates controversy among scholars and Drake buffs from British Columbia to southern California.

The question: How far north did the *Pelican (ne Golden Hind)* sail and where was it beached to tighten its seams for the return voyage to England? British diplomats asserted that Drake sailed as far as 38 degrees latitude while searching for the Northwest Passage. During this northern voyage Drake allegedly made landfall, claimed what he saw for England, repaired his ship and set sail across the Pacific, circumnavigating the world. Over the centuries, claims have been made for Drake's Bay, just north of San Francisco Bay, Whale Cove along the Oregon Coast, and most recently Vancouver Island.

More than 150 years would pass before Europeans again probed the waters of the Pacific Northwest. While the Spanish remained heavily involved in extracting gold and silver from New Spain, they still considered the Pacific Ocean a Spanish lake. But as with England, Russia, another European (and Asian) nation, did not recognize Spanish hegemony.

The Russians had by 1741 probed as far south as today's Kayak Island in Southeast Alaska launching fur trading activity in North

America that would not flag until 1867, when Russian-America was sold to the United States.

More than 30 years passed before the Spanish responded to the Russians. In 1774, the viceroy of New Spain dispatched *Santiago*, with pilot Juan Perez in command, north to divine how far south the Russians had probed. The vessel also was to seek sites for possible Spanish colonies. Perez sailed into Russian waters, doubled back and in the process made contact with the Haida people just north of Haida Gwaii (formerly the Queen Charlotte Islands). He also anchored in Nootka Sound, where he traded with the Nootkas, but did not go ashore. This so displeased the viceroy that he commissioned Capt. Bruno Heceta the following year to do what Perez could not – plant the Spanish flag. During this voyage, Heceta anchored in a bay full of vegetable matter and logs and deduced that it might be a river mouth. He named it *Bahia de Asuncion* and went on his way.

Three years later, the renowned British explorer, Capt. James Cook, called at Nootka Sound during his third epic voyage to explore and chart the Pacific Basin. This northern portion of the voyage was to determine, finally, if a Northwest Passage existed, either by river or saltwater channel. Cook noted then that the Indians were in possession of silver spoons of Spanish origin, but of even greater import, that the Nootkas were offering, in return for metal, otter pelts, which were far superior in quality to beaver pelts. The pelts commanded high prices in China, which ignited the maritime fur trade in the Pacific and underscored the second major British claim to the region.

The prospect of riches of the China trade enticed officers such as Lt. John Meares to leave the Royal Navy in pursuit of furs to trade with China. A blueprint had developed for merchant traders on the North Pacific coast whereby trading vessels would depart China in April heading north to the Sakhalin and Kurile islands, where food and water would be replenished. The ships then crossed the North Pacific. Initially the traders would end the season in October and head south to catch the southern trade winds back to China. This was a labor-intensive and risky pattern that saw crews spending the bulk of their time at sea rather than at trade. Eventually, captains followed the lead of Cook and took to wintering in the Hawaiian Islands before returning to the Pacific Northwest for another season. Not only did this Pacific "homeport" offer abundant food and water, in addition to a salubrious climate, but Hawaiians eager to earn money and move up the social ladder provided a labor pool that would be drawn upon by traders—including, by 1853, the Hudson's Bay Company farm on San Juan Island.

However, Meares went one better over his fellow traders by establishing a fortified factory ashore on Nootka Sound under the aegis of his Macao-based company—including a ship building and repair facility that produced the first European ship constructed on the Northwest Coast. Other British traders, hoping to sidestep British charter corporations such as the East India Company and the South Sea Company, later began shipping their cargoes of furs in ships flying the flag of the newly independent United States of America. But the first Yankee traders on the Northwest Coast were more interested in accumulating their own pelts directly from the Nootka and other groups along Vancouver Island's outer coast. These were Capts. Robert Gray and John Kendrick, of the *Lady Washington* and *Columbia Rediviva* respectively, who first sailed to the North Pacific in 1787 from Boston with Kendrick in overall command. Meares himself greeted Gray when the *Washington* arrived off Nootka Sound in September 1788 and found a thriving trade colony with Chinese shipwrights at work and a fortress under construction ashore. Gray told Meares that his vessel and the *Columbia* soon to follow had been dispatched...

> "under the patronage of Congress to examine the Coast of America and open a fur trade between New England and this part of the American continent, in order to provide funds for their China ships, to enable them to return home teas and China goods[2]

Meanwhile, word of increased Russian activity on the Northwest Coast at long last spurred Spain in 1788 to dispatch Capt. Esteban Martinez to reassert Spanish claims to the region—based upon, in addition to the Treaty of Tordesillas, Perez's 1774 expedition, on which Martinez was along. Martinez made contact with Russians along the shores of today's southeast Alaska, where he learned about British activities in Nootka Sound, which he reported to the viceroy on his return to New Spain. In May 1789 Martinez was again sent north, this time to establish a Spanish settlement in Nootka Sound to resist encroachment by Anglo Americans. Thus, the new Spanish claim was to include effective occupation, in addition to the right of prior discovery. Here arose the first conflict between contending European nations in the Pacific Northwest.[3]

Upon his arrival at Nootka in July, Martinez approached his work with relish, impounding four English ships, clapping the crews in irons, dispatching some to dungeons in Mexico and others to Macao in the hold of an American ship. The Americans Gray and Kendrick, though also trading in the sound, were left alone, presumably because they did not appear to be a threat. When the British learned of Martinez's rash act, they called their ambassador home from Madrid and prepared the fleet for war.

However, the Spanish fleet was not prepared to face Great Britain alone and thus agreed to the Nootka Convention of 1790, which, as historian Alan Frost writes, "...represented the last Spanish attempt to preserve exclusive rights in the Pacific basin as prescribed in the Treaty of Tordesillas."[4]

The agreement opened the region between Russian America and Spanish California to joint exploration until either side could establish effective occupation. Both nations agreed to dispatch missions to settle British claims for property confiscated by Martinez, as well as to explore and chart the region to lay foundations for future claims.

Meanwhile on the far side of the world the viceroy of New Spain, Conde Revillagigedo, ordered two more voyages north to retrench Spanish presence in the Strait of Juan de Fuca. In 1790, an expedition under Capt. Manuel Quimper, with pilot Juan Carasco, sailed from Nootka Sound and laid claim to being the first Europeans to sail up and compile the first accurate charts of the north shore of the Strait of Juan de Fuca. They probed to the mouth of Admiralty Inlet and Puget Sound, which they took to be a shallow bay and named *Seno de Santa Rosa*. They then came about and pushed north up the Haro Strait, named *Canal de Lopez de Haro* by Canasco. The following year Capt. Francisco Eliza passed through the Haro Strait north to today's Strait of Georgia, which he called *Canal de Nuestra Senora del Rosario*. He also named the San Juan Archipelago *Isla y Archipelago de San Juan*.[5]

These explorations were run concurrently with the Alessandro Malaspina expedition, which had been dispatched from Spain for the same purpose as the voyages of Cook to chart the Pacific Basin from Cape Horn to the Gulf of Alaska and beyond. While in Mexico, Malaspina in March 1792 detached the schooners (*goletas*) *Mexicana* and *Sutil*—under the command of Dionisio Alcala Galiano and Cayetano Valdes y Flores respectively—north to make more detailed charts of the Strait of Juan de Fuca.

Reaching Nootka Sound in May, the Spanish set out in June to chart the Strait of Georgia, where on June 13, 1792, they encountered HMS *Chatham* and then HMS *Discovery*, both under the command of Capt. George Vancouver, who had embarked from England more than a year before as the British representative to square the Nootka Convention. Vancouver may (or may not) have reported an encounter with Robert Gray who, in command of the *Columbia*, claimed to have discovered a great river several hundred miles to the south.

Gray had been a busy mariner over the previous two years. Following the departure of Martinez from Nootka with his spoils, the Yankee had switched vessels with Kendrick and in July 1789 proceeded to Macao, where he made a hefty profit from fur sales. He continued west to Boston around the Cape of Good Hope, completing the first circumnavigation of the globe by an American skipper. After only seven weeks rest from this three-year voyage, Gray was off again to make more money for his owners. He spent a year trading and charting in the Northwest, wintered in Macao, then returned to the Northwest for more trading in the spring of 1792.

On making the Northwest Coast in April, Gray sighted two capes with strong current and roiling surf at 46 degrees, which he surmised was the mouth of a great river. Gray sailed on and encountered HMS *Discovery* just south of the Strait of Juan de Fuca. Vancouver sent Lt. Peter Puget and surgeon/naturalist Archibald Menzies over to *Columbia* to divine whether Gray had earlier sailed up the strait in *Lady Washington*. Gray replied in the negative, but did mention the suspected river mouth to the south that he had already decided to revisit. Puget averred that *Discovery* had passed the same rough water a few days before, but they believed the formidable Columbia River bar was a line of surf and presumed that fresh water signs indicated a profusion of streams pouring into the sea.

The British continued on up the Strait of Juan de Fuca, while Gray turned south. Two weeks later the American crossed over the bar and named the river for his ship. Some weeks afterward he gave copies of his charts to the Spanish Nootka representative, Juan Francisco de la Bodega y Quadra, who shared them with a chagrined Vancouver. Consequently, five months later Lt. William Broughton, 29, conned *Chatham* over the bar and sailed up river as far as Washougal (east of today's Vancouver).

Broughton later claimed that Gray's chart was inaccurate, as the American had neglected to include the sand bar at the river mouth, though it is likely that the river volume was higher when Gray entered in the spring. While acknowledging Gray's discovery and accepting his chart, Vancouver contended that the British held right of claim because Broughton had sailed 100 miles upriver and, as an officer of the Royal Navy on the King's business, legitimately claimed the same for Britain. Unknown to Vancouver, Gray possessed a "Sea Letter," signed by Pres. George Washington, asking foreign ships to receive and grant "peaceful passage" to Gray and his ship. And according to John Boit, a 16 year-old fifth officer aboard *Columbia*, Gray did land and make a formal claim on behalf of the United States:[6]

> I landed abreast of the ship with Captain Gray to view the Country and take possession leaving charge with second officer—found much clear ground for cultivation and the woods mostly cleared of underbrush none of the natives came near us.[7]

Gray's primary interest were profits from otter pelts, but his discovery of the Columbia, the great river of legend, became the first U.S. claim to the region and eventually spurred the Lewis and Clark expedition. At least that was the way the Americans saw it, particularly the secretary of state of the new Yankee government, Thomas Jefferson. But Gray was not being paid in 1792 to claim territory, so after leaving copies of his charts, he sailed off for more immediately lucrative shores.

Vancouver, meanwhile, *was* making charts—extensive ones— of the entire Puget Sound basin and the complete coastline of Vancouver Island, as well as the navigable channel that ran from the Strait of Juan de Fuca between the mainland and a cluster of islands and islets to the Gulf of Georgia. The waterway was called Vancouver's Channel in honor of the explorer, but eventually would become accepted by its Spanish name, the one it carries today—Rosario Strait.

These charts would one day fuel the San Juan boundary

dispute, though Vancouver never entered the San Juan archipelago himself. That was left to Broughton, who in May 1792 charted the islands aboard *Chatham*. His sailing master, James Johnstone, left this description: "The land is delightful, being in many places clear and the soil so rich that the grass in several parts grew to man height..."

Vancouver left many place names in his wake, but most of the island nomenclature was left to the Spanish, among these San Juan, Orcas, and Lopez islands and most importantly for Americans, the Haro Strait, a wide, easily navigable channel that ran between that same cluster of islands and Vancouver's Island.[8]

Chapter 3

MANIFEST DESTINY
AND JOINT OCCUPATION

The 1790s were a time of ferment for the young United States, not least in the mind of Thomas Jefferson. While he was aware of Vancouver's and Gray's voyages, it was the overland explorations of the North West Company's Alexander Mackenzie, culminating with the Scotsman's arrival on the Pacific via the Bella Coola River in 1793, that moved Jefferson to propose U.S.-sponsored expeditions. The apparently vast, bountiful and virtually untouched continent stretching to the Pacific Ocean was the canvas upon which he would paint his vision of a yeoman democracy, expanding to meet each new challenge.

Jefferson's plans had to wait until his own presidency, when a combination of international events—primarily Napoleon's rise and fall and their effects on Spain—dropped the massive Louisiana Territory into his lap. A transcontinental expedition already was in the planning stages when the terms of the sale were being negotiated in 1803. It proceeded on May 14, 1804, under the leadership of Meriwether Lewis and William Clark.

It required two years for Lewis and Clark to make the round trip via the continental divide from St. Louis to the mouth of the Columbia River. But their efforts gave the United States another claim to the Oregon Country to add to Gray's. These claims were underscored in 1810 when the fur merchant John Jacob Astor sent missions overland and by sea to establish a fur post at the mouth of the Columbia. The Montreal-based North West Company, catching wind of Astor's doings, also dispatched a mission to the Columbia under astronomer/explorer David Thompson.

Much to Thompson's surprise, the Yankees got there first when Astor's bark *Tonquin* crossed the bar and established Fort Astoria. But the world caught up with Fort Astoria by 1813 when British trapper and trader John George McTavish appeared at the fort's gate one day and informed the occupants that Great Britain and the United States were at war. The Royal Navy was soon to arrive, McTavish said, so it would be best if they surrendered the fort to him before anyone got hurt.

At the outbreak of the War of 1812, North West Company officials had gone to the Admiralty and pressed for a naval force to capture Astoria as a prize of war. The Admiralty obliged in 1813 when they sent the warships *Phoebe*, *Cherub* and *Raccoon* to accompany the armed North West trade vessel *Isaac Todd*. In the South Atlantic, the flotilla's commander, Capt. David Hillyer of HMS *Phoebe*, learned that USS *Essex*, an American frigate commanded by Capt. David Porter, was raising havoc with British merchant and whaling ships in the South Pacific. Hillyer dispatched HMS *Raccoon* under Capt. William Black, and the *Todd* on to Astoria while retaining HMS *Cherub* to help deal with *Essex*. The British cornered Porter in the harbor of Valparaiso, Chile and the two British vessels stood off with their long guns and pounded the *Essex* into submission. It was one of the bloodiest battles in U.S. Navy history and resulted in British naval dominance of the Pacific that would endure into the 20th century. Meanwhile, the *Raccoon* and *Todd* pressed on to Astoria, the *Todd* disappearing en route. When the *Raccoon* launched boats and portaged the crews around the Columbia River bar, as McTavish warned, in November 1813, they discovered that the Astorians, ever seeking profit in adversity, had sold the post to the North Westers. Not to be denied, Black seized the fort as a prize anyway and renamed it Fort George.[1]

After the war, the British government, weary of contending with the rapidly expanding United States, returned Fort George to the U.S. (which Astor refused) and acceded to the joint occupation of the Oregon Country with the Anglo-American Convention of 1818. This included the establishment of the international border on the 49th parallel between the Lake of the Woods in Minnesota and the Rocky (or Stony) Mountains. Although the British had wanted a Columbia River boundary, the Americans balked, which prompted British Foreign Secretary Castleraugh to give ground, believing the overture "...an additional motive to cultivate (in the Americans) the arts of peace."

Thus it was decided that the largely undeveloped land from the Rocky Mountains to the Pacific, north of the 42nd parallel (California-Oregon border) and south of the Russian possessions (the 54th parallel or Southeast Alaska) would be shared. The agreement, subject to renewal in 1827, was similar to the 1790 Nootka Convention as it stipulated that possession of the region would be determined by "effective occupation," that is, established settlement and an active commerce.

The Hudson's Bay Company (HBC) bought out the North West Company in 1821 and quickly took the lead by establishing a network of fur trading posts on tributaries of the Columbia and along the Northwest Coast of British Columbia. Fort Vancouver, about 60 miles up the Columbia from Fort Astoria, became the primary post in the region, dominating the fur trade and administering agricultural colonies that provided foodstuffs for its outposts and for the Russian-America Company in exchange for furs. This alarmed the still largely agrarian Americans, who by the mid-1820s were beginning to think about organizing agricultural colonies of their own south of the Columbia.

What they could not establish in fact, the Americans tried to do on paper. In 1825, Secretary of State Albert Gallatin proposed that the 49th parallel divide British and American possessions across the continent, but the Hudson's Bay Company would have none of it. The Columbia was the main highway into their vast inland fur empire, and the company viewed it as a private canal. Therefore the British government countered the American proposal by again suggesting a border tracing the Columbia River from the 49th parallel south, then west to the Columbia River bar. The Americans would get the Olympic Peninsula, which would grant them access to Puget Sound, plus free navigation rights on the Columbia. The Americans declined and joint occupation continued.

Working in the field to make the British offer a foregone conclusion, Hudson's Bay Company Gov. George Simpson systematically undercut Yankee sea captains and fur traders from the Columbia to Alaska. First it was with the Indians, and then with the Russian America Company, as the HBC swapped dimension lumber and food products for prime otter and beaver pelts at good prices. As early as 1824, Simpson realized that the HBC would have to diversify if it was to maintain its economic dominance in the Oregon Country. He focused on three extraction industries—timber, fishing, farming—that formed the nucleus of the region's economy well into the late 20th century. To direct the company's farm activities, he established the subsidiary Puget Sound Agricultural Company with sites at Forts Nisqually and Vancouver, as well as a plantation near the Cowlitz River landing in today's southwestern Washington.[2]

Now American immigrants trying to subsist as farmers anywhere near HBC facilities were in the same fix as the sea captains, as the Company produced more for less. The Americans were effectively stymied, and those who managed to hold on in the area developed bitterness for the Company that would never be forgotten.

However, while the door to Yankee settlement may have seemed shut tight, a sizable crack remained. At Fort Vancouver, Factor Dr. John McLoughlin had a heart, to his eventual undoing and the undoing of his company south of the 49th parallel. Fort Vancouver was the regional center for supplies, news, medical care, and interesting company, and McLoughlin helped the American settlers who began to trickle in. This alarmed Simpson, who never liked the Fort Vancouver site because ships frequently sank crossing the Columbia River bar. By 1841 the American missionary movement embraced the Oregon Country, found the backing of Congress, and began to actively market settlement. It had become American's "Manifest Destiny" to extend democracy from coast to coast, but this visionary hoopla was fueled by practical considerations. The Panic of 1837 spurred many farm families west to beat low prices. Oregon was a second chance. McLoughlin helped them out with low interest loans, tools, and information. The dramatic results were typical of the patterns of American westward settlement that began with the first penetration of the Appalachians.

Western historian Ray Allen Billington argued that the British were only too happy to settle for the 49th parallel by 1846 for a couple of reasons. First there was the Walker Tariff, passed by the U.S. Congress and signed into law by President James Knox Polk in 1846, which lowered duties on British manufactured goods. Britain responded by repealing its protectionist Corn Laws the same year, opening British markets to U.S. farm crops from the West and Southeast. British business interests would have brought great pressure to bear on any foreign policy measure that might provoke hostilities with the United States.

> "(The tariff) mollified English opinion, long opposed to American high protection, and aided the government in its policy of compromise."[3]

Second, U.S. immigration into Oregon by land and sea had accelerated by startling proportions by 1845. A thousand people had arrived in 1843 alone and another 1,500 would settle in 1844. This was enough to prompt Missouri Sen. Thomas Hart Benton to declare, "Let the emigrants go on; and carry their rifles... Thirty thousand rifles in Oregon will annihilate the Hudson's Bay Company, drive them off our continent."

The British were less impressed by rifles than they were with the exponential growth in Yankee settlement. From 1841 to 1845 the American population in the Oregon Country skyrocketed from 300 to more than 8,000, most gravitating south of the Columbia to the fertile Willamette Valley.[4]

The incoming farmers helped drive out the fur trade, and by 1842 George Simpson decided to move the HBC's main Oregon Country post away from the Yankees and the Columbia River bar to a more accommodating site on Vancouver Island. Under the leadership of James Douglas the new fort was established in 1843 in an excellent natural harbor on the southern end of the island and named Fort Victoria. In five years, the once thriving factory and trading hub at Fort Vancouver would be reduced to a modest trading post that received two shipments of goods per year.

That meant since the British already were evacuating the area in dispute, British diplomacy could now yield gracefully and without the sacrifice of any important economic interest.[5]

Simpson, who wasn't much interested in diplomacy, disparaged the Americans on his way out the door as "worthless and lawless characters of every description."

And so the bitterness between the company and the American settlers cut both ways. Despite Company policies, HBC employees, especially James Douglas, would never get over being sold out by their own government and being shoved out of the Columbia River Valley.[6]

Chapter 4

THE TREATY OF OREGON

The Oregon Treaty of 1846 gave the United States undisputed possession of the Pacific Northwest south of the 49th parallel, with the western boundary extending to the "middle of the channel which separates the continent from Vancouver's Island…" However, while the treaty settled the larger boundary question, its wording left unclear who owned San Juan Islands. The seemingly endless diplomatic juggling that went on before a settlement was reached left both nations so desperate to get on with business that they were willing to overlook niggling details—such as the ownership of a relatively insignificant archipelago thousands of miles from the seats of power. As Lord Derby remarked to Lord Malmsbury as the Oregon problem festered more than a decade later: the only way to handle the Americans was "to be very civil, very firm, and to go our own way."

When the British proposed to settle the Oregon question once and for all in 1842, hoping against hope that the boundary might trace the Columbia River, they were well aware that such a boundary would deny the Americans a deep-water port in the region, a prospect totally unacceptable to the U.S. Government.

The British also knew that the as-yet-unpublished findings of the United States Exploring Expedition—which, under the command of U. S. Navy Lt. Charles Wilkes, had in 1841 charted a large stretch of the Oregon Country, including the San Juan

Islands—already were circulating in the corridors of power. Wilkes had written that the Columbia River bar "rendered the entrance of that river impracticable for large vessels during nine months of the year; and that the only harbor available along the whole coast was at the 'Strait of Juan de Fuca,' three degrees north of the Columbia, and of course within that portion of the territory which, according to any compromise of the Disputed Boundary, would belong exclusively to Great Britain."[1]

By August 1844, President John Tyler's second Secretary of State, John Calhoun, proposed a compromise of the 49th parallel. If the British accepted, he wrote, the U.S. might be willing to cede Vancouver Island and guarantee free navigation of the Strait of Juan de Fuca and other channels and inlets running south of the line. Instead, in late 1844, Britain countered with a proposal to submit the question to binding arbitration. Calhoun refused and it was back to square.

James Knox Polk was subsequently elected president on the crest of highly inflammatory campaign dialogue ("54-40 or Fight"), which favored setting the boundary north of Haida Gwaii (Queen Charlotte Islands). Reality had to yet set in by the time of his inaugural address, which was so bellicose it prompted the Admiralty to alert the Royal Navy to enforce British rights wherever and whenever threatened on the Northwest Coast:

> You will hold temperate, but firm language to members
> of the Government and to all those with whom you
> converse. We are still ready to adhere to the principle of
> equitable compromise; but we are perfectly determined
> to concede nothing to force or menace, and are fully
> prepared to maintain our rights.[2]

The Royal Navy already had been active throughout the election year, showing flag along the coast, and sending the 18-gun sloop HMS *Modeste* up the Columbia in July 1844.

In Washington City, the ever-tactful James Buchanan was appointed Polk's Secretary of State and despite Polk's posturing he was determined to settle the Oregon Question peaceably. On July 12, 1845, Buchanan submitted a proposal to the British, outlining what the United States would be willing to consider. It was backed by a windy summary, rehashing Calhoun's arguments going back to the Nootka Convention of 1790. He then offered the same compromise of the 49th parallel, providing that Britain accommodate free ports on Vancouver Island.

The British rejected the proposal, pointing out that it contained nothing about free navigation of the Columbia and that Britain already was entitled to all of Vancouver Island. Buchanan replied in August with another lengthy history lesson that included the myth-laden voyage of Juan de Fuca (Apostolos Valerianos the Greek also known as Ioánnis Fokás) on behalf of Spain in 1592. He cited Samuel Purchas's *Hakluytus Posthumus*, or *Purchas His Pilgrims*, published in 1625, as his primary source, as well as a personal interview with Fuca by the Englishman Michael Lok in Venice in 1596. He then withdrew the offer of the 49th.[3]

Finally on May 20, 1846, the U.S. resorted to brinksmanship, announcing that it intended to "put an end" to the Convention of 1827, which would effectively terminate the joint occupation. The British envoy in Washington, Richard Pakenham, was grudgingly urged by his government to renew his efforts at a settlement. Foreign Secretary George Hamilton-Gordon, the 4th Earl of Aberdeen, opined that the British government already had been conciliatory to the extreme: "Can it truly be said that the Government of the United States have advanced to meet us in the path of mutual concession?"

Aberdeen instructed Pakenham to propose to the U.S. that the 49th be the boundary from the "Rocky Mountains to the seacoast; and from thence in a southerly direction through the centre of King George's Sound and the Straits of Juan de Fuca to the Pacific

Ocean, leaving the whole of Vancouver's Island, with its ports and harbors, in possession of Great Britain."

The Columbia River was to remain "free and open" to the Hudson's Bay Company and to subjects of Great Britain trading with the company. The HBC also would be permitted to retain Fort Vancouver and other stations south of the 49th. The HBC subsidiary, Puget Sound Agricultural Company, also would be allowed to remain in business south of the 49th or be fairly compensated. The treaty was drafted at the British Foreign Office and was accepted by the U.S. as written.

The final, ambiguous passage concerning the water boundary between Vancouver Island and the mainland read:

> From the point on the forty-ninth parallel of north latitude where the boundary laid down in existing treaties and conventions between the United States and Great Britain terminates, the line of boundary between the territories of the United States and those of Her Britannic Majesty shall be continued westward along the said forty-ninth parallel of north latitude to the middle of the channel which separates the continent from Vancouver's Island; and thence southerly through the middle of the said channel, and of Fuca's Straits to the Pacific Ocean; provided however, that the navigation of the whole of said channel and Straits south of the forty-ninth parallel of north latitude remain free and open to both parties.[4]

Sir John H. Pelly, a governor of the HBC, reviewing the passage in its draft form, was immediately alarmed. Hudson's Bay officials knew there were two channels, not one, cutting south from the Gulf of Georgia. On May 16 he complained to Lord Aberdeen about the ambiguity, noting that it could have been avoided had the people who actually knew the area been consulted.

The treaty language, he pointed out, should read: "...to the centre of the Gulf of Georgia in that latitude; *and from that point south along the track of Vancouver* (today's Rosario Strait) till it meets a line drawn from the sea to the centre of the Straits of San Juan de Fuca, and from that point to the sea." The San Juan Islands should, without question, he wrote, belong to Great Britain and specifically to the HBC, according to Pelly, who attached a map to clarify matters.[5]

The map Pelly sent incorporated data from maps published by George Vancouver in 1798 and an 1848 map based on Vancouver's atlas, crafted by Charles Preuss, a German cartographer traveling with American explorer John C. Fremont in 1842-43, 1845, and 1848. The maps reveal the islands as vaguely familiar masses blocking the Strait of Georgia from which irregular passages noodle their way to the Strait of Juan de Fuca. While the Preuss map clearly labels the "Canal de Arro," the passage highlighted by a red line denoting the "true" north-south route—or "Vancouver's track"—is Vancouver's Strait, or Rosario Strait, as it is known today.[6]

Buchanan also expressed alarm when he read Article 1. In a June 6, 1846 letter to Louis McLane, the American minister in London, Buchanan contended that the article did not "provide that the line shall pass through the Canal de Arro (Haro) as stated in your Despatch. This would probably be the fair construction."

However, Buchanan's observation and Pelly's protests were ignored and the Treaty of Oregon was signed with minor adjustments by both nations on June 15. The Senate ratified it on June 18, and Parliament followed suit.

Either Congress and Parliament were unable to focus their attention on such an obscure part of the world or both governments were in a hurry to conclude the agreement and cool the growing crisis in the Northwest before it started to affect business.

The British government changed in June and Henry John Temple, the 3rd Viscount Palmerston became Foreign Minister.

Palmerston was considered more hard-nosed when it came to foreign policy, a trait cited more than once as another reason why the treaty was concluded in a hurry. After studying the treaty, Palmerston approached Pelly on July 30, requesting clarification of certain geographical details. Pelly again drew attention to the passage identifying the "channel" running between Vancouver Island and the mainland. He wrote that "...there are numerous islands, and, I believe, passages between them. I know there is one close round Vancouver's Island; but I believe the largest to be the one Vancouver sailed through, and coloured red in the tracing, and I think this is the one that should be the boundary."

In February 1847, George Simpson went to Washington to suggest a commission to adjust certain points in the treaty. He wrote:

> There are several channels separating the mainland from Vancouver's island (occasioned by islands); it is therefore very desirable that which is to form the line of demarcation should be determined, otherwise the sovereignty of those channel islands may very well soon become a source of dispute between British and American subjects.[7]

Pakenham dutifully submitted Simpson's observations to his government. Two British survey ships were at that instant exploring the area in question, he was told. The geography was still "imperfectly known" and adjustments should wait on the results of those surveys. Unfortunately the ships, HMS *Pandora* and HMS *Herald*, never made it beyond the entrance to the Strait of Haro, so the territory remained unknown to the powers that be.

The British legation secretary, John Crampton, was given instructions to approach the U.S. and suggest that each nation provide an officer of "scientific attainment and conciliatory character" to mark and survey the area and come up with a water boundary satisfactory to both nations. The word "channel" was key to reaching an accord. The final treaty said nothing about "Vancouver's track." The Foreign Ministry observed that in most treaties "channel" meant a "deep and navigable" waterway. Presumably this characterized the one charted by Vancouver in 1792. If it were adopted, the government presumed no "difficulty" would arise. And while it was true that selection of this waterway would attach the island to Great Britain it was doubted the U.S. would protest for "...these islets are of little or no value."

Buchanan interpreted "channel" to mean the "main navigable channel" wherever situated. But he had never examined Vancouver's charts, and though he was not prepared to contest the British claim, he declined to adopt the view without additional research and geographical evidence. Crampton then officially proposed a joint boundary commission to make the final determination.

On July 31, 1847, U.S. envoy in London, George Bancroft, forwarded to Palmerston the charts of Lieutenant Wilkes, who in addition to writing his observations of the Columbia River bar had extensively surveyed Puget Sound and other coastal waters, including the San Juan Island group. Violating an unwritten protocol among explorers of all nations, Wilkes had renamed most of the islands for U.S. War of 1812 naval heroes, ships and battles. Shaw, Decatur and Waldron islands, plus Mount Constitution and Mount Erie, remain Wilkes's lasting legacy.[8]

Most importantly, however, Wilkes's charts quite clearly show the San Juan Islands situated in the Strait of Georgia. The Haro Strait is labeled *Canal de Haro*, while Rosario (Vancouver's) Strait is labeled *Ringgold Strait*. Why this map was circulating among the inner circles of Washington, but was not used in boundary negotiations remains a mystery. It was certainly clear to Bancroft that the Haro Strait was the proper "channel." However, this was yesterday's news by then to Palmerston. The San Juan Islands were flyspecks on the great canvas of empire. Palmerston thanked Bancroft for the information and that was the last anyone in the halls of power had to say about the issue until December 1853 when local disputes began to percolate.

For Hudson's Bay Company factor and Vancouver Island Crown Colony Gov. James Douglas there was never any doubt as to the proper ownership of the islands. To his dying day he maintained the San Juans were the logical extension of Vancouver Island. And he was willing to stake his life and the lives of his countrymen on it.

Chapter 5

THE SAN JUAN SHEEP WAR

"San Juan is a fertile and beautiful island, with a large extent of open prairie land; but were it barren and rocky, and intrinsically worthless, it is of the utmost value to Great Britain, commanding as it does the channel of communications between Vancouver Island and British Columbia... in my opinion, it matters not if all the other islands between San Juan and the Continent pass to the United States, but San Juan is invaluable to our possession; it clearly is ours, both in right and in equity, and to yield it to the United States would be to depreciate our contiguous territory to an extent that someday might prove fatal to Her Majesty's possessions in this quarter of the globe."[1]

— James Prevost (July 23, 1859)

And so the protests of a few businessmen and bean-counting diplomats were shunted aside, the Treaty of Oregon was concluded, and it was business as usual again between the two governments. The view among the powerful was that the confusion over a few little islands on the other side of the world would work itself out. And why should the Americans care? They were warring with Mexico and would soon take possession of the entire American southwest?

The key word is "equity." Capt. James Prevost, RN, commander of the steam corvette, HMS *Satellite*, never wavered on the San Juan question in his role as water boundary commissioner for the British government. Set geographical arguments aside and he would still believe the San Juans were unquestionably British because that is what James Douglas believed.[2]

With the brief exception of the crisis period in mid-1859 when the Royal Navy intervened, James Douglas *was* the British government north of the 49th parallel from the founding of Fort Victoria until he retired in 1864. Vancouver Island had been conveyed to the Hudson's Bay Company by Royal Grant on Jan. 13, 1849, which placed the "Company of Adventurers" in the colony business. Hoping to match the tide of American immigration, the government told HBC to provide a suitable climate for British settlers. This required a major change in thinking.

Heretofore, the company had discouraged settlers because they were bad for business. They moved to the hinterlands, got sick, went broke, or were slaughtered by Indians. That meant the company had to spend good money to heal them, bail them out, buy them boat tickets home, or hire soldiers to protect the survivors.

If Douglas wasn't miffed enough by this prospect, the British government tweaked him further by sending someone else to be governor; someone who presumed he could tell Douglas what to do. The unfortunate Gov. Richard Blanshard's term lasted less than a year. On Sept. 1, 1851, James Douglas was Chief Factor of Fort Victoria and governor of the crown colony.

Born Aug. 15, 1803, in British Guiana (his father was Scottish, his mother African-Caribbean), James Douglas left home to make his fortune at 16, joining the old North West Company in 1819. When the North West Company merged with the HBC in 1821, Douglas remained. He arrived at Fort Vancouver in 1830, where he was made clerk. But in a few years he rose to become Chief Factor John McLoughlin's assistant, acting in his stead when McLoughlin went to England for a year in 1838. He became chief factor at Fort Vancouver in 1846 before moving to Fort Victoria, a post he'd founded in 1843. He also was appointed agent of the Puget Sound Agricultural Company affiliate in 1849. From the beginning, he considered the San Juans "a dependency of Vancouver's Island."

In many of his missives justifying the British claims to the island, the governor's principal argument was that HBC agents had claimed the island in July 1845 by placing an engraved wooden tablet on Mt. Finlayson ("an eminence near the Southeast point of the island"). Douglas was to flatly maintain years later that this act took place prior to 1846, when the royal grant permitted the HBC to establish facilities anywhere in the Oregon Country between Russian America and the California border. He exercised this view in 1851 when, on Blanshard's authority, he established a seasonal fish salting station on the southern end of San Juan Island. After that it was easy for him to violate his government's agreement with the United States and take formal possession of all the islands on behalf the Crown.

By late 1853 with the formation of Washington Territory and the expected arrival of an aggressive young governor and Mexican War hero, Isaac Stevens, Douglas knew more Americans would move north of the Columbia and snap up lands in the Puget Sound basin. Stevens already was on record in his belief that while American settlers, focusing on agriculture, represented civilization and progress, the HBC's preoccupation with trade placed them in league with the Indians. Stevens had not been in the territory a month when he sent letters to Peter Skene Ogden, who ran what remained of Fort Vancouver, and Dr. William Tolmie, the Puget

Sound Agricultural Company head at Fort Nisqually. The letters essentially contained the U.S. blueprint for jettisoning the HBC from the mainland south of the 49ᵗʰ parallel: The Company had to stop trading with the Indians and prepare to be "bought out" at a fair price.

The prospects were familiar to Douglas. The Americans would next push up to the 49ᵗʰ and those who knew anything about agriculture would grab the islands barren of trees but rich in topsoil. The American customs collector, Isaac Neff Ebey, already had claimed a prime homestead on Whidbey Island in Puget Sound. The San Juans with their acres of virgin prairie beckoned. Douglas advised the colonial office that the San Juans could "maintain a large population" because of the extent of timber, arable farmland, and fisheries.

In November 1853, Douglas decided to act. He wrote to the Duke of Newcastle that it was his intention to "assert the sovereignty of her majesty the Queen to all the islands of the Arro Archipelago" lying west of Cypress Island. If Washington and London were not prepared to settle on Rosario Strait as the boundary, Douglas would do it unilaterally. To support his action, Douglas contended (erroneously) that the Rosario Strait was the only navigable channel for sailing ships from the Strait of Juan de Fuca to the Georgia Strait. This was the channel to which the Americans agreed in the treaty, because the document also guaranteed British navigation rights. Douglas also cited the 1848 edition Preuss map to demonstrate his point. Preuss still had not consulted Wilkes's charts and had indicated Rosario as the sole channel and boundary. Douglas magnanimously proposed that the channel be open to both nations and free of collection of duties. Duties required on either shore would be paid on Vancouver Island or Olympia. Newcastle did not reply to this document; therefore Douglas took it upon himself to enforce Britain's claims, while discouraging American activity.

His first target was R. W. Cussans, an American citizen who had claimed a tract of land on Lopez Island, made $1,500 in improvements, and then cut and squared 30,000 board feet of lumber. As Capt. James Alden of the U.S. Cost Survey Steamer *Active* reported on Oct. 31, 1853, Cussans was "compelled" to apply for a license with Douglas and then ordered to clear customs in Victoria with the timber. The license was issued for six months from July 25, 1853. Cussans was to pay 10 pence sterling for each 50 cubic feet of lumber. On September 11 Cussans completed an affidavit for Alden swearing that he had occupied the land assuming it was U.S. territory. He also swore that he had never given security for the payment of any dues to the British government. Douglas told Alden that Cussans had claimed he was a British subject at the time of application.

Alden added in his dispatch that Douglas' choice of Rosario as the preferred channel was puzzling because "there is a channel much nearer home, better in almost every respect, and, to them, far more convenient I mean the Canal de Haro." Alden probably knew the San Juan waters as well as any U.S. Navy officer on the coast since he had been a junior lieutenant on Wilkes' survey of the islands in 1841.[3]

Douglas was quite proud of himself after his ejection of Cussans:

> "I have succeeded in defeating every attempt made to preoccupy the Arro Archipelago through the agency of American squatters, so that those islands will still remain a de facto dependency of Vancouver island *unoccupied* by any whites except a fishing station which was established some years ago by HBC on the island of San Juan.[4]

This was not entirely truthful. For even as he was penning the above dispatch Douglas finally decided to take his crown colony mandate seriously and open San Juan Island to British settlement. There was a problem, however. He had been so successful discouraging colonists, no was around to take him up on it. But Douglas refused to assume blame. Instead he wrote another dispatch lamenting that British settlers were scarce because he was not authorized to grant free land as the Americans were doing.

Douglas' settlement plans were not to be denied. After all, he was also chief factor of Fort Victoria. With a stroke of his pen, he cemented British presence in the San Juans by establishing a plantation on the island's southern end. On Dec. 15, 1853, a group of Kanaka (Hawaiian) herdsmen, led by freshly appointed chief agent Charles John Griffin, turned loose 1,369 sheep to graze on a sweeping prairie that gave onto the Strait of Juan de Fuca. Griffin also brought along seed for crops and farmyard animals, including several Berkshire boars. Gazing at the magnificent Olympic Mountains directly across the strait, Griffin appropriately called his prairie home "Belle Vue Sheep Farm." He also established sheep stations at three other points on the island, including Oak Prairie (today's San Juan Valley), another prairie just south of Roche Harbor, and a clearing above a sheltered bay on the island's east side (Friday Harbor).[5]

Douglas did not inform his government that a corporation and not British subjects had settled the island.

In April 1854 the governor's worst fears were realized when he heard through the grapevine that without advising Governor Stevens, the U.S. Customs Collector in Port Townsend, Isaac Neff Ebey, threatened seizure of British property on San Juan Island to collect duties. In Ebey's view, the San Juans were American possessions and not a duty-free zone. In a swiftly written dispatch, Douglas told his home government that he had no military forces at his disposal, but even if he had he would not use them. Instead he appointed Belle Vue Sheep Farm agent Griffin Justice of the Peace for the District of San Juan Island, at no pay. The American tax

collector was to be treated as a common offender if he attempted
to enforce his jurisdiction. Thus commenced the first standoff on
San Juan Island.

Ebey twice visited the island, the first time on April 21,
when he handed Griffin the duties bill and told the agent that he
should pay it because the sheep "...were liable to seizure" for being
smuggled into the territory. On May 3, Ebey returned to collect,
landing in an open boat about 6:30 p.m. He dispatched an Indian
to Griffin with an invitation to visit him in a tent he was sharing
with Henry Webber, his assistant. Griffin paid the call and "...after
several minutes spent in conversing on commonplace subjects, I at
once put the question to Colonel Ebey, 'What is the purport of your
visit?'" Before Ebey could answer, Griffin warned the American
of the penalties for molesting property or disturbing the peace, to
which Ebey replied, "I have done nothing."

Griffin returned to his cabin and noted in his journal, "I paid
them a visit without gleaning anything of importance from them."
He next dispatched a messenger aboard the *Otter*, another Hudson's
Bay Company steamer, to advise Douglas.[6]

Douglas steamed to the island the following morning,
accompanied by British customs inspector James Sangster. Standing
offshore, Douglas through his spyglass could see that Ebey's modest
party hardly constituted an invasion force and decided not to
land. Instead he called Griffin to the ship and was informed that
Ebey had encamped and seemed intent on remaining, probably to
collect duties. Douglas may have considered this an empty gesture
on Ebey's part and returned to Victoria. But Sangster was ordered
ashore with a British Union flag, which he was directed to run up
the Company flagpole.

Sangster then approached Ebey, who was again asked to state
his intentions. The American replied, "I am thinking of putting
an inspector on this island (Webber)." Sangster warned Ebey that
if he did so Webber would be arrested. Ebey was cavalier. If and

when he formally commissioned Webber and the British arrested him, he said he hoped Webber would be treated well when he was hauled off to Victoria.

The gauntlet was thrown the next day when Ebey and Webber called on Griffin whereupon Ebey read a proclamation naming Webber assistant collector of customs on San Juan Island. Ebey left soon thereafter and Webber pitched his tent "immediately" behind Griffin's cabin, garnishing the act by running up an American flag. That did it for Griffin. The next morning he issued a warrant for Webber's arrest and directed Thomas Holland, a Belle Vue herdsman acting as "constable" to serve the warrant and bring back the prisoner. Sangster went along to observe.

Webber was armed and belligerent.

> On the constable reading the warrant, and when in the act of raising his hand to arrest Mr. Webber, this gentleman instantaneously presented a revolver pistol at the breast of the constable, telling him if he touched him he would most certainly fire, giving as reason at the time that he did not consider the constable's office legal, as he was given to understand he, the constable, had not been sworn in before a bench of magistrates, and if he or any other man or men attempted to arrest him he should fire, and otherwise protect himself as long as a ball remained in any one of his pistols; he had two brace of pistols hung about his waste and breast, and a knife thrust in his boot at the knee.[7]

Sangster and Holland ran and got six men but Webber, determined as ever to resist, continued to menace them with his pistols. The constable returned to Griffin and asked if he could arm himself, but Griffin, abhorring violence, said no and ordered his men, Sangster included, to leave Webber alone with his knife and pistols. A disgusted Griffin wrote in his journal, "...Such a farce! If this is what is called law, then it plainly is rum law."[8]

After all that, Webber and Sangster left the next day, Webber to purchase supplies and report to Ebey, Sangster presumably to tell all to Douglas.

Webber returned, apparently to stay, on May 10. Opting for the high road, Douglas advised Griffin not to bother the American so long as he minded his own business and did not attempt to confiscate or molest property. Webber was to be treated not as a U.S. Government agent, but a private person "entitled to protection by Her Majesty's Government and subject to those same laws." If the American attempted to collect customs duties he was to be arrested. If he resisted arrest he would be held accountable in the Queen's courts.

Webber was likewise directed by Ebey not to collect, but to peacefully keep book on HBC property, for which he would be paid a rate of $5 a day. Webber was only too happy to comply and remained where he was at Belle Vue Sheep Farm, where, in what was to become a tradition among contending government officials on San Juan Island, he soon became fast friends with his neighbor Charles Griffin.

While friendship blossomed, letters were penned quickly (though delivered too slowly for the pace of events) between Ebey and Douglas and their respective governments. Douglas complained of American effrontery while Ebey, in a dispatch to Secretary of the Treasury James Guthrie, accused the HBC of violating U.S. revenue laws. His position that the San Juans belonged to the United States was shared, but for diplomatic reasons not enforced, by Governor Stevens. If Webber was detained, Ebey stated, he would simply replace him with another agent and appeal to the territorial government for help in obtaining Webber's release.

The British Foreign Office was not amused by Ebey's international boundary interpretation, or Webber's sourdough antics. In July they asked the U.S. Government in Washington City to "make inquiries" and order local officials to cease and desist.

Secretary of State William Marcy first wrote Guthrie, advising him that a commission would soon meet to decide the boundary. But he did not disabuse Ebey's opinion on American title. Far from it. In fact, he told Guthrie that U.S. authorities should continue to "hold possession" of the islands.

The colonial office was sending the same message to Douglas concerning the disputed isles: "...In conveying to the approval of HM Govt. of your proceedings with respect to the sovereignty of the islands in the Canal de Arro, I have to authorize you to continue to treat those islands as part of the British Dominions."[9]

Douglas embraced these instructions with relish over the next five years, though he still believed the reaction of his government had not been strong enough. Sir John Crampton, now British minister in Washington, cautioned Douglas not to "push matters to extremities, unless we are compelled to do so." The governor found this advisory "an unfortunate admission, showing a lamentable want of information on the question at issue, and yet it is a fact that may greatly embarrass Her Majesty's Government."

Ever the peacemaker, Secretary Marcy in late July wrote a soothing semi-apology to the British, stating that Governor Stevens (then in Washington City on business) told him that he had no reason to collect customs duties from the HBC. Displaying a sure grasp of the pulse of his territory and the character of its officials, Stevens told Marcy that while Ebey had probably posted an agent on the island, the agent likely had not been directed to make collections. In almost the same breath the governor suggested that the U.S. Army garrison at Fort Steilacoom be moved to Port Townsend, about 20 miles across the strait from San Juan Island.

By early 1855 the issue was academic as northern Indian raids drove the Americans, including Webber, away from the islands. Douglas, however, was still smarting from the Webber incident and was sensitive to any American act around the islands, no matter the purpose. In October 1854, for example, he reported that a U.S.

Revenue cutter mounting six guns and commanded by U.S. naval officers was lurking in the area. "They appear resolved to gain forcible possession of the *disputed* territory, and I hardly know how to prevent them," he wrote.

The ship probably was nearby, but more with an eye to intercepting Indian raiders who had struck Whatcom, Whidbey Island and points south throughout the year. These Northwest Coast groups had been operating in the Strait of Georgia and Puget Sound basin since Fort Victoria opened in 1843. They came in swift, high-prowed canoes, hitting Coast Salish and white communities alike without warning, taking slaves from the Indians, firearms, pots, and anything else not nailed downed from the whites. They also ritually decapitated their victims, carrying away the heads as trophies, which spooked white settlers (see note 6., this chapter). In response the Department of Oregon established military posts at Bellingham Bay, just east of the islands, as well as at Port Townsend.

Northwest Coast groups never attacked HBC posts for fear of immediate reprisal. The British had coined the term "forest diplomacy," whereby civilian posses or British warships found the village of the offending parties and burned it to the ground if the miscreants were not swiftly turned over to justice. This may explain why Webber and Charles Griffin became such close neighbors.[10]

But it was Americans, not Indians, who troubled Douglas most now. In January 1855, the governor wrote that he had "never been free from alarms." He complained about American newspapers and also about acting U.S. Territorial Gov. Charles H. Mason for landing on San Juan Island with troops from Fort Steilacoom in pursuit of northern Indians. These officials brought along "a large train of lawless followers." If that wasn't bad enough, U.S. Revenue cutters were continually threatening to enforce duties and now the fledgling government of Whatcom County was attempting to collect so-called "back taxes" on the HBC operation at Belle Vue Sheep Farm.

Whatcom County in those days embraced most of northwest Washington Territory from the Cascades to the San Juans. But its few white settlers lived in two small villages lying on either side of a waterfall giving on to Bellingham Bay, about 20 miles east of San Juan Island. With barely 40 citizens on the rolls, a complete county government had been elected, appointed, and hired, which resulted in 100 percent employment. One of the fortunate was County Commissioner William Cullen, an agent of the Puget Sound Mining Company, the San Francisco-based coal mining operation on the bay. Cullen believed San Juan Island was rightfully in the orbit of the county and thus the HBC operation had to pay its due. Being an Irishman full of spite for the English, he approached the issue with enthusiasm.

Starting in October 1854, Sheriff Ellis Barnes four times visited the island and ordered Griffin to pay $80.33 in back taxes or face a sheriff's sale, which would be conducted on the beach under his very nose. Griffin refused so Barnes posted tax sale notices in December and proceeded to the beach (presumably Grandma's Cove, which is just below the Belle Vue Sheep Farm site) to conduct an auction. No buyers appeared, Barnes went away and Griffin felt confident that he had seen the last of the sheriff. He was wrong.

An "armed party" composed of Cullen, Barnes, coal company manager (and county judge) Edmund Fitzhugh and five other prospective "bidders" in three rowboats landed on the beach on March 30, 1855. By some accounts it required the better part of two nights and one day at the oars to reach the island. Again they ordered Griffin to pay, and when he refused they rowed off, but only a short distance. They returned after midnight and spent the next several hours rounding up breeding rams on the prairie. They then built a makeshift pen on the beach, from which they completed a starlight auction. Forty-nine breeding rams were "sold," with Cullen buying a dozen for his personal use at 50 cents to one dollar a head. However, the Americans did not bring vessels enough to match their ambitions. In desperation they commandeered an Indian canoe and tried to coax the rams into it. The result was predictable. Deputies were butted, the canoe foundered and several rams galloped across the black prairie with Americans in stumbling pursuit.[11]

Somehow Griffin missed the racket. He got up as usual at dawn and left his cabin to check on one of the herds. He hadn't been out long when he was approached by an Indian boy bearing a hastily scrawled note from one of his herdsmen. The Americans had penned a flock of breeding rams, 34 of which had already been driven down to the beach. Another 24 sheep also were sold, sight unseen, he was advised, presumably to be snatched later "...I imagine by stealth."

Griffin rounded up several Kanakas and ran to the makeshift pen. After releasing the remaining animals, he scrambled down the bluff to the beach to stop the Americans. The boats already were pulling away with the rams aboard. Griffin and one man beat through the surf to the gunwales and attempted to untie the cords securing the animals. Three of the frustrated Americans, all armed, turned and pushed the HBC men away. Griffin and his assistant made another attempt, whereupon "...one of them drew from his belt a Revolver Pistol, which the moment I saw I expostulated with them, telling them I could not possibly contend against such a force... Seeing no other recourse I immediately left the spot. They as quickly left in two boats and one canoe."[12]

The American Sumas *Vidette* saw it differently. In its "eyewitness" version, the sheep buyers were leading the rams to the beach when "Griffin charged down the hill accompanied by about twenty Kanakas, who were armed with knives, and ordered that the sheep be cut loose. Dramatically, Sheriff Barnes ordered his men to protect the property 'in the name of the United States.' Since Barnes's men were armed with revolvers, the Kanakas retired and shortly afterward six of them in a canoe, started across the channel for Victoria."

One of the Americans spotted what he thought to be the *Beaver*, clearing the harbor at Victoria seven miles off.

> We did not wish to be taken prisoners and lie in jail until the boundary question could be settled by the two governments; we loaded about one-half of the sheep into our boats and "lit out." We were all worn out from loss of sleep and hard work, the tide was running very strong against us, our boats were heavily loaded, but we bent to the oars and like Wellington at Waterloo, prayed for 'night or Blucher to come to our relief...[13]

Griffin bent to the oars himself to report in Victoria the "theft" of the rams.

Douglas immediately complained to Governor Stevens, who once again learned of a San Juan action after the fact. Stevens disapproved of the ram auction but felt compelled to back Americans in asserting their rights south of the 49th parallel, disputed islands or not. Douglas also reported the incident to the Foreign Office. And once again, he neglected to define what he meant by "British property." The wronged party, he wrote, was not the Hudson's Bay Company, but Charles Griffin, a British subject "who had been menaced with violence and put in danger of his life."

This "exceedingly annoying affair" was especially frustrating to Douglas because the HBC could not muster the wherewithal to apprehend the Americans, even though the *Beaver*, the Company's legendary steamer, gave chase. The Americans were armed with six-shooter revolvers, while the HBC men carried single-shot, smoothbore North West Trade guns. Douglas reported 45 rams stolen, with 11 "having escaped" during the loading carnival.

It was July before British envoy Crampton made a claim on the United States on behalf of the HBC. According to his figures the Americans owed: £650 for 34 rams; £650:13 for 267 ewes and 142 lambs; £500 for the hire of the *Beaver*; and £1,000 for incidental losses for a grand total of £2,990:13—altogether about $15,000.[14]

All items of claim, aside from the rams, were condemned as "fraudulent and unfounded" by the writer of the account in the House documents. Douglas was not satisfied and wrote yet another letter of complaint to Lord John Russell, again neglecting to state that the wronged party was the HBC. This time he was called on it. Russell reminded Douglas that in November 1853 he had stated that the San Juan Islands should remain a "de facto" dependency of Vancouver Island, unoccupied by any whites except the fishing station. But the attached report from Griffin indicated a major agricultural operation on the island. The two statements did not gel and Douglas and the HBC were chided for masking their activities, and then asking for compensation as private citizens rather than as a corporation with a colonial charter.

Douglas apologized profusely in his next correspondence, admitting that he had "omitted to give information on certain points."[15]

On the American side, Secretary of State Marcy responded to the affair by instructing Governor Stevens to lay off:

> The President has instructed me to say to you that the officers of the territory should abstain from all acts, on the disputed grounds, which are calculated to provoke any conflict, so far as it can be done without implying the concession to the authorities of Great Britain of an exclusive right over the premises. The title ought to be settled before either party should attempt to exclude the other by force or exercise complete and exclusive sovereign rights with the fairly disputed limits. Application will be made to the British government to interpose with its local authorities on the Northern borders of our territory to abstain from like acts of

exclusive ownership, with an explicit understanding that any forbearance on either side to assert the rights respectively claimed shall not be to any concession to the adverse party.[16]

He followed this with a letter to Crampton on July 17 admitting to "some apprehension that a collision may take place between our citizens and British subjects in regard to the occupation of the disputed points along the line between Washington Territory and the British Possession on the north of it."[17]

He assured the Crampton that he would notify Stevens to use discretion, adding that he hoped the British would write a similar missive to Douglas. Crampton agreed and said he had dispatched copies of the letter to the Governor General of British North America, to George Simpson of HBC and by October, to Douglas.

The so-called "Marcy Letter" was thenceforth carried in the vest pocket of every British official in the old Oregon Country to be used as a club against any overreaching Yankee. However, while this "hands-off" message was recognized as the continuing policy of the U.S., Douglas did not feel bound to it, insisting to the end that the San Juans were British possessions and the U.S. had no rights nor legal claim to them.

The Royal Navy agreed in spirit with Douglas. The Pacific Station commander in 1855 was Rear Admiral H. W. Bruce. In his view the "serious difficulty" in the Northwest was "owing to the grasping spirit and habits of the neighboring Americans." The Admiralty urged caution, primarily because the U.S., at least in spirit, supported the Russians in the Crimea. But Bruce also was advised in 1856 to move his ships from Central America to Vancouver Island to secure British interests in case American filibusters made a move on British possessions.[18]

If it accomplished anything other than satisfying County Commissioner Cullen's Anglophobia, the Barnes incident prompted the U.S. Congress finally to move on appropriating money to pay for a boundary commission, which the British had proposed as far back as 1848. The money was allocated on Aug. 11, 1856, whereupon Archibald Campbell was appointed commissioner, with a chief astronomer and surveyor assigned to assist him in marking the boundary between the Rocky Mountains and the Pacific. The respective commissioners by agreement were supposed to exchange their instructions. But British commissioner Capt. James Prevost's orders included a caveat not intended for Campbell's eyes. Prevost was directed to press for the Rosario Strait, and failing that, to seek another channel within the archipelago that might conform to the language of the treaty. Above all,

> ...her Majesty's Government therefore desire that you should use your utmost efforts to induce the American commissioner to assent to the view which Her Majesty's Government have taken of the case.[19]

Prevost's position had been spelled out for him before a single measurement had been taken. Marcy's marching orders to Campbell were hardly less partisan, but they were not withheld from the British. When Campbell finally saw the secret verbiage two years later he decided that the water boundary proceedings had been prejudiced from the start.

The primary British argument for Rosario Strait was that it ran directly south from the 49th parallel through the Strait of Georgia, thus satisfying the language if not the spirit of the Treaty of Oregon. As early as 1846, British warships regularly used the Rosario Strait over the Haro Strait as a matter of policy, hoping to reinforce the British claim. The American position, as postulated by Campbell, was that if one drew a line directly south from the middle of the Strait of Georgia, it would run directly through the Haro Strait.

Prevost also was told to push for an accommodation on Point Roberts, that strange comma of land that dips below the 49th parallel from the British Columbia mainland into U.S. territorial waters. Most importantly for the British, "quiet possession" of Vancouver's Island was to be maintained, which Prevost interpreted as keeping the Americans away from Victoria's back porch, i.e. San Juan Island. That aim was reflected in all that passed from his lips or flowed from his pen over the next three years. San Juan would form a "wall of defence," he wrote, protecting Vancouver Island and the R.N. anchorage at Esquimalt.

The United States Board of Engineers in 1858 likewise concluded that "by establishing a military and naval station at Griffin Bay, on the southeastern shore of San Juan Island, she shall be able to overlook those inner waters equally with Great Britain from Esquimalt Harbor, and thus counterbalance the preponderance she is seeking to establish."

Prevost and Campbell met six times between June and December 1857, and to no one's surprise could not agree on a water boundary. Seeking a way to end dispute and continue to guard Victoria's flank, Prevost in November 1857 proposed President's and San Juan channels—soon to be called the "Middle Channel"—which divide San Juan Island and its satellites from Orcas and Shaw islands. This would award all the islands except San Juan to the United States.

Campbell declined.

Those who knew anything about the dynamics of Douglas, Isaac Stevens, or the land-hungry American miners trickling down from the diggings up the Fraser River Valley knew the climate was ripe for serious trouble.

For while letters were being written and surveys taken, the U.S. Revenue agents continued tabulating property at Belle Vue Sheep Farm. Between 1855 and 1859, taxes were assessed (but not collected) on the HBC. As of May 20, 1859, the HBC had 4,500 sheep, 40 cattle, 5 yoke of oxen, 35 horses and 40 hogs, plus 80 fenced acres under cultivation with oats, peas, and potatoes. Griffin had 19 employees, three of whom were naturalized American citizens who actually voted in the territorial election. There were 29 settlers altogether.

No Americans settled on the island until several frustrated miners drifted over from the Fraser River diggings between the summer of 1858 and January 1859. Indian fears had heretofore kept them away. For example, in April 1858 Deputy Collector of Customs Paul K. Hubbs, Jr., was shot at by a party of Clallams from the Olympic Peninsula encamped on the island. Capt. Granville O. Haller, commander of Co. I, Fourth Infantry at Fort Townsend, crossed the strait with a small guard to "capture the offenders." Griffin had helped Hubbs escape and was pleased to see Haller and his men. The Clallam fled.

Then in late February 1859, Griffin wrote Douglas that a party of Americans from Victoria had been there over a 10-day period surveying and laying out land in hopes of establishing preemption claims pending a U.S. takeover of the islands. A Capt. C. L. Denman and B.C. Gillette directed the surveying. Griffin reported he had heard Denman talking about bringing lumber because he wanted to buy "Webber's house" and finish it.

Douglas was aware of the enterprise and wrote the colonial office that he was continuing to regard San Juan Island as a dependency of Vancouver Island as per his instructions of Sept. 21, 1854, and he had appointed Griffin Justice of the Peace. Griffin's operation until recently had been "general and complete" as well as undisturbed by Americans. However, Douglas now feared that as a result of the surveys the "whole island will soon be occupied by a squatter population of American citizens if they do not receive an immediate check."

> ...This movement has, I have no doubt, been commenced by some designing person exciting and working upon the minds of the ignorant masses with

the view of hastening the settlement of the Boundary
Question and fortifying the claims of the United
States Government. The course is one full of danger,
and I fear that HM Govt. would not approve of my
adopting measures for the summary and forcible
ejection of squatters, while the sovereignty remains
avowedly in dispute; at the same time circumstances
may call for decisive action.[20]

Douglas wrote the new territorial governor, Richard Gholson,
proposing that Americans and British join together in ejecting
squatters until the boundary was settled. But he was also prepared
to unilaterally protect British interests. Two months later Douglas
received a dispatch from Colonial Secretary Lord Lytton. He was
astonished to read that Lytton not only shared his views, but also
had stressed that possession of the San Juan Islands was "essential
to British interests." The governor was ordered to "warn off"
squatters attempting to settle on British Dominions on San Juan
Island and maintain British rights by exercise of "civil power."

By taking this position the crown was courting the very trouble
it sought to avoid; for the territorial government in Olympia could
likewise view the HBC as an "alien squatter." Even more critical,
the colonial secretary's instructions ignored the Marcy agreement
of 1855.

Whose laws would be obeyed?

On May 12, Richard Bickerton Pemell Lyons, the 2nd Viscount
(Lord) Lyons, the new British envoy in Washington City, contacted
Secretary of State Lewis Cass. Pending the results of the ongoing
boundary survey, U.S. citizens should be restrained from settling
on San Juan Island, Lyons wrote. No mention was made of the
HBC sheep farm as the only British interest or of how Americans
could cause a local "collision."[21]

Charles Griffin's rail back pig had the answer to that.

Chapter 6

THE PIG INCIDENT

Lyman Cutlar warned Charles Griffin several times about the Company pig that was rooting up potatoes in his truck garden. Actually, it was a Berkshire boar, and contrary to local folklore, no record exists that it was ever a prize animal worth $100, an enormous sum in 1859. The name is more romantic than the animal, as Berkshire boars were commonly known on the frontier as "railbacks." They were then (and continue to be) renowned for rooting.

So much myth has grown up around this incident that visitors to San Juan Island National Historical Park continue to ask: "Who ate the pig?" And they wonder why two great nations would be willing to go to war over such an absurdity.

Cutlar arrived on San Juan Island in April 1859, according to a sworn deposition he gave later that year in Whatcom County superior court. He was 25 at the time, a failed miner from the United States looking for a place to "winter in" with his Indian wife and child. He had claimed the standard 160-acre homestead under preemption laws, though none applied to the disputed islands at that time. His opposite, Belle Vue Sheep Farm agent Charles Griffin, maintained that Cutlar was squatting on more like a third of an acre. Squatting is a derogatory expression used by those who own a lot of land to describe those who want to scratch out a living on a little piece of it.[1]

The "farm" was in the path of Griffin's main sheep-run that led to other sheep stations dotting the island from the Home Prairie on the island's southern reach to Roche Harbor on the northern end. According to several descriptions, it was a humble place with a garden that, as Griffin stated, was "imperfectly enclosed" by a crude fence. Most accounts describe the fence as having three sides. San Juan Island historian Boyd Pratt theorizes that the "enclosure" amounted to lines of stacked rocks fashioned by Cutlar's Indian wife, because that is how the Coast Salish women delineated their family camas root plots. Rocks, split rail, whatever, we'll never really know. Accounts given 40 to 50 years after the fact also have Cutlar rowing 40 miles to and from Port Townsend across the Strait of Juan de Fuca to buy seed potatoes. He then lugged them up the hill from today's Grandma's Cove, scene of the sheep incident, to about a mile and half from Belle Vue Sheep Farm before putting them in the ground.

Cutlar was not the only Yankee trying Griffin's patience. Others had taken advantage of the work of the self-proclaimed American surveyors in Victoria and were squatting about the prairies where Griffin grazed his sheep or encamped on Griffin Bay.

Griffin was growing more exasperated and he told Governor Douglas so:

> There are now upwards of 16 squatters who have recently come and established themselves on various parts of the island, all claiming to be Citizens of the United States and they have one and all taken up claims and making improvements/a log cabin and a potato patch/ on the most valuable prairies I have in possession of my herdsmen and stock.[2]

One settler had the temerity to land 20 or more head of cattle, the agent added. Griffin raised sheep, which required ample acreage to be profitable and now those lands were being carved up by a bunch of no-account miners trying to scratch out subsistence until something better came along. The simple fact was that the Americans were trespassers. The governor was going to have to do something about it.

That was Griffin's view in so many words. As for the facts, all we have are letters from Griffin and A.G. Dallas and a sworn affidavit from Cutlar.

Because of Cutlar's insufficient mystery fence, Griffin's cattle and pigs had "free access" to the potato patch. "One of the pigs, a very valuable boar, he shot this morning at some distance outside of this same patch and complains the animal was destroying this crop," Griffin stated in letter to Douglas, written that very day. His Belle Vue journal account was more succinct: "An American shot one of my pigs for trespassing!!!"[3]

Cutlar visited Griffin to confess the shooting and proceeded to offer "a remuneration which was so insignificant it only adds insult to injury, and likewise used the most insulting and threatening language and openly declared that he would shoot my cattle if they trespassed near his place."

Griffin wrote that Cutlar also said he "would just as soon shoot me as he would a hog if I trespassed on his claim," which prompted Griffin to retort that Cutlar had no right to squat on the island, "much less in the centre of the most valuable sheep run I have on the island."[4]

Cutlar countered that he had received assurances from American authorities in Washington Territory that he and all other Americans squatting or taking up claims on San Juan Island would be protected and their claims recognized as being established on American soil.

Lyman Cutlar gave his own account on Sept. 7, 1859, in the Whatcom County courthouse. He also wrote a letter to U.S. Deputy Collector of Customs Paul K. Hubbs, Jr.[5]

In each, Cutlar claimed he repeatedly drove off Griffin's "black Boar" and that the company was aware of it. He shot the hog on June 15, 1859, after being awakened by the laughter of Jacob, a Hawaiian herdsman—or as Cutlar termed him, "a colard man"—in Griffin's employ. [6] Cutlar followed the Hawaiian's gaze and saw the hog "up to his old game." Outraged by "...the independence of the Negro, knowing as he did my previous loss," Cutlar rushed into his cabin, reemerged with his rifle and shot the hog.[7] After awhile he felt badly about it and went to see Griffin and reported that he shot the pig in a "moment of irritation." He then offered to replace the animal or have Griffin select three men to determine a fair price. That's when Griffin told him the animal was worth $100.

"Mr. Griffin flew in a passion and said it is no more than I expected," Cutlar reported, "for you Americans are a nuisance on the island and you have no business here and I shall write Mr. Douglas and have you removed."

Cutlar replied, "I came here to settle for shooting your hog, not to argue the right of Americans on the island for I consider it American soil."

That evening (some say it was the next day) Griffin went to Cutlar's place accompanied by Dr. William Tolmie, founder of the Puget Sound Agricultural Company; Vancouver Council Member Donald Fraser; and Alexander Grant Dallas, governor of the Hudson's Bay Company west of the Rockies and Douglas's son-in-law. Dallas did the talking, according to Cutlar.

In a very "supercilious" manner Dallas asked Cutlar "how he dared to do it." Cutlar replied that he dared to do whatever he wanted and had no cause to feel guilty. He thought he was being virtuous by confessing the act and offering to pay, as the animal was so "worthless" that Griffin would not have missed it anyway. Dallas reminded Cutlar that he was on British soil and if he did not pay $100 he would have to go with them to Victoria; that the *Beaver* even then was awaiting them with a "possy" on board.

Cutlar snorted that he would not pay $100 for an animal that was not worth $10. If they brought their posse he would have his friends resist them. "I then told Mr. Dallas to crack his whip and left them," Cutlar wrote. As they rode off, Cutlar said they shouted back, "You will have to answer for this hereafter."

Dallas remembered it differently when he wrote Brig. Gen. William Selby Harney, commander of the U.S. Army Department of Oregon, on May 10, 1860[8]

According to Dallas, he and his associates (Tolmie and Fraser) dropped in on Griffin the afternoon of June 15. Dallas told Harney that they traveled to San Juan that day on the *Beaver* and found Griffin still seething.[9] They may have suggested a soothing horseback ride or perhaps it was "let's go up there and scare the bastard away." No one wrote it down.

In any case, the three approached Cutlar's dwelling, which Dallas described as a "hut or tent" adjoining "...what has been dignified by the name of his farm," which turned out to be "a very small patch of potatoes, partially fenced on three sides and entirely open on the fourth." It would be a virtual impossibility to keep more than 5,000 head of sheep and other ranging farm animals out of such a flimsy cantonment, he claimed.

Most critically the hog was not shot in the patch, Dallas contended, but in the woods bordering Cutlar's property. This shed an entirely different light on the matter as it was considered a capital offense to kill or rustle another man's livestock on the frontier. However:

> No demand of $100 or any sum of money was made upon him, nor did I threaten to apprehend him and take him to Victoria. On the contrary, I stated distinctly that I was a private individual and could not interfere with him.[10]

The Hudson's Bay Company had shown remarkable forbearance, all things considered, he added, despite his having given "scant notice" of the incident that summer.

Which brings us to Hubbs, the deputy collector of customs. He was probably the first person Cutlar told about the incident—the man who baited the lion with his blow-by-blow account to Harney.

Hubbs was a Tennessean with a genteel background. His father, Paul K. Hubbs, Sr., was a lawyer, former plantation owner, and a friend of Andrew Jackson, who once appointed him ambassador to the court of King Louis Philippe of France. The California Gold Rush pulled the entire family west. Following a bitter family dispute, which involved Paul Jr.'s loyalty to a mining camp rowdy named "Texas Jack," he abandoned the gold fields first for Honolulu, then Fort Vancouver. From there he drifted north to live, he said, among the Haida, with whom he claimed to have participated in their raids on other groups—acts which usually involved taking slaves and chopping off heads—before coming south in 1855-56 to fight for Washington Territory against the Klickitats and Nisqually in the White River War. The war availed him the opportunity to rub elbows with a lot of important people, which, combined with a considerable verbal ability, resulted in his being appointed deputy collector of customs on San Juan Island in April 1857. The younger Hubbs must have made peace with the family because Paul K. Hubbs, Sr. was living in Port Townsend at the time of the pig incident. The elder Hubbs was to become a political force in Washington Territory, being elected to the legislature and to the Board of Regents of the new University of Washington.[11]

As the ranking (and only) U.S. official on the island, the younger Hubbs took it upon himself to fire off, on June 23, a dispatch to his boss, Customs Collector Morris H. Frost. In the letter, actually dated June 2—*before* the incident—Hubbs complained vigorously about the Hudson's Bay Company, whose actions were "odious and intolerable." He frantically urged that either the boundary dispute be quickly settled or that "a large military force" be landed to protect American settlers.

Curiously enough, when Hubbs gave his affidavit at the Whatcom County Courthouse, the same day that Cutlar gave his, he offered only the bare facts with no embellishment. The deputy collector of customs swore, under oath, that he only told Harney what Cutlar told him and then dictated a dispassionate account much as a newspaper reporter would cover a city council meeting.

More than 30 years later Hubbs recalled that after the incident he rowed more than 20 miles to Fort Bellingham. There he met with his old White River War buddy, Capt. George Edward Pickett, the post commander, and told him Cutlar's story. Pickett assured Hubbs that he would relate the incident in detail when Harney inspected the fort in early July.[12]

Hubbs claimed that Pickett was true to his word, but Harney insisted that July 9, the day he visited San Juan Island, was the first he'd heard of the pig. Pickett never wrote of it and no official account is known to exist. The only other person who could have called his meeting into question was Pickett's then-second lieutenant at Fort Bellingham, James Forsyth. But in 1892 Forsyth, a brigadier general by then, was still trying to explain why his troops killed 150 Sioux men, women, and children at the "Battle" of Wounded Knee two years earlier.[13]

Meanwhile, the Americans on San Juan Island decided a show of support was in order for Lyman Cutlar. Former miners among them were probably bitter over their treatment around the upper Fraser River diggings. Unlike American gold strikes, where miners filed claims for exclusive rights, claims on British lands were reserved for the crown. Douglas not only stringently followed this rule but also forced the miners to pay a monthly fee and prohibited American retailers or ship owners from doing business in British territory. This incensed former Washington Territory Gov. Isaac Stevens, now a delegate for the territory to the U.S. House of

Representatives. When the gold strike turned out to be marginal, Stevens and the miners gave up, but they did not forget.

The American settlers on San Juan Island decided to show national solidarity by throwing an old-fashioned flag-raising party on the Fourth of July. Charles McKay in 1908 still remembered the celebration that preceded Harney's visit. All 14 Americans gathered at Hubbs's log cabin, about 100 yards on the rise above Belle Vue Farm.

"...We passed a resolution that each one of us had to make a speech," McKay recalled. In the course of the speechmaking a Welshman among the Americans, and no lover of the English, pointed out that the squatters should be independent of Great Britain.[14]

Hubbs also recalled the ceremony, but with considerably more detail, both in his 1892 Seattle *Post-Intelligencer* story and again in the Friday Harbor newspaper in 1909, a year before his death. The pole erected in front of his cabin was 55 feet high, and the flag soared to the masthead amidst "showers of bullets, and not withstanding its ducking and dodging was struck in its starry night, but 'got there all the same.'"

The Americans decided to leave the flag where it was—presumably near the site of the future redoubt, where it could be viewed by Charles Griffin and hopefully fellow Americans pushing up the strait.

Griffin took note and promptly raised the Union Jack over his cabin.

So what really happened? Whose account is correct? Hubbs's story of what transpired between Griffin, Dallas and Cutlar is unreliable given his lukewarm affidavit and the exaggerations evident in his newspaper articles. A.G. Dallas either forgot or lied outright to Harney when he claimed no one demanded $100 from Cutlar. He also twisted the truth a bit in claiming scant notice of the affair when on August 5, at the height of the crisis, he wrote a stormy letter to Douglas howling for blood. In the end, it is hard to believe that Dallas could walk away without satisfaction. He probably did threaten Cutlar.[15]

Wherever the truth lies, Dallas's threats to Cutlar were heavy enough to alarm and excite the other Americans on the island— particularly Hubbs.

Chapter 7

WILLIAM SELBY HARNEY

Contrary to what has been written by some 20th century historians, William Selby Harney was not a complete idiot. In fact, he was a skilled frontier army officer. He quelled an Indian uprising, attempted to hammer out a just peace, and did such a good job of it he was actually called out of retirement to offer advice to William Tecumseh Sherman—a man who seldom sought anyone's counsel. Nor was he completely uncultivated. He learned French, married a French woman, and lived abroad for a time.

Harney's problem was an active imagination, occasionally bordering on paranoia. He also had a propensity for focusing on nits and gnats best left to his chiefs of staff or lower ranking line officers. He hated taking orders from superior officers because he believed he had no superiors. He occasionally lied to achieve his ends.

There could not have been a Pig War without him.

Harney was born Aug. 22, 1800, in Haysboro, Tennessee. He was directly commissioned a second lieutenant in the First Infantry in 1818 (as opposed to attending West Point), thanks to the intercession of Andrew Jackson, who was Harney's patron as long as he lived. The influence of Old Hickory manifested itself time and again in Harney's stormy career. Jackson harbored a hatred for the British resulting from a trauma suffered as a boy during the Revolutionary War when a British officer slashed him for not cleaning his boots. Jackson subsequently smashed the British at New Orleans during the War of 1812, and spared no effort to check them on the southeastern frontier, at times without the permission of his government. Harney took notes and soon formed his own pathological hatred for all things British.[1]

Harney was more than six feet tall with blue eyes and red hair that eventually turned silver. As a young man he possessed "tremendous physical strength and endurance," according to Jefferson Davis, who as a young West Point graduate served with Harney on the plains. Davis particularly recalled Harney being a fleet runner who on many occasions bested the Indians in races. In fact, Harney once chased a dog that was tearing up his garden a mile and a half before catching and beating it.[2]

However, from the start he demonstrated a knack for trouble. At his first post—Fort Warren—near Boston, he brashly "took command" of the post when his commanding officer was away, for which he was court-martialed. But thanks to his powerful patron, was acquitted.

He next campaigned against the Winnebagos in 1827, and then against the Sauk and Fox in the Black Hawk War of 1831. He firmly believed the Black Hawk War was justified because the Indians did not follow the letter of the law, even though the law was unjust.

Throughout his professional life he employed the same reasoning, citing the letter of the law against any individual who disagreed with him. In an army composed of officers jealous and distrustful of each other, Harney was not above using the court martial as a means of revenge against his professional adversaries.[3]

When the Second Dragoons were created May 1836 in response to the Seminole uprising, then-Major Harney connived with by-then President Jackson to wrest the lieutenant colonelcy of the unit from the man to whom it already had been assigned. He justified these machinations by developing a reputation for dash and daring, which often resulted in the reckless endangerment of his men. Col. Stephen Watts Kearny of the rival First Dragoons wrote of him:

You know the opinion I have of Colonel Harney, that he has no more brains than a Greyhound. Yet, I consider that by his stupidity and repair in action, he has done more to inject the Indians with a fear of us and the desperate state of their cause, than all the other commanders.[4]

This was borne out in July 1839 when Harney and another small contingent were attacked and 11 of his dragoons were killed. He managed to escape with his slave and eight soldiers, vowing revenge, and was good on his word. Almost two years to the day he caught up with this same group of raiders, killing four and hanging five more following a kangaroo court.

He was in Texas fighting the Comanche when the Mexican War broke out in 1846. Gen. Zachary Taylor—too far away to oversee all matters on his own—gave Harney wide discretionary powers to protect the frontier and enlist volunteers if needed. This Harney did and more, taking it upon himself to raise an "invasion army" with seven volunteer units plus a band of Delaware Indians. Without authorization, he crossed the border, defeated a small Mexican force and occupied the town of Presidio. That's when Gen. John E. Wool ordered him back. Harney disputed the order and took his sweet time—five full days—before returning, leaving behind a company of volunteers whom the Mexicans eventually defeated.

Harney's actions exhibited "extreme imbecility and manifest incapacity," Wool reported to U.S. Army commander, Lt. Gen. Winfield Scott.[5]

Scott took note. When he decided in early 1847 that he needed the Second Dragoons for his push from Vera Cruz to Mexico City, he gave command of the regiment to another officer and ordered Harney to remain behind. Harney protested to his Democratic party patrons in Washington, among them Pres. James Knox Polk, another Tennessean called "Young Hickory" during his election campaign. Harney also refused to obey the order, which resulted in a court martial. But the court martial board was lenient, let him off with a reprimand and permitted him to go to Vera Cruz anyway, much to the mortification of Scott. In the board's judgment, Harney was merely displaying patriotic zeal.

Never known for bipartisanship, Polk wrote that Scott had "arbitrarily and without cause" throttled

> ...One of the most gallant and best officers in the service. He was not under any charges of any kind. He was, however, a Democrat in politics, was one of General Jackson's personal friends, and was appointed by him. I can conceive of no reason but this for the arbitrary and tyrannical conduct of General Scott in doing such gross injustice to this gallant officer.[6]

The president went on to write that Whig officers in Scott's and Taylor's camps had unjustly punished Democrats as well, and he was quite ready to check Scott's "tyrannical" course. He decided to send a letter ordering Harney's reinstatement even before hearing the results of the court martial board. Polk closed by writing: "...I am resolved that Col. Harney shall not be sacrificed to propitiate the personal and political malice of Gen. Scott..."

For all of this vinegar, Harney was just the officer Scott needed to lead his cavalry in Mexico. Harney continued to disobey orders, attacking without authorization Mexican positions outside of Vera Cruz. Scott stormed, but victory took Harney off the hook. He then performed heroically at Cerro Gordo—an entrenched Mexican position about halfway to Mexico City—using his dragoons as shock troops to dislodge Mexican infantry. The action won for him a brevet rank of brigadier general.

He went on to excel in several other minor engagements, though he did not have a prominent role in the final assault on Mexico City, as that was primarily an operation for infantry and artillery forces.

What he did do was hang a group of Irish-American deserters, who, unsatisfied of their lot with the U.S. Army and lacking confidence in the ultimate victory, went over to the Mexicans. With great flair Harney arranged to have the deserters trussed and positioned on the gallows so that they were facing Chapultepec castle in the distance. They were told that when the U.S. flag appeared over Chapultepec, signaling victory, the traps would be sprung one after another, which is exactly what happened. The officer who raised the flag, at least according to legend, was 1st. Lt. George Pickett of the Eighth Infantry.[7]

The upshot of Harney's Mexican service, especially the court martial and the snipes from Scott's staff, was bitterness toward officers whom he perceived to be his tormentors. This, coupled with the Democrat-Whig factionalism, eventually would permeate the officer corps and undermine morale throughout the service. The results were resignations by some of the best officers, among them George McClellan, Isaac Stevens, William Tecumseh Sherman, Thomas "Stonewall" Jackson, and Braxton Bragg. With few skills to attempt anything else, the Harneys and the Picketts stuck around.

Harney was reassigned to Texas and the Second Dragoons after the war, where he helped establish a line of border forts from the Oklahoma panhandle to the Rio Grande. One of these was Fort Gates, where Pickett would spend several years and lose his first wife in childbirth. There is no hard documentary evidence that the men had anything other than a casual relationship in Texas. Harney certainly was not a Pickett patron at that time.

Harney went to France with his wife of 20 years in 1854, but returned the next year to join the fight against the Brule Sioux on the northern plains. The war broke out when 1st Lt. Hugh Fleming, inexperienced on the plains, allowed a fresher second lieutenant to ride into a Sioux camp with a platoon of soldiers and a mountain howitzer to arrest an Indian for stealing a cow. The soldiers and the Sioux chief, Conquering Bear, were killed.[8]

Before leaving on the Brule campaign, Harney was said to
have remarked: "By God, I'm for battle—not peace," an utterance
that came to haunt him a few years later. In September 1855, his
combined infantry and cavalry forces attacked Little Thunder's
camp in a pincer movement at Blue Water Creek. The attack,
relentless pursuit and slaughter of refugees were exacted with a
ferociousness that earned him the name "Mad Bear" from the
Teton Sioux. Other nicknames from the Indians included "The
Butcher," "The Hornet," and "The Big Chief Who Swears."

He was an early proponent of winter campaigning against the
Indians (when they were most vulnerable), a tactic that would be
adopted by Phil Sheridan and executed by George Custer, Nelson
Miles, and others after the Civil War. However, like Miles and
even Custer, Harney could be magnanimous in victory. Despite
his ruthlessness in combat, he possessed a genuine empathy for the
plight of the Plains Indians, as he was to demonstrate in his later
years. He drafted his own peace treaty and cowed the Brules into
signing it, only to have it derailed by the Department of Indian
Affairs. The department had recently come under the aegis of the
civilian Department of the Interior. Harney did not view Indians
as equals, but he thought it unseemly to cheat a defeated people
who owned nothing but the clothes on their backs. He suspended
the activities of one crooked agent and sent him packing back to
Washington. The agent whined to Indian Affairs Commissioner
George W. Manypenny, who conspired with Congress to have
Harney's treaty rejected. Harney believed civilian efforts to
administrate Indian policy were doomed to failure. A strong, but
just hand—free of the corruption of Indian agents—was a better way
to go in his view and he made his opinions widely known.

But before a major confrontation arose Harney was sent to
Kansas, where he supervised the general elections and kept the
peace in that troubled state. In 1858 he was promoted to brigadier
general—a general officer died, opening a billet—and out of his job

as commander of the Second Dragoons. He was given the newly created Department of Oregon, where the War Department hoped he could use his skills to bring a quick end to the uprising of the tribes in eastern Washington Territory.

The Department of Oregon had been split off from the once-massive Department of the Pacific, recently under the command of his old nemesis, John E. Wool. Harney's slice encompassed present-day Washington, Idaho, Oregon, and parts of Montana and Wyoming. Spokanes, Palouses, Yakamas, and other Northern Plains groups in today's eastern Washington state still seethed over Isaac Stevens' whirlwind treaties and had risen in revolt. The murders of two miners brought the army. In May 1858, the Indians ambushed a 164-man cavalry and infantry contingent under Lt. Col. Edward Steptoe who abandoned his artillery—anathema for any commander—and slipped through the Indian lines under cover of darkness.

But before Harney cleared the Isthmus of Panama, regular army units led by Ninth Infantry commander Col. George Wright and Maj. Robert Garnett defeated the Indians in running battles in eastern and central Washington respectively. Harney arrived in time to make the peace with the help of the Jesuit Father Joseph de Smet. He also reopened the Walla Walla Valley to resettlement and set about making improvements to roads and river crossings.

However, without a serious challenge to occupy his mind, Harney lapsed into old patterns, imagining intrigue and insubordination where none existed. The junior officers at Vancouver Barracks bore the brunt of his wrath, frequently being placed under arrest for minor infractions. The commander of the U.S. Army intervened on the side of the junior officer in one case, pronouncing Harney's act "not discipline, but vengeance!"

It was in this frame of mind that William Selby Harney undertook his inspections of the northern forts in July 1859.

Chapter 8

THE PETITION

San Juan Island can be especially spectacular in July. The golden prairies on the Strait of Juan de Fuca shimmer in clear marine sunlight, while heavily forested uplands on Griffin Bay give onto saltwater marshes and rocky beaches teeming with shorebirds. Just off the western shore, orca whales engage in the timeless pursuit of salmon. Anyone with time on his hands and access to a steamer would be tempted to drop anchor.

But according to William Selby Harney, it was the American flag on Paul K. Hubbs' pole that caught his eye around noon on Saturday July 9, 1859, as he steamed up the Strait of Juan de Fuca bound for Admiralty Inlet and Port Townsend aboard the USS *Massachusetts*.[1]

The general had been on a tour of the Department of Oregon's northern outposts, which included Forts Bellingham and Townsend and the army camp at Semiahmoo on the 49th parallel, headquarters of the British and American boundary commissions. His last stop had been in Victoria on July 8-9, where he personally thanked Governor Douglas for helping American settlers during recent northern Indian raids. Ironically, in weeks past Harney had been demonstrating his Anglophobia by so harassing the remaining HBC operation at Fort Vancouver that the factor had protested to the home government. But Harney could not visit the area and not pay his respects to a governor who had been so generous and loyal to fellow members of the Anglo-Saxon race. The two apparently discussed a wide range of topics—with the notable exceptions of the boundary dispute, San Juan Island and stray pigs.[2]

According to various accounts, the *Massachusetts* rounded Cattle Point and heaved to a stop off the Hudson's Bay Company dock on Griffin Bay. Charles Griffin checked his watch and made an entry in his journal. It was 1 p.m.[3]

Harney was rowed ashore, where he was met on the beach by a contingent of American citizens. Among them was Charles McKay, a blacksmith who, after 1910, would claim the distinction of being the last survivor of Pig War. Hubbs also was along, having been the one who spotted the ship and rushed to run the flag up the pole.

McKay remembered "...seeing such a strange thing as a man of war coming into our harbor, we all went to see him land. So he said 'Are you Americans?'"[4]

"Yes."

"Is that your flag?"

"Yes."

"What are you doing here?"

Hubbs quickly told the story of the "hog scrape," while Harney strode purposefully up the hill from the dock. When the group reached the crest of the rise about where the redoubt would be built, the general spotted Belle Vue Sheep Farm and decided to leave. Barely 10 minutes had gone by and Hubbs probably knew he would have to talk fast and throw in a little spice to press his case. The Americans scrambled down the hill, Hubbs chattering away. Did the general know that northern Indians raided the islands last summer and fall, murdering and beheading two Americans on San Juan? It happened right under the noses of the vaunted Royal Navy in Victoria. True. HMS *Satellite*, the RN's newest and biggest steam corvette (21 guns), had captured or run off several war canoes in the strait in recent months. But it was hardly enough to make a dent.

Speaking of British ships: Did the general know that the *Beaver* brought Messrs. Dallas, Fraser, and Tolmie of the Hudson's Bay Company to arrest Lyman Cutlar, an American citizen? Did he know that the Hudson's Bay Company considered the Americans "trespassers" on crown lands and planned to evict them? Hubbs capped his tail by asking Harney to "...send us a company of soldiers to protect us from the Hudson's Bay Company's threats to take us prisoners," according to McKay.[5]

History blurs here. McKay claimed that Harney suggested the citizens draft a petition asking for protection from the northern Indians, although no record exists of his involvement. At any rate, Hubbs drafted and submitted the petition to the Americans on the island on July 11. Signed by 22 American citizens including Lyman Cutlar, it sought military protection against Northerners, and then *commended* the Hudson's Bay Company for helping American settlers in time of need—a line that somehow slipped Harney's mind weeks later. According to Henry Crosbie, then U.S. civil magistrate for Whatcom County, this was the second petition for troops submitted to Harney by the San Juan Americans. The first, seeking 20 soldiers, was sent in May following a raid by northern Indians on the Smith Island lighthouse, "which the general, with the usual reluctance of military officers to credit the alarms of citizens, withheld." Many of the recent Indian problems were restated in the petition, but oddly enough, nothing was said about the pig incident or threats of the Hudson's Bay Company. This could be taken as strong evidence that Harney coached the settlers. After all, marauding Indians offered more justification for placing troops on the island than a dead pig.[6]

Looking back over the years, Hubbs described Harney going back to the *Massachusetts* and firing a salute to the American flag waving over the log cabin. The general then:

> ...dismissed his staff officers, and in private communications the arrangements were made

which led to the occupation of the island by the
United States troops and hastened the long-delayed
question of sovereignty which took a Jackson or
Harney to consummate.[7]

Hubbs probably meant Old Hickory's illegal march into Florida
in 1818, when he captured the Spanish city of Pensacola without
the sanction of the president or the U.S. Congress. In the process
Jackson hanged two British subjects for "spying." He was the man
on horseback doing what politicians seldom had the nerve to do,
and Harney was cut of the same cloth, at least in Hubbs' estimation.

Hubbs maintained that Harney promptly steamed back to Fort
Bellingham to see Pickett, whereupon the two Southerners plotted
strategy. McKay also recalled this side trip, but the ship's log indicates
that the *Massachusetts* lumbered across to Fort Townsend and thence
up Puget Sound. The general returned to Fort Vancouver on July
13 after anchoring at Olympia, where he met with former Governor
Stevens. He then traveled overland to the Cowlitz River landing.

On the 18th Harney dispatched Special Orders No. 72, directing
Captain George E. Pickett to abandon Fort Bellingham and occupy
San Juan Island.

The next day he wrote the War Department to explain himself.
This letter is more revealing of Archibald Campbell's prejudices—
not to mention Isaac Stevens' views—than it was of current boundary
facts. Ten days earlier at Semiahmoo the commissioner had
presumably given the general a briefing on the dispute that likely
included his frustrations with the apparent duplicity of Prevost and
the British. Harney opened with a rehash of Manifest Destiny, as
it applied to the Oregon Country before the Treaty of 1846. The
British did not belong on Vancouver Island and environs because
they could not attract British settlers, he wrote. Already more Yanks
than Brits lived in Victoria and with "pressing necessities of our
commerce on this coast" the British would have to give ground. He

then stumbled into the realm of sociology, declaring it "common knowledge" that the British were "too exacting" to colonize so close to an American possession. More critical, Vancouver Island was as important in its proximity to the United States as Cuba was to Florida. He echoed the inflated estimations of San Juan Island's strategic value, as expressed by the U.S. Topographical Engineers report filed five years earlier.[8] His description is remarkably similar to Capt. James Prevost's version:

> SJI contains good water, timber and grass and is the most commanding position we posses on that Sound—the most suitable point to prevent the northern Indians from visiting the settlements to the south of it. At the Southeastern end one of the finest harbors on the coast is to be found, completely sheltered, offering the best location for a naval station on the Pacific Coast.[9]

The general's central reason for dispatching Pickett surfaced when he turned his attention to the settlers' petition and the Hudson's Bay Company. Despite the petition's emphasis on northern Indians, Harney made only passing reference to them, dwelling instead on the pig incident and the harassment of Cutlar. Northern Indians were a problem, but the settlers needed protection especially from the "oppressive interference of the authorities of the Hudson's Bay Company at Victoria..."[10] This was fueled by Hubbs, who revealed the depth of his resentment of the HBC—and offers a hint of his July 19 discussion with Harney— in his June 23 letter to U.S. Collector of Customs Morris H. Frost:

> The monopoly of the Hudson's Bay Co. is intolerable & odious to the (American) settlers. Collision is imminent and that of such a character as may produce the most serious result to the two Governments. It is in the desire to prevent this and in what I deem a

legitimate discharge of my duty that I forward this to
you Sir who have some Knowledge of the threatened
difficulties that can only be avoided by a settlement
of the Boundary question, or if not settled the
placing immediately (sic) a large military force to
protect the American settlers from being carried off
at will of the Hudson's Bay Co., and shut up in the
prison of the British Colony somewhat worse than
the Dartmoor was in 1813.[11]

Harney was particularly outraged that "...Mr. Dallas, son-in-
law of Governor Douglas, came to island in the British sloop-of-
war *Satellite*, and threatened to take one of the Americans by force to
Victoria, for shooting a pig of the company." Over the next several
weeks Harney would persist in claiming a warship brought Dallas
to the island to punish Cutlar, despite the fact that Hubbs insisted
he told Harney it was the *Beaver*. It would become "...a necessary part
of Harney's case that a warship brought A.G. Dallas to the island,"
one historian wrote. "...without the supposed use of such a vessel
of war, arguments based on threats of Dallas would not have been
very impressive." Pacific Station records indicated that no warships
called at San Juan between May 7 and July 27.[12]

Harney closed his letter by stressing that he dispatched Pickett
to San Juan Island to "...prevent a repetition of this outrage."
Orders also were sent to Lt. Col. Silas Casey, deputy commander
of the Ninth Infantry Regiment. Since January 1856 Casey had
commanded all U.S. military forces from the Puget Sound to the
49th parallel from his base at Fort Steilacoom, south of today's
Tacoma, Washington.

Harney neglected to mention that Pickett and Casey each
received a different version of the order and were not copied to one
another. While Pickett was directed to abandon Fort Bellingham
and reestablish his company on San Juan Island in a "suitable
position near the harbor at the southeastern extremity," Casey was

ordered to provide support via the *Massachusetts*. The ship, under
lease to the army, would cruise the archipelago and northern
sound and with her 32-pounder naval guns turn back any northern
Indians heading south. But she would first sail to Bellingham, pick
up Company D, drop them at San Juan, and then embark Company
I, Fourth Infantry, at Fort Townsend—20 miles across the Strait of
Juan de Fuca from San Juan Island—and stand by in case hostilities
broke out with the British.

Much has been made of how Casey, a higher-ranking officer,
was reduced to a support role for George Pickett, who was given
independent command over a vast domain. Most of it comes from
San Juan and Secession, a paper delivered to the Loyal Legion of Seattle
in 1896 by Granville Owen Haller. The author was not an unbiased
source. In 1859 he was commander of Company I. Moreover, he
outranked Pickett by time in grade and held a brevet (honorary)
rank of major. But instead of getting the San Juan command he had
been ordered to abandon his post, steam about the straits aboard
the *Massachusetts* and render assistance if needed to Pickett, whom, by
the tone of his prose, he intensely disliked. His temper already was
shortened by the popular (and unjust) phrase, "Haller's Defeat,"
which in Washington Territory identified one of the opening
engagements of the Indian War of 1855.[13]

Casey's "demotion" also has been cited as key to an intrigue
perpetrated by Harney and Pickett, the two Southerners. One
source on the incident—albeit a dubious one, as he wasn't within
two thousand miles of San Juan Island or even in the army at the
time—was George B. McClellan, Pickett's West Point classmate and
lifelong friend. McClellan claimed that Harney and Pickett nobly
entered a cabal to start a war with Great Britain in hopes it would
unite North and South in common purpose and thereby head off
civil war. Haller debunked McClellan's theory. In his opinion
Pickett and Harney schemed to start a war all right, but with the
far darker motive of distracting the North so the South could

achieve independence. No records exist, in either official or private correspondence, to validate either theory.[14]

In fact, Casey was not subordinated to Pickett. The *Massachusetts* and *Haller* were placed under Casey's command for "better protection and supervision of the waters of Puget Sound." Casey also was given latitude to deviate from the order based upon his considerable military experience. (His textbook on infantry tactics was standard issue in Union Army units during the Civil War.)

It was not unusual for a company commander to exercise independent command on the frontier where regiments rarely assembled as units. Pickett simply relocated his company from Fort Bellingham to San Juan Island for the purpose of providing direct protection to American citizens—something he had been incapable of doing on the mainland. If Haller had landed his troops to reinforce Pickett then he would have assumed command by virtue of his rank, as Casey would do two weeks later. Very much aware of this, Pickett refused Haller's help at every turn.

Meanwhile on San Juan Island, Pickett had been ordered to find a site suitable for four to six companies, preferably in a defensible location. However, when he landed his troops in a driving rain on the morning of Wednesday July 27, Pickett ordered his tents pitched on about 300 square yards of open hillside about 100 yards east of the HBC dock on Griffin Bay, flanked by woodlands. The crest of the hill overlooking today's American Camp prairie was directly in his rear, leaving him vulnerable to naval bombardment.

While the camp was going up, Pickett ordered his second lieutenant, James W. Forsyth, to post a proclamation stating the army's intentions. It was this proclamation, more than the landing of troops, that set off James Douglas. The offending passage read:

> III. This being United States territory, no laws other than those of the United States, nor courts,

except such as are held by virtue of said laws, will be recognized or allowed on this island.[15]

The origin of this proviso remains a mystery. Harney, at least on paper, ordered Pickett to protect American citizens and resist all attempts at interference, by "intimidation or force," by British authorities on Vancouver Island. Any grievances the British had with American citizens were to be handled "under our own laws," Harney specified. The order said nothing about assuming jurisdiction over the entire island.

Pickett's proclamation was posted just in time for the British magistrate, the one-eyed British Army veteran and future Irish peer, John de Courcy, to see it when he arrived from Victoria that very day at 6 p.m. aboard *Satellite*. On rowing out to the ship Griffin learned that de Courcy, until then a notorious Victoria Police Court judge, had replaced him as Justice of the Peace and held a new title of "Stipendiary Magistrate" for the District of San Juan to deal with "complaints of squatters disturbances." These undoubtedly included the pig incident.

De Courcy's appointment—made more than a month before, Douglas later claimed—underscored the governor's confidence in his authority to take action on San Juan Island. Even more, by insisting that de Courcy be transported to the island aboard a ship of war, Douglas presumed the Royal Navy would back him.

De Courcy's instructions, issued July 23, were to restore possession of squatters' properties to HBC, arraign trespassers and collect bail from them to insure they reported to court in Victoria, and seek assistance from naval and military authorities if necessary. Employment of armed forces was to be a last resort. At all times he was to be "most careful to avoid giving any occasion that might lead to acts of violence."

These instructions were read aloud at the HBC flag post the following day (July 28), but not before de Courcy approached

Pickett's camp at 3 p.m. The Irishman, a distant cousin of Capt. Michael de Courcy, the senior Royal Navy officer in Victoria at the time, was neither intimidated by the odds, nor the bizarre nature of his mission. He had, after all, led a band of Turkish guerilla fighters during the Crimean War. De Courcy boldly strode to the camp perimeter and ordered the sentry to point out his commanding officer. Once Pickett was located, de Courcy approached and introduced himself in his official capacity.[16]

Pickett knew precisely who de Courcy was and what he was doing on San Juan. The ubiquitous Hubbs had warned him almost immediately upon the landing that Douglas had appointed a new justice of the peace and other "civil officers" to deal with the Americans.

De Courcy described his initial encounter with Pickett in this July 29 dispatch to Douglas:

> I asked him, 'By what right or for what reason he had landed and occupied this island.' To which he answered that he did not consider that I, or any other person, had the right to ask such a question; but as it was generally known to everyone about, he had no objection to state that he occupied and landed on the island by order of his *Government.* I then informed him that his acts were illegal; that he was trespassing, and that it was my duty to warn him off the premises and island.[17]

Pickett responded by calling over Henry Crosbie, and introducing him as the "Resident Stipendiary Magistrate" of the island for the United States. Crosbie told de Courcy that, having no authority on the island, he would be in serious trouble if he attempted to enforce the law. At this de Courcy excused himself and left to read his commission at the HBC flagpole. He returned to the camp later on and overheard Pickett promise protection

"…to any and every American citizen who might wish to squat on this island. He further said that they had a right to squat on every part of the island."

John de Courcy's commission has been open to debate over the years. Michael de Courcy, the naval officer soon to play a prominent role in the incident, maintained that Douglas appointed his "cousin" in anticipation of Pickett's landing. But Douglas claimed he appointed John de Courcy to enforce British law on San Juan Island because of the unrest caused by the American squatters and then the pig incident. It probably would have better served Douglas to go along with Michael de Courcy's interpretation. By sticking to his story, Douglas revealed that he fully intended to enforce jurisdiction over the island as Harney charged, which, in essence, validated Pickett's landing as a necessary American counterstroke.

This is confirmed by a July 28 letter from A.G. Dallas to Griffin that "in accordance of the wishes of the Governor" Griffin was to lodge a complaint against Cutlar for shooting the boar and for being a trespasser. The latter charge also was to be directed at any other "squatter" on the island, who would presumably be evicted. Dallas then suggested to Griffin that de Courcy seek room and board away from Belle Vue Sheep Farm:

> We are particularly anxious to disconnect ourselves from the Government in the eyes of the world. In the meantime you will charge Major De Courcy, while staying with you at the rate of £100 per annum for board and explain to him that we are actuated by no feeling of inhospitality to him as a private individual. In his public official capacity the Government has no claims on us.[18]

Cutlar, in his September 7 affidavit, stated that he believed a process had been issued and that de Courcy came expressly to arrest him for trespassing on the sheep run. A "Captain Gordon of the constabulary" came to Cutlar's cabin with a posse on the 29th, Cutlar stated, but that he was not at home because he had spent the night in Pickett's camp. Charles McKay, Hubbs and others had urged him to hide and Pickett had promised protection. Cutlar later stated that if Pickett and his soldiers had not been there, he would have been taken to Victoria.[19]

Hubbs's memoir is more imaginative: Pickett, tongue in cheek, suggested to Crosbie that he issue a warrant for Cutlar's arrest and have Hubbs serve it, after which the two would come to the army camp. Hubbs approached Cutlar's cabin the morning of the 28th and told the miner he was under arrest. Cutlar laughed and said, "I surrender." Armed with six shooters, the two negotiated a mile and a half of enemy country and en route encountered "Major De Courcy and two other British officers." A showdown seemed imminent, but the British officers politely stepped aside and allowed the Americans to pass. Hubbs and Cutlar were soon having a whisky and enjoying a laugh with Pickett and company.

Crosbie reported a few weeks later that no process was served. But he also believed the HBC and Victoria government intended to evict all American settlers from the sheep runs, effectively denying them access to arable farmland. He concluded, "...the only inference that can be drawn is had there been no probability of at once an active resistance to the execution of the process the original intention would have been carried out." If John de Courcy had not arrived at Pickett's camp commission in hand, Crosbie wrote, he would have left San Juan Island to Pickett, the squatters and Griffin's sheep. Ironically, as with Webber and Griffin in 1854, Crosbie and de Courcy would become friends and number among the few involved who maintained effective communication. Each would praise the other's restraint.

While conviviality was brewing ashore, Prevost and his boundary commission counterpart, Archibald Campbell, were exchanging amicable visits in the harbor and somehow avoiding the main topic at hand, at least according to the claims of the commissioners. This would come back to haunt them both.[20]

By contrast, despite his bold talk, Pickett had come away a troubled man from his initial encounters with the British. In a letter dated July 27 to Capt. Alfred Pleasonton, Harney's acting adjutant, Pickett groused that HMS *Satellite* had not fired the accustomed ceremonial salute on arrival and that de Courcy and Prevost had not advised him they were coming ashore. The "very great want of courtesy towards us by these 'Bulls'" threatened his authority and did not set well with his considerable ego. "You know I am a peaceable man, but we cannot stand everything." As a result he was going to be firm. "As a matter of course I shall not allow (de Courcy) to take any official action; should he attempt to exercise any authority, I shall at once inform him that I do not recognize him and prohibit the opening of any court except those authorized by U.S. laws." However, this bravado was laced with insecurities as evidenced by his final entreaty to his old Mexican War comrade: "Please, my dear *amigo mio*, tell me anything-*entre nous*-what you think ought to be done."

True enough, the situation seemed certain to escalate and Pickett would soon have his mettle tested by the Royal Navy. The performance of his company over the last three years could hardly have inspired confidence.[21]

Chapter 9

GEORGE PICKETT AND
THE FRONTIER ARMY

Maria Roberts was alone on her farm when the brig *George Emery* dropped anchor in Bellingham Bay on Aug. 26, 1856. A long boat made for shore, full of armed men in blue uniforms. Company D, Ninth Infantry, Capt. George E. Pickett commanding, had arrived from Fort Steilacoom with all of the gear requisite to establishing an army post—including several head of beef and some milk cows.

The captain approached Maria, removed his hat, introduced himself, and then politely informed her that he was going to evict her from her property, tear down her house and build a fort. She and her husband would be paid for the property, of course, after it had been appraised.[1]

This was the long-promised fort for which a federal survey team had visited the bay and selected the site a year before. It was to serve as a deterrent against northern Indian raids and lend the community the essential perception of solidity required to attract capital and people to dig coal. It also would serve notice of a strong American presence to the British in Victoria and only 15 miles to the north on the mainland.

Ninth Infantry deputy commander, Lt. Col. Silas Casey's orders to Pickett on August 16 prescribed that a fortress be established on the Robert's claim at the mouth of the Nooksack River on

Bellingham Bay. Pickett's initial command included 1st Lt. Robert H. Davis, the nephew of Secretary of War (and future Confederate president) Jefferson Davis; 2nd. Lt. Hugh B. Fleming, late of the Brule Sioux War (see Chapter 7), and 57 enlisted men.[2]

At this point—through the commotion of soldiers scurrying about setting up a temporary camp and sailors shoving cows overboard to swim to shore—Maria Roberts could have cared less about northern Indians. The U.S. Government was committing thievery, not the Indians. And she was no shrinking violet either.

This "large, courageous motherly woman of dark complexion" thought nothing of packing a Colt's revolver and hoofing it to town on her own when the Northerners weren't around. With a heavy German accent, she ordered Pickett and his men off her property.

Ever the Southern gentleman, Pickett again courteously informed Maria that she had to leave, that the federal government was claiming the entire plateau—640 total acres—and that she would have to move into town. Nothing doing, she said. Her husband was away and she wasn't going anywhere. She was heavily pregnant and almost due. Unmoved, Pickett next ordered a work party to remove the roof of her home (much as British constables evicted families from their cottages during Ireland's potato famine) and then had her bodily removed to just beyond her property line. There was nothing left for her do but hike the trail to Whatcom and wait for her husband to return.

Charles Roberts indeed had words with Pickett, but to no avail. However, Pickett gave the family permission to rebuild their cabin off federal property on the beach below, where Maria Roberts and her daughter would remain, unmolested, until the government finally relinquished the claim in 1868.

Who was this Capt. George Pickett, with the fancy manners, the English-style accent, and hair that smelled like the women on San Francisco's Barbary Coast?[3]

George Edward Pickett was born on Jan. 25, 1825, at Turkey Island Plantation, Virginia, home to one of the Virginia Tidewater's most respected families—the "Fighting Picketts of Fauquier County." When the family fortunes declined following the Panic of 1837, George was sent to Quincy, Illinois, a Mississippi River town where his maternal uncle, Andrew Johnston, practiced law. Pickett's parents made this arrangement for the expressed purpose of obtaining a West Point appointment for George, who could not compete with others of the Virginia gentry. U.S. Rep. John Todd Stuart, a close friend of his Uncle Andrew (and a kinsman of Mary Todd Lincoln) would bestow the appointment. It was from this connection that Sally Pickett, his third wife and widow, concocted the fiction that Abraham Lincoln had engineered Pickett's appointment in 1842, as Lincoln was Stuart's junior law partner from 1837 to 1841.

It was hoped a little of Uncle Andrew's industry would rub off on the young man, but George was bored with his studies and spent more time fishing the river and learning to play the banjo than he did with the books. Pickett did scrape through the West Point entrance examination and then barely survived the four-year course, managing to graduate 59th, dead last, in the illustrious Class of 1846—a class that included future stars such as George McClellan, Thomas "Stonewall" Jackson and Ambrose Powell Hill (though the latter was held over a year after falling ill). As always, Pickett was quicker with a song or a prank than he was with mathematics or military thought. Indeed, one classmate called him "...a jolly good fellow with fine natural gifts sadly neglected."[4]

Nevertheless, when war broke out with Mexico almost immediately following graduation, Pickett was a brevet second lieutenant in the Eighth Infantry. His regiment included several other Southerners, among them the stolid Capt. James Longstreet and 1st Lt. Lewis Armistead, men with whom Pickett's life would be inexorably entwined for the rest of his career.

In the fall of 1847, George distinguished himself during Winfield Scott's campaign against Mexico City. He was promoted to first lieutenant after showing reckless bravery at Churabusco and was made brevet captain for snatching the regimental colors from a wounded Longstreet and carrying them over the wall during the final assault on Chapultepec Castle.

Following the war he went with the Eighth to Fort Gates, Texas, where in 1851 he brought his new bride, childhood neighbor Sally Minge. Sally and his infant son would die in childbirth a year later.

By June 1855, Pickett was ready for a change and got it when he was assigned as a company commander with the Ninth Infantry regiment, authorized by Congress in March and reforming at Fortress Monroe, Virginia. Once in fighting trim, the unit was to be dispatched to Washington Territory to quell the Indian uprisings and establish peace on the frontier.

Pickett's Indian war was limited. In an all-too-common practice of the time, he was detached from his company in November and sent to Florida for court martial duty. There he would remain until the end of March 1856. By the time he crossed the Columbia River bar, the Ninth had been split. Eight companies went east of the Cascades with regimental commander Col. George Wright, while Casey took two companies to Fort Steilacoom. There, Casey consolidated his companies with elements of the Fourth Infantry and Third Artillery to fight Puget Sound Indian groups outraged by treaty terms. Pickett arrived at Steilacoom in time to participate in a brief engagement on the White River in the Cascade foothills. A few weeks later Company D was sent to Bellingham Bay.

Chilly mornings heavy with dew, warm afternoons, and spectacular sunsets over the San Juan Islands characterize Bellingham Bay in mid-September. Occasional light winds blow up from the south, but it's not hard to spend the day outdoors. It is easy to imagine Pickett's men doffing their heavy woolen uniform coats, rolling their white cotton muslin shirts to the elbow, and with forage caps pulled over the eyes, digging, digging, digging in the eternal rhythm of soldiers; digging latrines, digging garbage pits, and most important, digging the trenches into which the palisades would be set.

Through it all hammers barked and whips snapped as horses strained to pull loads up the track from the beach. Pickett hired three civilians from Whatcom at $4 per day ($84.83 per month), who performed finish carpentry through the end of the year, after which he retained one on duty through June.

These facts are known to posterity thanks to monthly "Post Returns," documents through which local commanders reported the activities of their posts. Pickett's comments, entered in a looping scrawl, are terse and to the point: "Nineteen on extra duty" (meaning digging or hammering), "Ran out of report forms," "Still need horses." No mention was made of the night 1st Lt. Robert Davis challenged Edmund Fitzhugh, a distant kinsman of Pickett's who managed the local coal company, to a duel over a card game. It was well known that both men were hotheads and nothing ever came of it. Nor did anyone bother to note the death of the civilian who was attempting to fire his rifle on the Fourth of July. The man was the first to be buried in the post cemetery.[5]

Such was life in the antebellum frontier army.

By 1856, the U.S. Army had fought three major wars against foreign powers since the nation's birth 80 years before. All but 12 of those years were spent paving the way for westward-bound settlers in the form of exploring and mapping the wilderness, building roads and bridges, and fighting, protecting, and then containing Indians.

Legislators who stumped for expansion across the continent were less willing to expand the budgets of the army and the newly formed (1849) Department of the Interior. Believing that peace could be maintained on the frontier with a "suitable number" of

Indian agents, Congress slashed the authorized strength of the post-Mexican War Regular Army to 10,000 officers and enlisted men. However, as territory was added and more and more settlers hit the trails, reality set in and spurred by Secretary of War Jefferson Davis, the Army was expanded to 18,000 by 1855. Still the Army rarely had enough men to do the job.[6]

The Army's lineup by 1859 consisted of four artillery, 10 infantry and five mounted regiments. Regiments were organized into 10 companies, each run by a captain, who was assisted by a first and second lieutenant plus an orderly sergeant. Companies were then broken down into four squads, each headed by a sergeant and a corporal.

West Point graduates who had proved their mettle in the Mexican War largely led the Regulars on the company level. Many, such as Pickett, were products of the Plantation South and therefore exhibited the qualities of gentlemen in the French and English upper-class traditions. As time went on, many of these officers, not to mention the higher quality enlisted men, left for greener pastures. No wonder.

An enlisted infantryman signed to a five-year hitch started at $7 a month, rising to $13 a month if he ever made sergeant. Officers earned from $25 a month for second lieutenants to $75 a month for colonels. Extra pay was allotted for quarters, remote service and food, but the stipend overall paled in comparison to the civilian world and was certainly less dependable. In his five years as Company D commander, Pickett's most consistent lament was that his men had not been paid. The paymaster was to call every two months but at times the men were six months or more without money. This left them at the mercy of the post sutler, who dispensed canned goods, beverages, writing paper and other necessaries and sundries on accounts that were collected when the pay arrived. Some soldiers never caught up or were able to save a dime.

Lieutenant Davis, a nephew of the secretary of war/senator and future Confederate States president, became so fed up with the pay, the discipline, and military life in general that he resigned his commission, took an Indian wife and made a living hunting deer.

This was probably viewed as a step up in society, as the peacetime army could hardly count on the regard of a grateful nation. Officers such as Davis were adjudged parasites of the public purse, "sustained by a laboring people, fed from the public crib, but doing nothing whatever to support themselves or increase the wealth of the nation." Enlisted men were rated just below dogs on the social ladder, considered too lazy to work for living.[7]

They ate only slightly better than dogs. In 1855 daily rations consisted of fresh or salt beef or pork, fresh bread or hardtack, coffee, and beans, peas, or rice. Soldiers serving on the West Coast usually found hardtack alive with weevils and salt meats spoiled as rations were shipped around the horn from Baltimore. Some relief was drawn from truck gardens, authorized in 1851 at the discretion of post commanders. But most commanders considered gardens more trouble than they were worth, except for Pickett, who inherited a thriving patch from the Roberts family. Pickett and his officers expanded the garden and did so well that Fort Bellingham produce was sold as far south as Fort Steilacoom. Enterprising souls with their own firearms also could vary the bill of fare by bagging an elk or wild turkey. Use of government firearms and ammunition for hunting was forbidden, so hunting was mainly the province of officers.

Soldiers saw more of the butt end of an ax than they did of a rifle. Frontier soldiers felled trees, dug ditches, and performed countless other tasks of drudgery more suitable to civilians than fighting men.

Discipline was harsh. The Articles of War left punishment to the discretion of court martial boards, which prescribed whippings and other forms of torture ranging from hauling a ball and wearing a spiked iron collar to being strung up by wrists and thumbs on a

pole and marched around the parade ground. Deserters could be
shot or hung. But they were more often flogged raw, branded on the
hip with a "D," and sent packing while the regimental band played
the "Rogue's March."

The punishment for desertion was of little deterrence, since
it only applied if you were caught. In 1856, the year of Fort
Bellingham's founding, 3,223 out of 15,000 U.S. Army regulars
deserted. And of the first 500 men enlisted in the new Tenth
Infantry, 275 deserted before completing their five-year terms.

Fort Bellingham's first desertion in September 1856 followed
five in November, eventually numbering 50 over the fort's three-
year history. It was not uncommon for soldiers to desert in groups,
especially in view of the boredom that drove many a soldier to drink.
If any statistic runs consistently throughout Fort Bellingham's
returns it is the number of men in confinement in the uplands
blockhouse.

From December 1856 through July 1857 the post never had
fewer than nine in the guardhouse, with as many as 13 in irons in
June. When the fledgling community of Whatcom was threatened
by northern Indian raids in the Spring of 1857, Edmund Fitzhugh
wrote Washington Territory Gov. Isaac Stevens: "We might all be
killed as we expect no assistance from the Military Post, they having
as much as they can do to protect their perimeter, their pickets
not being finished and many of the soldiers being in irons in the
guardhouse."[8]

U.S. Army Inspector General Col. Joseph K. F. Mansfield,
taking the measure of Company I, Fourth Infantry at Fort Townsend
in 1858, attributed disciplinary problems not so much to punitive
officers as to taking peasant boys directly off the immigrant ships
and dropping them into uniform. The 1860 census reveals that
40 of 57 enlisted men in Pickett's company listed Ireland as their
country of origin.[9]

It was Wellington's "scum of the earth" dictum all over again.

More than 74 soldiers had deserted from that post in three years. This was attributable to poor instruction and lack of discipline at time of recruitment; the vicinity of the posts to gold diggings in Colville and British Columbia; mistreatment at the hands of sergeants; but most of all "the worthless unprincipled character" of the recruits themselves. Fort Townsend had 13 in irons that December and since the post's last payday there had been 18 desertions. Six of the deserters told Mansfield they'd been driven away by a cruel first sergeant, bad food and pitiful clothing. One soldier was so desperate he deserted while on guard duty, taking his prisoner with him.

"I have to remark that there must be great neglect, or want of attention, at the recruiting depot at Philadelphia, and at the General Depot," Mansfield wrote.[10]

The Fourth had been recruited separately from the Ninth, but there were many similarities. Despite prescribed training periods, Western troops were uniformly ill trained for military duties, lacking in discipline and full of defects, acquired as well as congenital. Two Irish recruits—one who could barely walk and the other with a useless right arm—had been enlisted. A German soldier in the guardhouse for desertion could not speak English and required an interpreter. At other posts he'd found soldiers nearsighted, lame, and left-handed. "Awkward left-handed men are quite common," he wrote "...I do not think a left handed man should be enlisted. He cannot fire efficiently by the right shoulder in the ranks."

Unfortunately for national security, righties were little better. The troops at both forts spent so much time taming the wilderness that they had little time to be soldiers. At Fort Bellingham, for example, "extra duty" meant just that; one dug, hammered, hefted and cultivated the post's abundant truck garden in addition to marching, drilling and standing inspection.

The result was disastrous, especially when Mansfield tested the Fort Bellingham soldiers' marksmanship with the aging Harper's Ferry musket.

> This company ... fired at the target 6' x 22" at 200 yards distant, one round per 40 men, and put only one shot in the target," he wrote. "This only showed the want of instruction and practice... Like all posts in this new country the soldiers work more than they drill and they need instruction here as well as other posts in target firing, rifle drills and bayonet exercises.[10]

The skirmishers—theoretically the best shots in the company who would move in advance of the formation during a battle— fared little better when put to the test. Their performance was only "tolerable," Mansfield reported.

The pay was good enough that only "good and active men and men of good habits should be allowed to enter the service," Mansfield believed. And despite its 50 desertions in three years, Mansfield actually considered the Bellingham company "in a good state of discipline," noting that 20 of the desertions were in San Francisco, long before the troops arrived in Bellingham.[11]

Most of the credit for the company's showing goes to 2nd Lt. James W. Forsyth and other subordinates, who were left in charge while Pickett was on extended leave in Virginia in 1858. When not on leave, the Virginian was snugly ensconced with his Northwest Coast wife in a house he'd had built in Whatcom, three miles south of the fort. The woman gave birth to a healthy baby boy in December 1857, who was named James Tilton Pickett, for the adjutant general of Washington Territory, James Tilton. The woman died shortly after childbirth and the boy was placed in the care of the Collins family who lived in Grand Mound, just south of Olympia, Pickett providing a stipend.

These were the troops and leaders who prepared to face off against the might of the Royal Navy: Bad shots who were more familiar with cultivating cabbages and hammering nails than with drill, and who could barely read and write. Either George Pickett was not spending enough time at his own post to realize how unprepared he was, or he was counting on employing the techniques he learned as a youth appearing in amateur theatricals in Quincy and at West Point (where he preferred the female roles, incidentally).

In any case, what John de Courcy, Governor Douglas, and the Royal Navy did not know certainly would not hurt the Americans. Pickett was obviously prepared to bluff until it was called.

Chapter 10

GOVERNOR DOUGLAS RESPONDS

James Douglas was aware of Pickett's landing even before *Satellite* returned to Victoria on the evening of July 28 with an alarming report from Magistrate John de Courcy. Telegraph communications were nonexistent in the Pacific Northwest. But steamship traffic had increased dramatically in the past two years so word of an imminent landing had spread from Semiahmoo to Olympia before Pickett's foot hit the beach.

Headlines in the July 27 Victoria *Colonist* screamed "San Juan Island Invaded By American Troops," the accompanying story replete with details of troops dispatched by General Harney. The Olympia *Pioneer and Democrat* took a decidedly chauvinistic view two days later, observing:

> We suppose our neighbors may grumble a little at this summary way of settling the disputed title, but then it is the privilege of John Bull to grumble and the motley crowd of native born British subjects congregated in those new colonies can just grumble away.[1]

The Olympia crowd should have known Douglas better. Before the ink was dry on the Treaty of Oregon he had been enforcing Great Britain's claim to the San Juan Islands. First it was the logger Cussans, then Ebey, Webber and Sheriff Barnes. Nothing could shake his belief that the San Juan Islands belonged to the HBC and the Crown. As for Pickett, the governor had dealt with him before and was convinced the captain had no grasp of geography, let alone international law. In December 1856 his Fort Bellingham subordinate, 1ˢᵗ Lt. Hugh Fleming, appeared on the Victoria docks with an armed detail, all in uniform and fully equipped. When Douglas stormed to the waterfront demanding an explanation, Fleming, speaking for Pickett, asked the governor to deliver to him some recent deserters from the fort. If the governor did not wish to do it himself, Fleming would do it for him. Douglas ordered him to leave.[2]

Now in his (largely honorary) position of acting vice admiral while the Pacific Station commander, Rear Adm. R. Lambert Baynes, was away, Douglas had the authority to act. Even before the latest edition of the *Colonist* appeared urging action, the governor ordered Capt. Michael de Courcy, the senior naval officer in Barnes's absence, to dispatch at once a warship to San Juan Island. De Courcy ordered HMS *Tribune*, a 31-gun steam frigate, to prepare for sea. He also assigned more Royal Marines to the ship including one lieutenant, three noncoms and 19 privates.

Tribune's commander, Capt. Geoffrey Phipps Hornby, was ordered to prevent the landing of further armed parties of U.S. soldiers for the purposes of occupation, and not allow erection of fortifications. But Douglas' orders also contained a frustrating dichotomy. Hornby was to use force if necessary, but *not* provoke the Americans into a "collision," according to Royal Navy Lt. Richard Mayne of HMS *Plumper*, who claimed to be aboard the *Tribune* when Hornby received the order.[3]

Hornby was well suited to the task. The son of Admiral of the Fleet Phipps Hornby, a former Pacific Station commander, Geoffrey Hornby, at 33, was one of the more highly regarded young officers in the Royal Navy, quiet but firm and an excellent sailor. He was given command of *Tribune* in London in the spring of 1858 during the height of the Fraser River Gold Rush. As with many English gentlemen of the age, his yearning for adventure took him overland across Europe, and then by sea from Marseilles via Cairo and Suez, before he finally joined his ship in Hong Kong in October. Hornby would prove his mettle as a sailor and captain on the voyage. On one "wild night" on the leg to Japan, he scrambled up the mizzen to help the crew furl the mizzen topsail. "It was the first and only time I ever saw a captain go 'above the dead-eye,'" said one of his lieutenants, Francis M. Norman. More than 600 men were stuffed into a vessel that was only 192 feet from stem to stern, which created no end of disciplinary problems. The crew being "slack" from too many months in port, Hornby literally cracked the whip to bring order. This and the attraction of gold resulted in more than 40 desertions of sailors and marines in the weeks following their arrival at Esquimalt Harbor in February 1859.[4]

With *Tribune* there were now five British warships in the area. The others were the *Ganges, Pylades, Satellite,* and *Plumper*—a total of 167 guns and 1,940 men. The numbers, initially tabulated and presented to Harney by Silas Casey, are impressive at first glance. They have been cited by everyone who has written on the topic, the first being Harney himself who elevated the number of "fighting men" to 2,140.

The reports are somewhat misleading, however.

First, *Ganges* may have been an 84-gun ship-of-the-line, a "second rate" in Royal Navy parlance. But she was a sailing vessel—the last of her class in the Royal Navy—and that made her a lumbering dinosaur in the age of steam. She was probably towed into Esquimalt Harbor and would have been nearly useless in Griffin Bay or anywhere in the interior waters of the San Juans.[5]

Second, the number of fighting men may be grossly inflated. Most of the 1,940 men listed are sailors. Ships' companies were comprised of able seaman, coal stokers, wipers and gunners, not infantry. How many blue jackets could be armed and sent ashore against Pickett's forces is unknown, but had to be limited. Why else would Hornby worry about not having enough men in ensuing days? About 400 marines and Royal Engineers were scattered on ships and shore stations in and about Vancouver Island and British Columbia. Hornby's initial allocation of infantry was 23 marines. He was promised 46 more marines, plus 15 Royal Engineers, which were to be sent to him from New Westminster, British Columbia, on the mainland. While Hornby was unaware that Pickett's men were bad shots and might bolt at the first volley, he understood that a company of infantry with rifled muskets could do a lot of damage.

Hornby left Victoria at 5 p.m., on Friday, July 29, arriving on San Juan Island at 9 p.m. Also on board *Tribune* were A.G. Dallas and George Hunter Cary, the attorney general for Vancouver Island, sent at the last minute to monitor John de Courcy's actions.

Douglas hoped the presence of a first-class British warship, with more on the horizon, would intimidate the Americans and encourage them to leave or at the very least modify their behavior. Such tactics had worked in the past in the Pacific, which the British had dominated since the War of 1812. He also believed that should hostilities break out, it would be easier to deal with Pickett's lone company rather than the bulk of the Ninth and Fourth Infantry and Third Artillery—close to 2,000 soldiers—who had so quickly and skillfully dispatched the Indians in eastern Washington Territory the year before under George Wright.[6]

Hornby steamed out of Esquimalt and likely beat north up the Haro Strait along the rocky west side of San Juan Island. The black frigate, cutting a white wake and trailing smoke through the blue water, rounded the northern reach of the island, then pushed south through San Juan Channel. Skirting the island's heavily wooded eastern shoreline—where midway the survey ship HMS *Plumper* had charted a deepwater bay and named it for a Hawaiian shepherd called "Friday"—*Tribune* soon entered the flat expanse of Griffin Bay. Even at 9 p.m., it was still light enough for Hornby to spot the inoffensive American lighthouse tender *Shubrick*, still riding at anchor with Commissioner Campbell aboard. Pickett had asked Campbell if he might remain on the bay for another three days to "...give him the benefit of my council on locating a (camp) site, which I concluded to do." The commissioner was probably enjoying the sunset in anticipation of a pleasant journey the next day through the islands to his headquarters at Semiahmoo on the 49th parallel. In late July the sky would be turning lavender, laced with clouds of almost incandescent pink reflected in silver waters. Panning his glass from ship to shore, Hornby spotted a cluster of white tents at the foot of a straw-colored clearing on a hill that rolled gently into the bay. Through the smoke of the cooking fires, his trained eye at once noted the camp was neither fortified nor entrenched! He could easily sweep the hillside with his guns and drive the Americans into the woods on both sides of the clearing. He wondered at a man who would establish such a vulnerable camp. The following July 30 report came from Hornby via the HBC steamer *Beaver* to Capt. Michael de Courcy:

> This morning, I perceive the Americans have formed a camp about 200 yards from the beach, in which they have two howitzers; the ground rises considerably behind the camp, and on either side, at a distance of 300 yards, it is flanked by woods... I am assured that the force at the disposal of the American captain consists of 50 soldiers, with the two howitzers above mentioned, and about the same number of armed civilians; and if they take to the bush, the Magistrate does not see how they could be arrested, at the same time they might be expected to commit serious depredations on the cattle of the Hudson's Bay Company.[7]

Magistrate John de Courcy planted this seed in Hornby shortly after *Tribune* dropped anchor, explaining that, as per his instructions of the 23rd, George Pickett, "an American," (de Courcy's underscore) must be warned off Hudson's Bay Company lands or be arrested as a trespasser. If he did not leave, then de Courcy would have to arrest Pickett and anyone "aiding him in resistance." By now, that "anyone" meant Company D. As a past and future military man— he was frequently addressed as "Major"—de Courcy knew he could hardly suppress infantry with a revolver and Griffin's Hawaiian shepherds. The Royal Navy would have to back him up. This stated, de Courcy confessed that he did not feel justified in asking Hornby to act unless Hornby had a larger force "sufficient, in fact, to line the bush…" He spun a vision of Royal Marines chasing panicky farmers and soldiers through the woods. They would be fools to press the point, he said. They needed more men, or better yet, time to allow matters to cool.

Cary and Dallas also advised the governor on July 30 that the Americans were much stronger than expected, in fact too strong for Hornby to bully at this point. Both men pressed Douglas to dispatch another ship. In the matter of the warrant, Cary recommended issuing a "summons" to Pickett instead. The actual arrest warrant should be postponed until Sunday (July 31). By then, reinforcements should arrive and "might would make right."

Douglas agreed and ordered Capt. Michael de Courcy to take the steam corvette HMS *Pylades* to San Juan "trusting that the exhibition of an overwhelming force might prevent resistance and the probable effusion of blood."

That's when the Royal Navy balked.

As the acting senior naval officer in Victoria, de Courcy had received his own report from Hornby. He also had spoken with *Satellite* Capt. James Prevost, freshly arrived from the scene and thoroughly dismayed by Pickett's actions. Realizing the incident was moving into deadly ground, Captain de Courcy—accompanied by Capt. George H. Richards of the *Plumper*—went to the governor that evening (July 30) to urge restraint. While de Courcy probably had a sincere desire to avoid bloodshed, he also was moved by practical considerations. His boss, Rear Admiral Baynes, was away. Douglas, as vice admiral, was nominally in charge, but de Courcy still had to answer to Baynes, who was personally and professionally committed to the Royal Navy's global policies. Those being: "deterrence through possession of overwhelming force, the protection of British commercial interests and the safe use of the seas."

"British policy in the mid-Victorian era was one of restraint. Britain was secure at home and abroad," writes historian Barry Gough. "She sought no self-aggrandizement. Naval commanders on foreign stations during this period frequently served as interpreters of the policy of 'minimum intervention.'"

That meant it was up to individual commanders to decide how and why and when to employ force in guarding British commercial and territorial interests.

> Sometimes, as in the San Juan crisis, British citizens at the scene of contention considered these officers overly cautious. But their actions conformed to their government's foreign policy. No officer dared to intervene where powerful nations had claims to the same territory unless British rights were in grave danger; if he did so without cause, he would face censorship of Parliament, the Foreign Office, the Admiralty and the British public.[8]

Not so Douglas. He believed the American act was no more than an invasion by freebooters who had to be dealt with in kind. If his policy had prevailed, war would have been inevitable.

No sooner were the captains seated in the Douglas parlor than Captain de Courcy asked Douglas for "more specific instructions," particularly "when I was to resort to force." The captain said he realized the islands were in dispute and wanted to do all he could to avoid conflict with the United States—especially as it appeared Great Britain could become involved in a European war. Unbeknownst to him, France and Austria, the latter Britain's ally, were at that moment engaged in the Battle of Solferino in northern Italy. France would win, upsetting the balance of power in Europe.

The captains expressed "very strong" reservations about the deployment of British ships against the U.S. troops and suggested "milder measures" at first. The "civil process" of arresting Pickett should be abandoned, they urged, but a detachment of marines could be dispatched and held at ready just in case. The message was clear: Douglas could issue orders, but the navy would not obey them.

De Courcy then recommended a formal meeting between Prevost and U.S. Boundary Commissioner Campbell to divine if the boundary dispute had been settled. Perhaps British messengers had been delayed. If the boundary had not been settled, then perhaps Campbell would know why the U.S. troops were camped on disputed ground. It is hard to believe Prevost did not already know why the Americans were encamped since he met with Campbell on Griffin Bay on the 27th and 28th. Campbell may have assured Prevost that the American troops were there only to protect the American squatters from northern Indians, as adjutant Capt. Alfred Pleasonton had advised him a few weeks before. But in a July 27 letter to Maj. Granville O. Haller at Fort Townsend, Campbell surmised that Prevost would misconstrue his presence on the island simultaneous with the arrival of Pickett's company. Whatever was said between the two commissioners, Campbell's presence in the harbor during Pickett's landing now made him suspect in the minds of the British.[9]

Overwhelmed and perhaps a bit intimidated by the captains' solidarity, Douglas agreed that Pickett's arrest should be postponed or, as he put it, "adjourned." If the warrant had not been served, they were not to serve it; if it had been served it was not to be enforced. He also canceled Hornby's orders to prevent the Americans from landing more troops and erecting fortifications, and agreed to a meeting between Prevost and Archibald Campbell. Perhaps

Campbell could influence Harney. Prevost left for Semiahmoo the next morning in hopes of finding his counterpart.

Douglas wanted de Courcy to go to San Juan Island as well with *Pylades* to supervise events, but not before Monday, August 1. Richards and the *Plumper*, meanwhile, would go fetch Royal Marines from New Westminster.

On San Juan Island, George Pickett was involved in high drama as was his wont. It began the afternoon of the 29th when 1st Lt. John Howard burst into Pickett's tent and before several civilians (including Magistrate Crosby) pointed a "cocked" revolver at the Virginian's chest, declaring, "I'm going to have satisfaction." In an instant Pickett stepped forward, disarmed Howard, grabbed him by his collar and thrust him out of the tent. (One witness reported that they wrestled on the ground.) He then returned the pistol to Howard and ordered him back to his quarters. After a few steps, Howard turned and shouted, "You have no authority over me."

This remark stemmed from Howard's erroneous assumption that because he'd been suspended from rank and pay since April— for of all things slugging an enlisted man while escorting prisoners by sea to a court martial at Fort Vancouver—he wasn't on active duty and could do what he pleased. Pickett had brought Howard along to San Juan because, as he confessed at Howard's court martial that September, he hadn't a clue what to do with him.[10]

A few hours later, Paul K. Hubbs's "black sea monster" (*Tribune*) dropped anchor, then turned on her chains until a broadside (about fifteen guns) was trained on Pickett's camp. She then whistled down her boats. Forty years on, Hubbs, compressing several days into one evening, jotted down this stirring dialogue:

"Captain," said the writer, "this looks uncomfortable."

"Not in the least," was Pickett's reply. "Stay here while I speak to my men."

At that moment a boat landed with several British officers. The most prominent was Captain Hornby, who advanced to the tent and asked for the commanding officer. Half a minute later appeared the hero of Gettysburg, cool and courteous as a French dancing master and never did an officer appear to a greater advantage, for he was now about to be in the element of his glory. The following words took place in the writer's hearing:

> Hornby: I have 1,100 men on board to land tonight.
>
> Pickett: Captain, you have a force to land, but if you undertake it, I will fight you as long as I have a man.
>
> Hornby: Very well; I shall land them at once.
>
> Pickett: If you will give me forty-eight hours, till I hear from my commanding officer, my orders may be countermanded. If you do not you must be responsible for the blood that follows.
>
> "Not one minute" was Hornby's reply.

Pickett, turning to the writer, said:

> "Summon your men and take the hill. Fire one-third at a time at close range. As you fire, wheel your men to the left and join me at the road. We'll make a Bunker Hill of it. I will not leave you and don't be afraid of their big guns."[11]

Actually, Pickett did not meet with Hornby until Sunday the 31st, *after* Hornby had received his orders from Prevost not to interfere with the Americans in any way. Nevertheless, the Virginian was plenty worried. The British seemed to be closing in, which made him feel even more isolated and still at loss over what to do next. In a letter dashed off to Casey on the 30th, Pickett wrote:

> From the threatening attitude of affairs at present, I deem it my duty to request the *Massachusetts* may be sent at once to this point. I do not know that an actual collision will take place, but it is not comfortable to be lying within range of a couple of war steamers. The *Tribune*, a 30-gun frigate, is lying broadside to our camp and from present indications everything leads me to suppose that they will attempt to prevent my carrying out my instructions."[12]

He enclosed an exchange of letters between himself and Charles Griffin, who at this late date, lodged a written protest and ordered Pickett off the premises, perhaps to lend weight to any actions taken by John de Courcy. Pickett responded that he was on the island under orders from his *government*. This statement would generate more confusion and uncertainty among Douglas, the Vancouver Council and the Royal Navy. The letter was signed "in haste…"

Pickett may have been anxious, but the Olympia *Pioneer and Democrat* had every confidence in him. A July 29 article boasted: "Captain Pickett is just the man to be put in command. With every attribute of the gentleman, he is a perfect soldier; a man of great prudence and self-command, and with decision, promptitude and energy, he will be equal to any emergency that may arise." The newspaper began referring to San Juan Island as a "Seat of War."[13]

Aboard the *Tribune*, Hornby was using his Sunday to catch up with personal correspondence while awaiting American reinforcements, or for Pickett's men to start digging or both. In a July 31 letter to his wife he mused that the "hot-headed Hearney (sic)" had hopes of winning the presidency. Despite the reservations he stated in his letter to Michael de Courcy, he strutted a bit for his woman. He wanted to "…bundle these fellows off neck and crop," he wrote. But the governor had forced him to follow a "medium" course, urging him to avoid a collision, which would be impossible under the circumstances. The idea of issuing Pickett a summons was as ridiculous to him as it was to John de Courcy. It must have seemed to Hornby another timeless example of civilians meddling in military and naval affairs.[14]

But then, almost midline, Hornby received the urgent communication from Michael de Courcy, modifying his orders:

> ...I have received fresh order to take no steps against these men at present, or prevent others from landing. The object now seems to be to avoid a collision at all hazards until we hear from the American authorities, but I fear if the marines (from New Westminster) are landed, it will inevitably produce one sooner or later. We have had one lucky escape. The Governor told me it would be well if I called on the commanding officer (Pickett) and told him what my orders were. When I called he was away, and before he returned my visit I had received my counter-orders, so I have not the disgust of having blustered, and then been obliged to haul in my horns.[15]

Pickett did visit *Tribune* later that day, but not before he was overwhelmed by a swarm of "tourists" and a couple of newspaper editors from Victoria, including one named *Amour De Cosmos*. They poked around the soldiers' tents and visited the ships in the harbor. De Cosmos claimed to have shared "refreshments" with Pickett himself. Several of the "sovereigns," as Pickett called them, turned bellicose a few refreshments on, but Pickett later assured adjutant Pleasonton that he had used "a great deal of my peacemaking disposition" to restrain them.[16]

Hornby's impression of the Virginian was not entirely unfavorable. He viewed Pickett as "more quiet than most of his countrymen, but he seems to have just the notion they all have of getting a name by some audacious act." The Englishman also thought Pickett sounded more like "a Devonshire man than a Yankee." Little comes down to us of what was said in the meeting. Hornby wrote that Pickett "...dropped one or two things which may be useful for us to know, and I hope did not get much information out of me." Painfully polite as the encounter may have been, it resolved nothing. Hornby urged Pickett to leave. Pickett refused, and that was that.

However, the frigate's big guns and the crispness of the sailors at gun drills must have unnerved the American. When he returned to shore he ordered his men to pull up stakes. They would move across the neck of the peninsula to a new location on South Beach. The level expanse of prairie there would easily accommodate reinforcements if needed... and they were far away from *Tribune's* guns.[17]

The waters of the Pacific Northwest were in motion on Monday, August 1.

While Pickett saw to the details of moving his camp, the *Massachusetts* with Company I, Fourth Infantry on board, was steaming toward San Juan Island. Alarmed by Pickett's letter, Casey honored Pickett's plea for the ship, but was at a loss to offer advice because, as he wrote Pleasonton, he had not been informed of the "tenor of Captain Pickett's instructions."[18]

That afternoon, Prevost, after a fruitless overnight trip to Semiahmoo in search of Campbell, steamed into a harbor full of ships on Griffin Bay. Along with *Tribune* and *Plumper* were the *Massachusetts*, *Constitution*—an American merchant steamer Pickett had requisitioned to haul stores, not to be confused with "Old Ironsides"—and the ubiquitous revenue cutter *Jefferson Davis*. Firsthand accounts differ as to the order of arrival. Some have *Satellite* showing up last, others *Massachusetts*, while still others claim *Plumper*, apparently stopping off on route to fetch the Royal Marines and Royal Engineer sappers.

Many of the officers already were ashore, including Haller and

Plumper's Richards. Thirty-seven years later Haller wrote that in a heated private meeting with Pickett he criticized Pickett's actions, then offered to land his troops, which Pickett refused. Haller said he next warned Pickett that he was jeopardizing his career by pursuing Harney's agenda. His actions, though ordered by Harney, were unlawful and provocative and Pickett was bound to the higher law of U.S. policy. Pickett waved him off and Haller, joined by Richards, visited Belle Vue Sheep Farm, where he inspected Griffin's roses and told Lt. Col. Richard Clement Moody of the Royal Engineers what he knew about events in Europe. In 1896, Haller claimed that it was *this briefing* about what had happened at Solferino that swayed the British into a position of restraint on San Juan.[19]

. Two British officers took a different view of Haller's presence on San Juan on August 1. According to David Boyle, first lieutenant on *Tribune*, *Massachusetts* steamed into the harbor while Prevost and Hornby were seeking Pickett ashore. The Royal Navy, he wrote, had not yet received the order to stand down from opposing troop landings. Moreover, Boyle claimed that he warned the *Massachusetts's* skipper, William Fauntleroy, that the British would prevent the Americans from so doing. Haller's troops—more than 120 according to some accounts—disembarked anyway and Boyle was about to beat to quarters when *Plumper* arrived with the fresh orders. Francis Norman, a sub-lieutenant aboard *Tribune*, later claimed this disembarkation from the *Massachusetts* illustrated perfidy on Pickett's part. The Virginian had denuded the British quarterdecks by inviting the officers, Hornby and Prevost included, to a picnic at the new Spring Camp site above South Beach. However, even Haller insisted that he went ashore alone and Hornby himself reported to Douglas that U.S. troops had arrived in the harbor on August 1 but left the same day without landing. No U.S. reinforcements were landed until Silas Casey arrived on August 10.[20]

While ashore Prevost, in the absence of Campbell (who had continued on to Orcas aboard *Shubrick*), decided to interrogate

Pickett. They had been acquainted since 1857 when the boundary commission teams were organizing at Semiahmoo. Pickett was humble with Prevost, contending, "...he was merely a subordinate carrying out the orders of his superiors." He was there to protect citizens of the United States and to allow U.S. civil powers to enforce the law. He assured Prevost that he and Magistrate Crosbie would approach their duties delicately to avoid "misunderstanding." However, he firmly believed San Juan Island belonged to the U.S., and therefore U.S. Army officers "were perfectly justified in all their acts with regard to it, and that the strictest orders had been given to protect and respect the property of settlers on the island, British or otherwise."

Prevost, in turn, insisted the islands were British: "...and as the line of boundary was still in abeyance, the act of violence committed by landing an armed force without any communications with me, or with British authorities was as discourteous as it was unjustifiable."

If Pickett's company remained, Prevost warned, the British might be forced to land the Royal Marines as a defensive measure; to which Pickett replied that British subjects and property would be protected and that Crosbie and himself would act with the greatest "caution and latitude."

This is the same man who said, "We'll make a Bunker Hill of it," or so claimed Hubbs. It is hard to believe this George Pickett was part of a "southern cabal" to start a war. He could have been prevaricating, but it seems unlikely.

Pickett then took Prevost by surprise by relating that Crosbie had "held court" and fined Cutlar for shooting the boar. Not only that, the fine would be turned over to the HBC. This must have been connected with Hubbs's "arrest" at Cutlar's cabin. Word got around, for John de Courcy also reported August 1 that this judgment against Cutlar had taken place the day before. Crosbie himself made no record of the action, nor did Cutlar mention it in his affidavit.[21]

Prevost finished with Pickett, and steamed to Victoria to file his report with Douglas. He arrived at the tail-end of a meeting that included Douglas, Captain de Courcy, members of the Vancouver Island Council and Lt. Col. John S. Hawkins of the Royal Engineers, the British land boundary commissioner. Still believing that *Pylades* was to join *Tribune*, Douglas that morning sent instructions to de Courcy reminding him that, while he would "deplore" any act the would disrupt the peace, de Courcy was to enforce Great Britain's claim to the islands. If it was necessary to land the Royal Marines to back that claim then so be it.

Before de Courcy weighed anchor, Hawkins rapped on his cabin door. The colonel thought the home government should immediately be informed and he volunteered to make the long journey to England. He would have to leave at once to catch the mail packet out of San Francisco for Panama. The two men went to the governor, who liked the idea and immediately summoned the council (led by his long-time associate Roderick Finlayson), which quickly approved the mission. The council also urged Douglas to recall Magistrate John de Courcy and avoid landing marines, as that might bring on a collision.[22]

The group must have eagerly turned toward the late-arriving Prevost hoping that he bore some explanation from Campbell. The captain lamented he could not locate Campbell, but that he had written him a letter and dropped it at Semiahmoo—a letter that, from the reaction it received, would have been better left in a drawer overnight.[23]

The meeting concluded with the council recommending that all British subjects residing on San Juan Island leave in protest of the American invasion. Hornby was designated the senior naval officer until Michael de Courcy returned from San Francisco, or Admiral Baynes arrived from Valparaiso. Before departing de Courcy urged Douglas to send "specific" instructions to Hornby, which Prevost would deliver before continuing his search for Campbell.

Blessed by another spectacular sunset, those aboard ships on Griffin Bay probably heard the soldiers ashore at their campfires, while the soldiers marked the ships' bells tolling the hours. Sentries and lookouts paced, probably wondering at the hubbub over a speck of rock in the middle of nowhere, let alone some farmer's infernal pig. Tobacco, whisky, and other sundries had been exchanged between the Americans and British shore parties. Almost everyone spoke the same language and seemed nice. Thank goodness no one had started anything yet.

But like soldiers and sailors of any time, anywhere, they knew they were powerless to shape events. They would keep their powder dry, do what they were told, and pray for the protection of a merciful God.

James Douglas and William Selby Harney would do the rest.

Chapter 11

"TUT, TUT, NO, NO, THE DAMN FOOLS."

No doubt James Douglas had a sleepless night, the events of August 1 looping in his head. How it must have galled him. First the captains questioned his actions, then the council and, of all people, Finlayson, backed the captains and urged him not to post Royal Marines on the island. The Hudson's Bay Company and Great Britain—then one and the same in the Pacific Northwest—had suffered the indignity of being shoved out of Oregon. Douglas retrenched on Vancouver Island, of which the San Juan Islands had always been considered a part. He acted decisively to save New Caledonia, now called *British* Columbia, during the Fraser River Gold Rush. He was not about to be overrun again by the rapacious Yanks. His mind was settled. If Pickett's soldiers remained on San Juan Island, he would land the marines as a counterbalance. British claims would be preserved and the clarity of joint martial law would replace the passions and uncertainties of civil law, often enforced on the frontier by self-interested parties.

This "mature reflection" spurred Douglas to reject the council's suggestions and on August 2 he decided to land British troops so "that the occupation at least might be a joint one." He fired off letters to Magistrate John de Courcy and Hornby, advising them of his intentions.

To Hornby:

Circumstances beyond my control and too various
for explanation in this form compelled me to assert
to the first modification of your orders revoking
the authority given you to prevent the landing of
U.S. troops and the erection of Military Works by
the detachment occupying San Juan Island... I place
the fullest reliance on your firmness of temper and
discretion and I trust that Captain Pickett will be
reasonable and mitigate as much as possible the
evils that must necessarily arise out of conflicting
jurisdiction of a joint occupation, I hope they will
not seek to force a quarrel upon us, in that case,
however the sin will rest upon their own heads.
I have written De Courcy (the magistrate) to be
cautious and not to push matters in his department
to extremes, wishing you well.[1]

That was precisely what concerned Hornby. He had written to
Capt. Michael de Courcy the day before, worrying that he could not
assist the magistrate ashore without avoiding a fight with Pickett.
The island was in a state. Griffin was complaining about soldiers
trampling his crops and stampeding his sheep. Tourists were poking
about. The slightest spark could ignite a collision, in Hornby's view,
so landing troops on any pretense would be folly.[2]

De Courcy was en route to San Francisco by then, so Douglas
wrote a second, "informal" letter to Hornby addressing his
concerns. The last thing he wanted was to provoke the U.S. soldiers
on San Juan, but he could not allow them to harm British subjects
or property and sacrifice "the honor and dignity of Her Majesty's
Government." Nor was he going to abandon the island to a military
occupation and "a Squatter population of American citizens." He
urged Hornby to enter into a "full and frank communication"

with Pickett to avoid hostilities. The occupation was contemptible and violated every agreement between the two nations, but he was willing to dismiss it if an equal number of Royal Marines set up housekeeping:

> If the joint occupation were wholly a military one I conceive that peace and good understanding might be preserved provided the officers in command were mutually desirous of maintaining friendly relations, and you might if you saw fit opportunity without weakening our position or committing us in any way propose that the Civil Magistrates should be withdrawn on both sides...

He stressed five points to justify landing British troops:

1. maintain the integrity of the British claim

2. maintain national honor and dignity

3. maintain control and influence over Indian tribes

4. protect British subjects and property

5. carry out any action which circumstances may hereafter compel you to take.[3]

Hornby must have flinched at the last proviso, which may have convinced him of his future course. Douglas attached his formal protest to the U.S. authorities, which stressed that because the islands always had been "undeviatingly" claimed to be in the Crown of Great Britain, he did "formally and solemnly protest against the occupation." It was signed, "By James Douglas of the most honorable Order of the Bath, Governor and Commander-in-Chief in and over the Colony of Vancouver Island and its dependencies, Vice

Admiral of the same etc., etc."

On August 2, a Tuesday, the *Plumper* arrived on Griffin Bay from New Westminster with 46 marines and 15 Royal Engineers, Colonel Moody commanding. *Satellite* returned the next day. By then Hornby had mulled over Douglas' instructions and decided to meet with Pickett at his camp.

Pickett worried Hornby. Nothing he had done thus far had inspired confidence in anything approaching consistent behavior. He was still puzzled by Pickett reestablishing his camp across the prairie near the springs above South Beach. It belied military thought and made moot Douglas' orders to stop the erection of fortifications.

> The Americans, he wrote, "do not seem inclined to strengthen nor have any preparations for intrenching or other defence been made by them, though the camp has been shifted from its first site to one close to the sea on the other side of the island and equally exposed to the fire of Ships, as was their original one."[4]

Hornby was evidently unaware that Pickett had graduated last in his class at West Point.

Pickett, Hornby, Prevost and Richards met in Pickett's tent at South Beach at 2 p.m., Wednesday. Hornby did all the talking and wasted little time on pleasantries. He again wanted know why, and on whose authority, Pickett occupied the island. Pickett replied "by the general commanding," whose orders came directly from Washington City. He expressed an "equal desire" that a collision be avoided and he was certain U.S. citizens would not provoke one. However, if the British landed, Pickett warned that "...his orders as a Soldier gave him no other discretion but to seize a small force, attack an equal one, and go down fighting if outnumbered." He concluded by observing—probably more cleverly than intended—that the British so outnumbered him that they did not *need* to land. They could achieve their end by merely standing off shore and the world would not think the less of them.[5]

If Hornby concurred with the last point, he did not say so on paper. He handed Pickett Douglas' formal protest to convey to Harney, explaining that because the United States placed troops and a magistrate on the island, Great Britain *could* do the same. This would involve considerable risk as magistrates could call upon military forces at any time to enforce the law. He then played Douglas' card. Why not get rid of the magistrates, suspend the courts, and have a joint military occupation, the officers on both sides adjudicating the affairs of their countrymen? No other course would avoid bloodshed, save of course Pickett pulling up stakes and vacating the island.

It was too much for Pickett to digest. Throughout his military career he had been inclined to sniff at authority on the one hand and crave its security on the other. The Virginian said he could not condone a joint military occupation until he received direction from Harney. He asked for time to send a dispatch. Perhaps, he added, Hornby should do the same with Douglas.[6]

Hornby lost patience. He warned Pickett that because his occupation was illegal the onus was on him to avoid "necessary evils" and accept this clearly equitable solution. The marines would land anyway if he thought the "honor of the flag" or protection of British rights was at stake. As the meeting broke up and the guests moved to the tent flap, Hornby and Pickett continued to joust over who would be blamed if fighting broke out. If Hornby forced a landing it would be his fault. If Pickett did not allow a landing he would be to blame. As the frustrated Hornby prepared to leave, Pickett stopped him and asked if he would write him a letter offering his interpretation of their conversation and reiterating the British position. Hornby consented and went on his way with Prevost and Richards.[7]

That evening Pickett sent a dispatch to Pleasonton via the *Shubrick*.

His correspondence continued to register surprise and chagrin at the British response to his landing. He had been "WARNED OFF" [his capitals] by the Hudson's Bay Company agent and forced to deal with three captains, though he nobly "thought it better to take the brunt of it." A joint military occupation had been offered, but Pickett "declined anything of the kind." He admitted that the British could land anywhere, anytime they wanted and he could do little to stop them, as his force was a "mere mouthful" for the warships in the bay. He had been as diplomatic as possible under the circumstances, and had put them off by giving them a "pill" to swallow. He also "...endeavored to impress them with the idea that my authority comes directly through you from Washington," he wrote, but the British were not impressed.

> ...(the British) seem to doubt the authority of the general Commanding, and do not wish to acknowledge his right to occupy this island, which they say is in dispute, unless the United States Government have decided the question with Great Britain. I have so far staved them off, by saying that the two governments have without a doubt settled this affair; but this state of affairs cannot last, therefore I must ask that an express be sent to me immediately on my future guidance. I do not think there are moments to waste.[8]

This letter reveals that, far from being one of the principals in a conspiracy, or even a scheme to grab the islands, George Pickett, until his meeting with Hornby, was apparently ignorant of even the most fundamental background of the Treaty of Oregon; thought Harney's orders came from Washington; was shocked that the British doubted the general's authority; and, most troubling, seemed unaware the islands were in dispute. He thought they were U.S. territory!

This was obvious to Douglas, who told a joint meeting of the colony's Legislative Council and House Assembly that Pickett's act was "originated in error, and been undertaken without the authority of that government." By contrast, Douglas claimed his government, arrest warrants and timber permits aside, had "abstained from exercising exclusive sovereignty over the islands." Finally, ever accustomed to being obeyed, Douglas proclaimed, even as Hornby and Pickett were meeting, that British troops would be landed.[9]

Hornby had other ideas.

British policy weighed heavily on his mind. He also was convinced that Pickett's orders originated with Harney and were not sanctioned by the U.S. Government. This was confirmed when Hornby produced his copy of the 1855 "Marcy Letter" (in which the Secretary of State had pledged that U.S. officials would not provoke the British over the San Juan Islands) and Pickett professed ignorance of the document.

Hornby also was aware of Pacific Station directives, which reflected the British government's policy of restraint—especially in view of the rising industrial might of the United States. And he was one of the few players involved who had a realistic idea of the risks. He had heard stories of blood-washed quarterdecks from his father and Admiral Baynes. He had seen for himself hospital ships crammed with the human wreckage of the Crimean War. Even farcical conflicts have real victims.

Above all, he knew Pickett was not bluffing. Anyone so obtuse about the implications of his acts; anyone so clearly unsure of himself made Hornby's course clear. He would hold the marines aboard ship and await Admiral Baynes. He dipped his pen and wrote two letters to Douglas; one was an official report justifying his actions, the other a more informal appeal to the governor.

In the official document he outlined the gist of his conversation with Pickett and then listed, in four points, his reasons for not landing troops. First, the British were powerful enough to blow Pickett from his prairie camp and Pickett knew it, therefore if the British chose not to fight, it was by virtue of restraint and the flag was not "compromised" (essentially Pickett's point); second, remaining on the bay gave them mobile striking power, unlike the Americans who were wed to their camp; third, they could hardly protest the landing of an armed force if they also put one ashore; and finally, just because the Americans demeaned themselves, did not mean the British had to follow suit.

The other letter was more a candid and personal appeal.

"It seems undesirable to have an open rupture here, until they can have heard of and replied to our case at home," Hornby wrote. Pickett and Company D had been on San Juan Island for a week. It would be "undignified" to land the marines after the *Massachusetts* sailed off without landing a single soldier from Haller's company. If the British chose to land, it would have to be with a superior force, which would prompt the Americans to counter. Taking a plunge into political waters—always dangerous for a military man—he stated that Lord Palmerston never had, and never would, enforce the British claim against the U.S. If Washington pressed London to give up the land, London would comply. What a "mess" they would all be in if the government had already done so. As far as Hornby knew, Pickett's modest force was all there was likely to be on San Juan. Surely the British could afford forbearance in the face of a motley collection of expatriate Irishmen led by a posturing Southerner.[10]

But to Douglas, Hornby's letters evinced insubordination, not common sense. The governor could not shape events without military force, which the captains had denied him. His orders from the home government were clear: Hang on to the San Juans. Now his own navy was standing in his way while the legislature and newspapers were howling for his scalp:

> The House would therefore inquire why British forces were not landed, to assert our just right to the island in question, and uphold the honor of the

country and our Queen.[11]

Washington Territory's *Pioneer and Democrat* proclaimed: "...there are thirty Americans on the island, and they are fairly made set of chaps, not easily scared." Paul K. Hubbs, Jr., was quoted: "The monopoly of the HBC is intolerable and odious to most settlers. Collision is imminent, and of such character as may produce the most serious result to the two governments."[12]

Somewhere along the way—we're not certain because in all his correspondence he never offers a date—Archibald Campbell visited Pickett's camp to divine his true intentions. From the first, the commissioner had watched Pickett's doings with a mixture of curiosity and alarm. As far as is known, he still believed Pickett was on San Juan as another futile exercise against the northern Indians, although the guns, the tents, the lumber for buildings, and heavy gun platforms puzzled him. In the past, a squad of light infantry would slip in aboard a revenue cutter, camp for the night and leave.

The commissioner asked to see Pickett's orders. Pickett produced them, adding proudly that he had not only enforced them to the letter but was determined to hold the island no matter what—which included repelling a potential British landing! Campbell read the orders and blinked, especially the passage that read: "*... resist all attempts at interference by the British... by intimidation or force.*" Either the world had turned upside down while he was gunk holing, or Pickett was indulging in a dangerous fiction. In an August 14 letter to Harney, Campbell questioned why the British could not land the same as the Americans. They were certainly justified under the terms of the standing agreement between the two nations, but:

> ...I found Captain Pickett had different views, derived from your instructions, which he confidentially showed to me. I perceived that they were susceptible of the interpretation he gave them, though they were not directly mandatory on the subject.[13]

Despite his concern, Campbell was reluctant to interfere in a military matter, especially if fresh orders from the War Department had reached Harney without Campbell's knowledge. He returned to Semiahmoo on August 1—missing Prevost by a day—to prepare for an expedition deep into the Cascade Mountains along the 49th parallel. Prevost and *Satellite* finally caught up with him at Semiahmoo on August 4.

As Campbell had feared, Prevost believed he had been deceived during their meetings in Griffin Bay while John de Courcy was ashore challenging Pickett. Their gentlemanly disagreement over the proper water boundary—Haro or Rosario—in recent weeks had degenerated into an exchange of petulant letters loaded with double-talk as both men viewed their roles with growing frustration. This was compounded when Campbell accused Prevost of coming to the table armed with a "secret" instruction not to consider the American claim. Is it any wonder that the commissioners did not meet personally to discuss Pickett's landing, but exchanged a series of letters with *Satellite* anchored in Drayton Bay?[14]

Prevost right off wanted to know if Campbell knew beforehand that troops were going to be landed, and, if so, did the U.S. Government sanction the landing. If not, he invited Campbell to join him in urging Harney to withdraw the troops not only to avoid war, but also to keep from spoiling business opportunities on both sides of the Atlantic. Not to be undone by Campbell's wordiness and exaggeration, Prevost concluded:

> ...that an act so unprecedented in the history of civilized and enlightened nations, and so contrary to that natural courtesy which is due from one great nation to another, cannot be productive of good, and may in the end entail such serious consequences, that I am sure both you and I would deplore to the last hour of our existence any hesitation or neglect on our parts to do all that lies in our power to avert pending evil...[15]

Campbell in turn accused Prevost of overstepping his bounds by pressing a boundary colleague about military matters over which he had no control. Not only did Campbell refuse to acknowledge any questions about the landing, he further lambasted Prevost for making threats:

> ...Notwithstanding the apparent air of moderation with which you have clothed your words, there pervades in your whole communication a vein of assumption and an attempt at intimidation by exciting apprehensions of evil, not well calculated to produce the effect you profess so ardently to desire...[16]

More exchanges followed. Prevost stubbornly demanded answers and accused Campbell of evasion and subterfuge. Campbell denied he was evading anything, since Prevost had no right to question him. On and on it went throughout the 4th and 5th, until they both gave up and complained about one other to their superiors. Prevost was so convinced Campbell was in collusion with Harney that he refused to have anything more to do with him.[17]

While the commissioners were hurling barbs, Lt. Cmdr. James Alden and the side-wheel U.S. Coast Survey Steamer *Active* dropped anchor in Griffin Bay on Thursday, August 4 for the 1859 survey, which on the Northwest Coast was usually performed from July to October. As a naval assistant, Alden took his orders from Coast Survey director Alexander Dallas Bache (a great-grandson of Benjamin Franklin). But Alden's first loyalty was always to the navy so he immediately offered to intercede on Pickett's behalf, divine British intentions and defuse the crisis. He had known Douglas since his first trip to the region in 1853 and was friendly with several of the Royal Navy officers. Alden reported the highlights of the meeting (liberally embellished) to Bache:

> I asked (Douglas) what Captain Hornby's orders were and if he was ordered to land why didn't he? In

reply to this the Governor said that if the Magistrate called upon Captain Hornby for assistance in the proper execution of the laws he would land

"Then," said I, "there must be a collision, for Captain Pickett will not permit it."

"What," said his Excellency, "Captain Pickett has only about 50 men? Would he fire upon six hundred?"

"Yes," said I, "six thousand."

"Oh!" said Captain Richards, R.N., who was present, "that would be madness."

"Call it anything you like," I replied, "madness or anything else. Captain Pickett has made up his mind to do it and I pledge you upon my honor he will, if he should be (to use a rather inelegant expression, but one very much to the purpose) 'wiped out' the next moment."

The *Active* remained in the area throughout the imbroglio, abandoning the largely "unfinished" hydrographic mission for more than a month to serve as a messenger and military stores ship. Harney cited Alden in dispatches, which was soon to become a dubious honor.[18]

Meanwhile, *Pylades* under Captain de Courcy was beating against a terrific southwest storm, not uncommon in August off the Washington coast. Even under steam, the ship could not make headway enough to get Colonel Hawkins to San Francisco in time to catch the mail boat to Panama City. De Courcy decided to come about and make for Victoria where Hawkins could board a commercial steamer and catch the next mail boat south when the weather calmed. Running with the wind, de Courcy spotted a tall ship on the horizon. It was the old HMS *Ganges* with Rear Adm. R. Lambert Baynes on board. De Courcy ordered a boat and braved the wild seas to consult with Baynes aboard the flagship.

At first sight, the Pacific Station commander belied the image of career fighting sailor, who, as a midshipman, had seen action at New Orleans during the War of 1812. He was in his 60s by then, short, slight of build and balding, with his graying hair combed over to hide a shiny pate. He fancied top hats, high collars and elaborate bow ties with his sea uniform—consistent with a well-known and appreciated sense of humor. He had been an admiral since 1855 and in his current job since 1858. Hudson's Bay Company factor Angus McDonald summed him up best: "...plain, little, big-hearted, unassuming, lowland Scotsman, lame but full of salt and fresh fun." The admiral's cool demeanor was in sharp contrast to Douglas or Harney. Most critical to the situation, he had a low tolerance for idiotic behavior. He is purported to have said when informed of the crisis, "Tut, tut, no, no, the damn fools."[19]

Ganges dropped anchor in Esquimalt on Friday, August 5, whereupon Baynes approved Hornby's course, but it was not until August 13 that he put it in writing. Hornby was commended for avoiding a potentially disastrous situation by refusing to land the marines. Moreover, Baynes agreed with Hornby (and Pickett) that the Royal Navy remaining on alert on Griffin Bay rather than forcing the issue ashore would not compromise the British claim to the island. He formally cancelled Douglas' orders, and directed Hornby to "strictly avoid all interference" with Pickett's force and "by every means in your power to prevent the risk of collision taking place." As insurance against this possibility, Hornby was ordered not to assist Magistrate John de Courcy unless it was absolutely necessary. Douglas, in turn, was asked to advise the magistrate not to act against the Americans without consulting Hornby.[20]

Douglas was furious. Hornby was praised for rank insubordination! He struck off a letter to Baynes pointing out that, quite the contrary, if Hornby had "vigorously carried out" his instructions the British would have maintained jurisdiction and the U.S. troops would have been withdrawn or reduced in number. And yet, as matters stood, he had no objections to Baynes's orders as Captain de Courcy had previously urged this same course.[21]

Despite his conciliatory attitude toward Baynes, Douglas remained angry enough to dispatch a hot letter to Colonial Secretary Lord Lytton:

> Hornby did not deem it advisable to carry out my instructions... the absence of movement of this kind has not only increased the confidence of the occupying party; and it places me in a difficult position, for so much time having elapsed the carrying out of the movement of this period, deprives it of most of its force.

He would have driven them out "...had it not been for the opposition of the civil and military authorities of this Colony." Now he was forced to act "as circumstances demand."[22]

Braced for the governor's criticisms, Hornby wrote a letter for the record to Baynes, stating that his forces at that time consisted of 69 marines, 15 engineers and the ship's company, whom he believed could land and contend with Pickett. But he promised Baynes that he would not do as the Americans had done, "violating" territory under negotiation between the two nations.

Hornby need not have worried. He was later praised for his forbearance in several quarters, including the Royal Engineers commander, Colonel Moody. In a letter to British Army Gen. Sir John Fox Burgoyne (a descendent of the Revolutionary War general of the same name), Moody remarked that it was lucky for Great

Britain that Hornby was on San Juan. The captain had performed superbly despite the fact that "...the governor wrote a very clever letter indirectly ordering him to land troops, but throwing the responsibility on him. Hornby has far too much 'mother wit' to be caught that way—of course he did not land them."

When Douglas was portrayed as a peacemaker in the incident some months later, Hornby commented to his wife:

> I hear that Governor Douglas has got much praise in England for keeping peace with the Yankees. That is rather good, when one knows that he would hear of nothing but shooting them all at first and that, after all, peace was only preserved by my not complying with his wishes, as I felt he was all wrong from the first. I got the abuse for saying that San Juan was not more our island than the Americans; and that we should be equally wrong in landing troops there.

And so fighting had been averted. If there was any one moment when Great Britain and the United States could have plunged into war, it was the encounter between Hornby and Pickett on Griffin Bay. They were far removed from their respective seats of power, pushed by immediate superiors who had lost all sense of perspective and by local populations clamoring for war.

Over the years George Pickett has been described as everything from Hubbs's great captain ready to take on the British Empire to Winfield Scott's mediocrity, stumbling through matters of which he possessed only a modest grasp. Conversely, Geoffrey Phipps Hornby is consistently remembered as a courageous man who would rather disobey orders than start a war.

The record shows George Pickett liberally misinterpreted his orders, and then held to a rigid path, refusing to make a commitment without confirmation from his superiors. The prospect of being on the point of U.S. foreign policy must have been a thrilling antidote to dreary frontier duty. However, he was ignorant of even the most rudimentary facts about the Treaty of Oregon, inexcusable for a man poised to shape events on an international scale. Once he sensed the gravity of his acts, his indignation over perceived slights was supplanted by high anxiety. After that he sought a peaceful course, despite his posturing with Hornby, his superiors and civilians such as Hubbs. In reality he was not prepared in any fashion to contend the British Empire. George Pickett would much rather have lunched and held forth with Geoff Hornby than fight him.

Hornby sincerely wanted to avoid war. Owing to his family connections, he was familiar with the nuances of foreign policy and the importance of Great Britain's economic ties to the United States. He also was aware of the Pacific Station policy of restraint and the views of his superior, Admiral Baynes. To commence hostilities without exhausting every avenue—especially checking first with the admiral—may have damaged his career.

More than anyone, Admiral Baynes deserves credit that the only casualty of this first stage of the Pig War was a pig. That's why he was knighted the following year.

But the crisis was far from over. While Baynes was attempting to restore calm, William Selby Harney, having had time to digest Pickett's letter, was preparing to send reinforcements.

Chapter 12

REINFORCEMENTS

The day after the *Shubrick* left with Pickett's dispatch to Harney, Griffin Bay again settled into conviviality. Pickett and Hornby stopped posturing and exchanged visits while British sailors and marines and American soldiers—many of the latter recent expatriate Europeans—mingled, swapped newspapers and cigars, and talked about home. Tourists continued to pour off the boats from Victoria and all the while a new town was being born.

Pickett's first tent stake was barely hammered when the first liquor establishment rose in a wall tent about 25 yards off above the Hudson's Bay Company dock. This was San Juan Village. Soon barges appeared with shacks from the abandoned mining camp on Bellingham Bay followed by rotgut whisky, cots, dirty curtains, and young Indian women. The women were mostly escaped slaves, or slaves being worked for a profit, or simply hopeless girls cast adrift from their groups. Soldiers, sailors, and marines were ready and willing, much to the chagrin of their respective commanding officers.

The *Victoria Gazette's* reporter (who called himself *Curioso*) wrote that "some three or four persons had started little groggeries near the landing from the harbor and several parties had been in a state of drunkenness the night before." Charles Griffin was amazed: "Soldiers, Inds. & Men all were determined to be drunk together. Never saw anything like it."[1]

This was not the tension-wrought island William Selby Harney envisioned. In his mind, British ships were lying offshore; guns run out, marines at ready near the boats, waiting for a false move from the gallant Virginian. Pickett had shown pluck, so Harney recommended him for brevet promotion. Soon the army, with the backing of the locals, would come to Pickett's aid. Even the newspaper in Olympia opined that the government had at last done the right thing.[2]

San Juan Island was not Harney's only concern. He was having trouble with his junior officers, a rebellious lot who, in his view, had required whipping into line. In recent weeks they had questioned his judgment in using soldier labor to build a private residence for himself off post. One officer resigned from the service over it. Inflammatory letters began to appear in the *Pioneer and Democrat*, the *Colonist*, *Gazette* and even the *New York Times*. An anonymous letter, allegedly written by an officer, stated: "General Harney, who is here called 'Goliah' for two reasons, first, that he is a very large man; and second, that he is all matter and no mind - ought I think to be court-martialed, and dismissed from the service for his conduct in this case." Another officer, who claimed to be stationed at San Juan, proclaimed Harney "one of the weakest officers and most arrogant humbugs in the army, and not all qualified for his position. He is a laughingstock, wherever he goes; and his administration is a series of blunders and mistakes. He is as callous as a pot-house politician, and insensible, I am afraid, to shame."[3]

The San Juan officers were aghast at this attack and circulated a petition denying any part of the letter. However, Capt. Lewis Cass Hunt, commander of Company C, Fourth Infantry, in a letter to a lady friend, boasted about submitting articles detailing Harney's failings (see Chapter 14).

With personal tensions and frustrations building, Harney received Pickett's August 3 letter outlining his encounter with

Hornby, and describing British ships "...lying in a menacing attitude in the harbor."[4]

He must have fulminated by the time he got to Douglas's proclamation, which gravely condemned the American occupation and stated that the islands had always been "undeviatingly claimed to in the Crown of Great Britain."

Never one to be surpassed in righteous indignation, Harney replied on August 6, chastising the governor for sending a warship "...to convey the chief factor of the Hudson's Bay Company (Dallas) for the purpose of seizing an American citizen and forcibly transporting him to Vancouver's island to be tried by British laws." Until Harney's government received "proper redress" from Douglas—in what form was not stated—the soldiers would remain. The general did not mention anything about sending more soldiers, which he already decided to do.[5]

Harney wrote the War Department the next morning to advise them he was sending Lt. Col. Silas Casey from Fort Steilacoom to San Juan Island with reinforcements. If dispatching Casey with three more companies, plus naval guns, was not escalation enough, Harney's prose was so incendiary it must have raised Pres. James Buchanan right out of his chair. After reiterating Hubbs's view of the pig incident, the general once more complained that the Royal Navy was intimidating American citizens in collusion with the Hudson's Bay Company; that the HBC "pretended" to own the island, but only had a few shacks to show for it; and that the company had threatened "at different times, to send the northern Indians down upon (American settlers) and drive them for the island." If this wasn't enough to generate alarm about his diplomatic skills, Harney confirmed it by declaring,

> ...It would be well for the British government to know the American people of this coast will never sanction any claim they may assert to any other

island in the Puget Sound than that of Vancouver's,
south of the 49th parallel, and east of the Canal de
Haro; any attempt at possession by them will be
followed by a collision.

If Harney raised the president's hopes in the next paragraph
by stating "...no one is more desirous than myself for an amicable
settlement," he quickly dashed them again by concluding that
the British had forfeited their rights to the island for being so
"perfidious." The president could rest assured that Harney would
"use all the means" at his command to hold on to the San Juans.[6]

Harney's letter may have been laced with gross exaggerations and
a couple of outright lies, but the underlying truth was that Douglas
had claimed the San Juan Islands for Great Britain. In fact, he had
been attempting to enforce British jurisdiction for more than eight
years going back to the Cussans lumber incident on Lopez Island.
He had dispatched Magistrate John de Courcy to San Juan to eject
American "trespassers." This was solid ground upon which Harney
could have built a case. It would have satisfied even the President of
the United States. Acting Secretary of War William Drinkard said
as much a few weeks later.

After finishing off the Douglas reply, Harney ordered
Pleasonton to write Pickett and endorse his actions on San Juan.
Pickett was to continue to reject a joint military occupation and stop
the British magistrate from enforcing civil law-even over British
subjects. "...No joint occupation nor any civil jurisdiction will
be permitted on San Juan island by the British authorities under
any circumstances," Pleasonton stated. This oddly enough placed
Harney in accord with Baynes, but for entirely different reasons.
Pleasonton completed the missive by advising Pickett that Casey was
on the way with reinforcements... and would assume command.[7]

Casey's orders were to reinforce Pickett and take command
on San Juan Island, leaving only one officer and a detachment to

mind "public property" at Fort Steilacoom. He was to take all of his ammunition and field guns and leave promptly aboard private steamers as "British authorities threaten to force Pickett's position." If need be, Casey was authorized to call out the "Volunteers," presumably the American settlers, to defend San Juan Island. "This authority the General is confident you will exercise with judgment and discretion," Pleasonton cautioned. No regular officer relished attempting to control armed civilians with a thirst for real estate.

To impress the British that the Americans intended to remain in force, Casey was to remove the eight, 32-pound naval guns aboard *Massachusetts* and place them in position to protect the harbor. Pickett would turn over his instructions to Casey: "Their substance may be stated: in not allowing any joint occupation of San Juan Island, either civil or military and that the right of our citizens on the Island will be respected as on American soil."[8]

Still another mail pouch was dispatched on August 8 with letters explaining Harney's actions to the Adjutant General of the U.S. Army, Col. Samuel Cooper in Washington City, and Department of Pacific commander Brig. Gen. Newman S. Clarke in San Francisco.

The Clarke letter included an enclosure addressed to the "Senior Officer of the United States Navy, Commanding Squadron on the Pacific Coast." This was a plea for naval support in the San Juan Islands. While Harney did not expect the British to attack his soldiers, he expressed hoped for something better than the slow moving and soon-to-be toothless *Massachusetts* to observe the Brits.[9]

Harney's letter to Cooper (which, by army protocol, was really intended for Lt. Gen. Winfield Scott), though brief, contained more half-truths and exaggerations to justify sending reinforcements. According to Harney, the islands had been under Whatcom County jurisdiction for "months" and "foreigners" as well American citizens on San Juan had paid county taxes. He neglected to mention that the only taxes ever paid by "foreigners" had four legs and had been wrestled into canoes in the dead of night. Because Whatcom County was clearly in charge, he stated, the British never attempted to "exercise authority" over the island except clandestinely, as in the case of the pig. This changed when Magistrate John de Courcy and other "civil authorities" were commissioned and dispatched by warship to enforce British laws after learning of Pickett's landing.[10]

At Fort Steilacoom, Casey wasted no time, setting off the next day aboard the requisitioned sternwheeler *Julia* bound for Port Townsend. He barely cleared the Tacoma Narrows when Lt. Comdr. James Alden, aboard the survey steamer *Active*, intercepted him. Alden breathlessly reported that he had steamed at full throttle to warn Casey that if he attempted to land his troops and guns HMS *Tribune*, anchored in Griffin Bay, would open fire.[11] This information came from Pickett who—unaware that the British had decided not to oppose reinforcements and that Hornby had opted not to press the issue of a joint occupation—believed a landing near the HBC wharf would be "interfered with." Casey weighed Pickett's penchant for drama with what he knew of the Royal Navy, or as he termed it, the "quasi enemy" in the Pacific Northwest, and decided to continue.[12]

He anchored that evening at Port Townsend where he encountered Archibald Campbell, the U.S. boundary commissioner, who by now was specializing in being the "last to know." The sight of 180 fully equipped infantry, coupled with the knowledge that 100 more troops, plus artillery, were on the way, troubled him enough to accept Casey's invitation to come along and observe the landing. The colonel hoped Campbell's presence would lend weight to negotiations he hoped to set in motion. Little did Casey know that Campbell had become *persona non grata* in Victoria.

The following morning a heavy fog rolled up the Strait of Juan de Fuca and smothered the island, which made negotiating Cattle Pass on the southern end almost impossible. The *Julia's* captain told Casey that, by his reckoning, they were just off a long pebble beach not far from Pickett's camp. He suggested Casey land the troops and the howitzers (small cannon used for high, plunging fire) on the beach and when the fog burned off unload the freight in Griffin Bay. As a sternwheeler, the *Julia* could be beached at the head and planks run ashore. Casey thought it a splendid idea and ordered it done, while the *Active* and *Shubrick* stood by. The troops trudged through the heavy sand and rock and up a low bluff, beyond which Pickett's camp occupied the level prairie. Pickett's soldiers told their newly arrived mates that Griffin Bay and the British warships were enveloped in the fog about a half-mile distant off the bayside shore.

While his troops were settling, Casey and the *Julia* rounded the point and as the fog lifted steamed into the harbor. *Tribune* was anchored several hundred yards out, broadside to shore, with gun ports open, just as Alden had described her. The *Julia* dropped anchor and the crew and several soldiers left behind unloaded Casey's stores, including ammunition for the howitzers, food, tents and other provisions. Contrary to Pickett's warning, the British "did not interfere with the landing of our freight," Casey reported. "Whether they would have interfered with the landing of the troops I cannot say. It is Captain Pickett's opinion that they would."[13]

Indeed. While the *Julia* exhaled her last and lowered her boats not far from *Tribune*, another warship was steaming toward South Beach from the direction of Victoria. Despite several days of amicable relations with British officials, Pickett's imagination was again generating catastrophe. He sent a messenger to the *Julia* with an urgent message for Casey to land and proceed immediately to Pickett's camp at South Beach. The ship (later identified as *Satellite*) was adjacent to his camp and appeared to be ready to open fire! Once it did, the marines and sailors from *Tribune* would likely land on the harbor side and assault the American position. If so attacked, they should fire the howitzers, spike the guns, loose a volley of musketry and high tail it for the woods.

Hubbs vividly recalled the strategy. Soldiers from the Ninth and Fourth Infantry and Third Artillery dotted the hills east of the camp (rather than emerging from the beach) in their "blue coats and brass buttons" while Casey's howitzers joined Pickett's on the crest of the hill overlooking Griffin Bay. Casey sought out Hubbs and told him that he hoped to avoid bloodshed. At the sound of the first shot Hubbs was to mount his horse and guide Casey "across the retreating grounds." This did not set well with Hubbs, who 33 years on, professed that while the British outnumbered the Americans two to one, the Americans could have held them off if the "Hero of Gettysburg" had remained in command:

> Things looked very different since Pickett had been superseded in command, and from what we afterward experienced the British forces would have been allowed to land unmolested, for a little fever and ague struck the new officers now in command.[14]

Casey actually was hesitant to countermand Pickett's orders, having so recently arrived. However, *Tribune* had not reacted when he unloaded his stores, which prompted Casey to ask Hornby for a meeting. Several hours later Hornby arrived at Casey's camp with the respective commissioners, Prevost and Campbell. Casey later claimed that he admonished Hornby for threatening Pickett with deadly force. When he asked Hornby from whom he received his instructions, Hornby replied Admiral Baynes. If Casey wanted to confront Baynes he would have to go to Esquimalt Harbor.

Changing to dress uniforms, resplendent with plums and epaulets, Casey and Pickett, joined by Campbell, departed the next morning aboard the *Shubrick*. The meeting fell through over protocol when Baynes refused to leave his 84-gun ship of the line to wait upon Casey aboard a lighthouse tender with a single 24-pounder mounted on the bow. Baynes had shown forbearance in leaving the island to the U.S. Army until diplomats settled the question. But he would not call upon a lower ranking officer aboard a tin-pot steamer a third the size of his own ship. Several hours went by as they haggled over the venue—Pickett serving as messenger boy— until Casey finally gave up and returned to San Juan Island.

The following day in a report to Harney, Casey explained that he went to Esquimalt of his own volition to avoid a collision. Had Baynes promised not to threaten Pickett, Casey would have recommended withdrawal of reinforcements in anticipation of a diplomatic solution. He then recounted the protocol flap, which probably explained why Royal Navy officers had not contacted him since his return to San Juan. The chilly response spurred him to seek four more companies of soldiers, plus a detachment of engineers to build fortifications. It was not pleasant, Casey wrote, "...to be at the mercy of anyone who is liable at any moment to become your enemy." He also suggested contacting the U.S. Navy in San Francisco Bay. In the meantime, he promised to "resist any attack they may make upon my position."[15]

Casey's requests for more troops and heavy guns were approved, along with brief instructions to build semi permanent fortifications that included entrenchments and gun platforms. Pleasonton relayed Harney's displeasure with the lieutenant colonel for his attempt at international diplomacy. But he also commended him for making the peaceful gesture and urged him to treat British subjects with the same courtesy as American citizens.[16]

Douglas shared Harney's unhappiness over the blown meeting. He was aboard *Ganges* during one of Pickett's shuttles and asked the Virginian why it had been Baynes and not himself to whom Casey applied. Pickett at first said Casey was unaware the governor was present. But in the next breath squandered his diplomatic points by stating that Casey preferred Baynes over Douglas as Baynes was the senior official in the colony (at least in military matters). Pickett had a way with the governor.

In measured tones, Douglas went to the source and vented his

ever-growing frustration with Harney, whose letter he had received
two days before, writing the Colonial Secretary, Lord Lytton on
August 12:

> It has now been clearly established that the Military
> occupation of San Juan Island has been undertaken
> without the knowledge or authority of the government
> of the United States, and upon grounds that are
> entirely false, both in fact and in principle...

Douglas felt certain that once the American government did
find out, Harney's actions would be rejected, which must have set
well with Lytton, who coined the phrase, "...the pen is mightier
than the sword."[17]

The governor next wrote Harney, hoping to convince him that
the HBC had no jurisdiction over the islands, even to the point
of claiming the Company lacked any influence whatever with the
government on Vancouver Island. He gave an "unhesitating and
unqualified" denial to the charges of threatening Cutlar with
arrest, though he did not mention the pig incident. He asserted that
no ship of war had "ever been sent to convey the chief factor or any
other officer of Hudson's Bay Company to San Juan for the purpose
of seizing an American Citizen."[18] He then referred Harney to an
enclosed copy of the Marcy letter, contending that his government
had never deviated from the spirit of the document. He claimed
to have dismissed accounts of a depredation committed against
HBC property, stressed that had he decided to act, he would have
first applied to the authorities in Olympia. And finally, he pointed
out that if Harney knew of Cutlar's "fancied grievance" when he
visited Victoria, he should have asked the governor about it before
dispatching Pickett from Fort Bellingham. In closing, Douglas
asked that troops be withdrawn.[19]

Two days later Archibald Campbell finally posted his own letter
of inquiry to Harney. The commissioner mainly wanted to know why

he had not known beforehand that Pickett's landing was something more than chasing Indians. Judging from Pickett's orders, he initially thought Washington had issued fresh instructions to Harney, so he decided not to interfere despite Prevost's urgings. While he agreed the San Juan Islands rightfully belonged to the United States, he no longer thought the dispute had been resolved, and that meant trouble. Unless the general had:

> ...some intimation from the War Department which has governed your action, I fear that the decided action that you have taken in declaring the island American territory may somewhat embarrass the question. I will be greatly relieved to learn that you have some authority from the government for the decisive step you have taken, though I do not pretend to ask or desire the information in my official capacity...[20]

Harney apologized to Campbell for the briefing oversight. He thought the commissioner already had left for Washington City (which does not explain the Pleasonton briefing about "northern Indians"). His actions had nothing to do with the boundary dispute, Harney claimed. The British were attempting to enforce their laws over American citizens. He closed by wishing Campbell well in the commission's work and pledged to support it. [21]

A mollified Campbell replied, excusing himself for being presumptuous. He then defended the general in a September 3 report to Secretary of State Lewis Cass, taking the opportunity to castigate Prevost and his government once more for obfuscating and delaying the boundary settlement. It was clear the British government had ordered the Vancouver Island government to treat the islands as "British dominions," in violation of the standing agreement, he wrote. The HBC had long coveted the island; therefore was it any wonder that they would contest a military occupation by the rightful owners?[22]

On San Juan Island, two capital class warships were aiming their guns at Casey, who was unaware Baynes had decided not to attack. He entrenched his camp in a secure location, as per instructions, and erected an earthwork for the naval guns that would give the British pause. Over the next several days more than 300,000 board feet of lumber was landed, enough for several gun platforms, barracks and other structures. Casey also managed to land the *Massachusetts'* guns on the beach without the means to move or emplace them. To underscore his alarm he itemized the British forces available in the Strait of Juan de Fuca: five ships, 167 guns and 1,940 sailors, marines, and sappers—enough to blow him off the island.[23]

The guns eventually were manhandled to the top of the ridge overlooking the Hudson's Bay dock and Griffin Bay. On August 17, Casey's reinforcements arrived, including four batteries (companies) of the Third Artillery, who disembarked on the Hudson's Bay Company wharf, marched up Charles Griffin's road and over the ridge to the prairie camp, accompanied by a patchwork military band. The new arrivals boosted Casey's forces to 15 officers and 424 enlisted men, plus 50 civilian laborers engaged to build the new camp.

Hornby was dismayed, especially after his assurances to Douglas and Baynes that no American reinforcements were forthcoming. "Six of their heavy guns are placed on the ridge of the hill overlooking the harbour; and by throwing up a parapet (the guns) would command the harbor; even in their present condition they would be difficult to silence," he wrote Baynes. "The other two heavy guns and field pieces are placed to defend their camp." This did not appear to be a force designed to repel raiding Indians. Rather, "they seemed not only prepared to defend themselves, but to threaten us."

The captain wondered what would happen if the Whatcom County Sheriff returned and tried to collect taxes from the HBC. And worse, rumor had it that Harney himself was coming with 400 more soldiers. "They are continually landing supplies of all sorts, and have now on the beach large quantities of lumber for gun platforms. Scantling of Barracks, etc., so that there is every symptom of their occupation being permanent." As matters stood, Hornby wrote, he could neither protect the magistrate nor enforce British laws. The Americans had demonstrated to him that they would take what they wanted when they wanted, regardless of prior agreement or international law. If they forced the magistrate to strike his flag and stopped him from doing his duty, Hornby, by previous instructions, would evacuate the magistrate. He would then fire on the American camp to "resent the insult to the flag and... this I should do unless I hear from you to the contrary."[24]

Baynes was so alarmed by Hornby's state of mind that his reply of August 16 was swift, specific, and firm:

> In my memorandum to you of the 13th of August I desired you by every means in your power to avoid a collision with the troops of the United States. It is now my positive order that you do not, on any account whatever, take the initiative in commencing hostilities by firing on them or any work they may have thrown up... Should the troops of the United States commit any aggressive act by firing on the *Tribune* or any of Her Majesty's ships or boats, you are at full liberty to resent the insult by adopting such measures as you think [desirable] informing me of the circumstances as quickly as possible.[25]

The admiral's remarkable calm and forbearance in the face of bluff and bluster (from both sides) quelled the initial excitement of the occupation, and the standoff began to wane by mid-August.

The respective magistrates, Crosbie and de Courcy, presaged the eventual joint occupation by acting jointly in banning the sale of liquor on the island. The soldiers may have been Americans, but a good many rabble-rousers were venturing over from Victoria to get in on the fun.

Then cooperation between peace officers almost came to naught when Deputy Collector of Customs Hubbs refused to allow passengers from Victoria ashore, and then required all ships to clear customs at Port Townsend before landing at San Juan. His growing appetite for power peaked when he quarantined John de Courcy's baggage. In his memoir, Hubbs recalled ordering de Courcy, James Forsyth, and a U.S. Mail agent, Capt. John Scranton, to pay duty on their return from a shopping trip to Victoria. All three refused, and though Forysth and Scranton were allowed to land anyway, Hubbs refused to budge on de Courcy's property. The Irishman, at least according to Hubbs, blustered that he would unload his gear under *Satellite's* guns and signaled the ship to send a boat. That's when, at Casey's direction, Pickett interceded and de Courcy finally was permitted to bring his baggage ashore. This reaffirmed Hubbs' opinion that the U.S. Army was next to useless with Silas Casey (and not Pickett) in command.[26]

By Sunday, August 21, all was quiet. Casey attended services aboard *Satellite* and posted general orders that soldiers were not to disturb Belle Vue Sheep Farm. This was probably in response to a letter of complaint to Douglas written two weeks earlier by Dallas.

> Our sheep, cattle and horses are disturbed at their
> pasturage, and driven from their drinking springs,
> in the vicinity of which the troops are encamped.
> Much of the pasturage has been destroyed. In a
> future day I shall be prepared to bring forward a
> claim against the United States Government...

In the near term Dallas wanted to know how Douglas would protect the plantation "...of which we have had till now, almost undisturbed possession during the last six years."[27]

No question. Times had changed for Belle Vue Sheep Farm

with more changes on the way. Casey intended to move next door. If the colonel had ever wondered why Pickett graduated last in his West Point class, his curiosity was satisfied after spending several nights at the Spring Camp site. It was as vulnerable to Mother Nature as it was to naval bombardment.

> We are encamped in rather exposed situation with regard to the wind, being at the entrance of the Straits of Fuca. The weather at times is already quite inclement." Gale force winds two nights running nearly blew the old colonel out of his tent. [28]

On August 22, Casey ordered his growing force (now about 450 men) to move camp to the north slope of the ridge near the HBC barns—once home to the errant pig that started the whole mess. Large, conical Sibley tents were shipped from Fort Steilacoom to the new site, which he considered "a very good position for an entrenched camp." The tents supplemented the box-frame buildings Pickett had already brought from Fort Bellingham, among these the hospital, barracks, laundress and officers' quarters.

Casey also saw to camp defenses, outlined in a letter to acting adjutant Alfred Pleasonton: "I shall put my heavy guns in position to bear on the harbor, and also on vessels that might take a position on the other side. Shells from the shipping might be able to reach us, and we may not be able to protect the camp from there; but I shall try."[29]

On the 23rd, a combat engineering team (called sappers), led by Corps of Engineers 2nd. Lt. Henry Martyn Robert, arrived to design and supervise construction of an earthen fortification on a bare ridge running east of the new camp and sloping into the prairie that divided Griffin Bay from the Strait of Juan de Fuca. The site had a commanding view of both strait and bay.

Throughout the work, William A. Peck, Jr., a private soldier on the team, kept a diary of his experiences on San Juan Island and in the Pacific Northwest. On disembarking from the *Massachusetts* at San Juan, he first tasted British humor: "While they were shoving off in their boats, the men pulled directly under the guns of the H.B.M. Sloop of War *Satellite* and the musicians played 'Yankee Doodle' for dear life." By August 25 Peck recorded that his team was engaged in "laying out the works for a fort all day." Because no teams of dray horses or oxen were available, the team supervised infantry and artillery troops not engaged in drilling.[30]

All of the work was done by pick and shovel, as per Alfred Pleasonton's instructions:

> ...Have platforms made for your heavy guns, and cover your camp as much as possible by entrenchment, placing your heavy guns in battery on the most exposed approaches... select your position with the greatest care to avoid fire from the British ship(s).[31]

Robert took advantage of the site's natural features, laying out his gun platforms and ramparts with a precision still evident today. The British officers were impressed. They especially knew how a formal fieldwork could alter the situation on San Juan Island. A fortress not only provided a means of last-ditch defense, but properly sited, also would permit a smaller force—even with inferior troops—to resist a larger one until help arrived. "(Casey's camp) is very strongly placed in the most commanding position at this end of the island, well sheltered in the rear and one side by the Forest and on the other side by a Commanding eminence," wrote Prevost.[32]

While the soldiers dug, guests arrived, among them Washington Territorial Gov. Richard D. Gholson. The governor held his hat over his heart while nine companies, led by Colonel Casey on horseback, passed in review for him at the old spring campsite on the prairie. Not to be outdone, the British invited the governor to witness gun drills and have tea aboard *Satellite*. Another visitor was former Gov. Isaac Stevens, the newly elected Delegate for Washington Territory to the U.S. Congress.[33]

Others from all walks of life came as well. Some, such as Matthew Macfie, a British subject, relied on the eloquence of facts rather than bombast to describe what they saw. Macfie visited San Juan at the height of the crisis, catching the *Shubrick* over from Port Townsend. His ship dropped anchor at 6 p.m. in Griffin Bay.

> ...H.M.S. *Satellite* was lying off with guns shotted, and pointed in the direction of the American camp, which was about a mile and a half from the beach. A boat came to us from the British man-of-war for letters, and I was introduced to the midshipman in charge as a 'clergyman' from England. This term, in British parlance, having a technical meaning— which it has not in America—and not being applied by my host in the British sense, the young officer was pleased to draw gratuitous conclusions, by which I seemed likely to be placed-innocently-in a position as false as it was delicate.

Macfie tabulated about 500 men and was not far off. With the arrival of Robert and his team the U.S. force had swelled to 461 officers and men. He described the earthworks under construction and mounted with cannon, which moved him to remark: "Judging from appearances, I am not sure that our nation has ever been so nearly precipitated into a war with 'Brother Jonathan' since 1812." He casually visited the tents of American officers, who "spoke freely of the international 'difficulty' that had arisen, and confessed that while convinced of the justice of their cause, they occupied their present position reluctantly. There was none of that thirst for war with England manifested by them which characterizes the less cultivated portion of American citizens."

He was next invited to Casey's tent:

...The venerable colonel, a man of about 65, seemed
more concerned if possible than his brother officers
that harmony should be maintained between the two
countries, and assured me that he was using all his
influence on the side of peace. He regarded it, he said,
as the greatest calamity that could befall the cause
of civilization all over the world, that two nations,
allied by community of race, language, laws, and
religion, should be plunged into hostilities. This was
saying a great deal of amna whose fortune was war.
Little then did my excellent friend apprehend the
melancholy consequences of civil tumult with which
his own country was so soon to be visited. I must
express the surprise and gratification I felt at seeing
one in the colonel's station having a reputation for
sober and reflective piety. He told me he was in the
habit of repairing to the British ship of war to attend
divine service every Sunday, and I learned that by a
pleasing coincidence, Captain Prevost of the *Satellite*
was a man of the same character.

No matter. Casey promised that if "a single shot" were fired
from a British vessel his troops would shoot back. "...'It is almost
certain,' said he, 'that in that case your ships would blow our
handful of men here to atoms, but 300,000 men would instantly
pour in from the states to take our place.' "

No wonder Macfie expressed relief when Admiral Baynes
returned from Valparaiso. "I have no hesitation in saying that
but for the timely arrival of Admiral Baynes, war was inevitable."
Had Douglas remained in charge, Macfie was certain that burial
parties would be working under flags of truce. In his view, Douglas
was still bitter over the loss of Oregon and "...from that moment
imbibed inimical prejudices toward them that only wanted a
suitable occasion for its manifestation."[34]

Those prejudices were still at work in the governor's mind and his exasperation was growing thanks to a stinging article in the *Colonist* on August 17. Following the usual florid opening, the editor cut to the lead: "An error has been committed by somebody." The government—civil and naval arms alike—was being wishy-washy in response to the American landing. Douglas must have choked when he read:

> Either the Administration should have been satisfied with a pacific policy, manifested by serving the United States authorities with a formal protest or an assertion of our sovereignty in the first place, and to have allowed the matter to rest until despatches (sic) were received from the imperial government, or it should have at once landed troops on the island without making such a display of force or asking permission. We confess that we are not disposed to accept peace at any price; for if that were the case cowardice would be the safest policy.[35]

Douglas again vented his frustration on Hornby. That same day he wrote Baynes that a "passive" and "retrograde" policy would not work with Americans. He was familiar with the "American Character" after his many years in the Pacific Northwest. As such he believed that if the naval officers had obeyed his original instructions no bloodshed would have ensued. Now the Americans were dug in and there would be the devil to pay getting them out.

> Had that (joint) occupation been effected as I intended, I feel confident in my own mind that no further reinforcements of American troops would have been landed, no fortifications would have been thrown up, and all of the action in the case would have been in perfect accordance with our national character and feeling.

He reminded Baynes of his "clear and definite instruction" from the Commonwealth office about treating the San Juans as British dominions. Compromise now would only imperil British rights here just as it had on the Columbia River. The British were in a "complicated and humiliating" position, which by no means guaranteed peace. He concluded by advising the admiral that he was going to complain to the home government about the Royal Navy.[36]

Baynes was unmoved. If Douglas had wanted San Juan to remain British he should not have allowed the American "squatters" to settle on the island in the first place, the admiral countercharged in an August 19 letter to the Admiralty. (He did not bother to reply to Douglas.) Several paragraphs were devoted to Douglas's bluster over embattled British "subjects," observing that British subjects on the island were largely in the employ of the Hudson's Bay Company. He blamed the scarcity of British settlers on the "confined and narrow views of the Hudson's Bay Company. A few American squatters, as before-mentioned, have established themselves from the opposite coast." Baynes also questioned Douglas's judgment during the pig affair when he sent a Justice of the Peace (Magistrate de Courcy) with the dubious mission of arresting the officer in command of the U.S. troops. Even worse, if the officer resisted, de Courcy was to seek assistance from the Royal Navy:

> The officer was summoned, but fortunately no further proceedings took place, the Governor having revoked the order... had this been carried out, I fear the result would have been a serious collision, as an officer in command of a company of soldiers was not likely to surrender himself without resistance.[37]

How could Douglas treat the islands as British when their possession was under review by both governments? This gave the British the perfect excuse to demonstrate restraint, for

...it cannot be said we have withdrawn from San Juan Island, consequently there has been no compromise of dignity or honor... if the authorities of the United States have taken a false step, it renders it all the more necessary that we should avoid doing so, and endeavor, if possible, not to complicate the boundary question still more and embroil the two nations.

Baynes saw two courses open to him. He could eject the Americans from the island by force and risk war; or protest the occupation and leave a ship of war in the harbor to oversee British interests, pending a decision on the boundary. "Had they been filibusters and not Federal troops, the case would be very different... I was decidedly adverse to a joint military occupation, which could in no way strengthen our claim, and was very likely, from various causes, to bring about a collision."[38]

Simple arithmetic moved Baynes not only to avoid challenging the Americans militarily on land, but also to discourage a joint occupation. As stated above, most of the British numbers were sailors, who could not hope to contend with infantry, of which the U.S. had ample supply. And these soldiers were "ready to embark."

It was Baynes's views not Douglas's that the British government accepted in the end. On October 21, these instructions were dispatched to Douglas from the Duke of Newcastle, the colonial secretary:

...in consequence of the opposite views to which your despatch refers as being entertained by Admiral Baynes and yourself in regard to the policy which you think ought to have been pursued toward the Americans, I must point out to you that the fact of overwhelming force of the British Navy, which was so rapidly summoned to the spot, as compared with the force of the United States, removed any possibility of misunderstanding the reasons of Her Majesty's Government for adopting the moderate course of remonstrance instead of violent measures.[39]

Harney was drafting his own letters of justification, including one to Douglas on August 24 after a delay of more than 10 days from the receipt of the governor's last, and to Adjutant General Cooper in New York City.

To Douglas, he again vehemently denied having prior knowledge of the pig incident before visiting the governor in July. The general was willing to accept that Douglas had no knowledge of the acts toward Cutlar, but he was not convinced that the British would do anything to head off another such occurrence. The warships in the harbor provided little reassurance in the minds of most Americans that Americans' rights would be protected. That's why his soldiers had to stay.[40]

However, the general again revealed his ignorance of San Juan background when he confessed to Cooper that Douglas's enclosure was the first he had seen of the famous Marcy letter. It also was in this same correspondence that Harney seriously began to twist the truth, relaying every xenophobic sentiment at work among American settlers in the young territory to justify his acts. He must have known that he had miscalculated in dispatching close to 500 men, plus heavy guns to an island one could cross on foot in an afternoon. But he could not admit it. He pressed on.

He had reviewed the Marcy letter's provisos and of course they were sound. He had not beefed up the American military presence in Puget Sound until this unfortunate incident. But the British, in the guise of the Hudson's Bay Company, had taken a page from the Revolutionary War and War of 1812 and unleashed the northern Indians upon American settlers in Puget Sound.

Time and again our lighthouses were attacked, and the wives and children of our settlers on that coast were brutally murdered by British Indians. Reports reached me that these Indians had been instigated toward these acts by the Hudson's Bay Company in order to drive them from the lands which this immense establishment covet for their own purpose. I am well aware of the extent and power of this great commercial monopoly, second only to the East India Company which has crushed out the liberties and existence of so many nations in Asia, committed barbarities and atrocities for which the annals of crime have no parallel.

And more Northerners were on the way, Harney claimed, because he had it on good authority that A.G. Dallas was threatening to set them upon the Americans on San Juan. This jelled with what he had been told by Captain Alden of the *Active*, viz. "in the event of a collision between the forces of the two countries, he would not be able to prevent the northern Indians from driving our people from the island."[41]

Harney offered to include affidavits from witnesses (mainly American citizens) offering proof of this grasping, aggressive, and inhumane behavior. But he neglected to include the petition from the San Juan settlers that incited the incident—the one that lauds the HBC for saving them from northern Indians.

Clearly these British acts were contrived to grab the islands, Harney contended, while U.S. forces stood on the defensive and were "influenced by no other motives in placing troops upon the islands." In fact, the British were so impressed by the island's strategic virtues that they were now calling it the "Cronstadt of the Pacific," of which Harney was in complete accord. That's why the British were after them. But he had studied the Treaty of Oregon, and there was no doubt in his mind that these critical islands clearly belonged to the United States.[42]

The very next day Harney sent yet another report to Cooper stating he had heard a rumor that Admiral Baynes had countermanded Douglas's orders and that the British would not land troops. He quickly added, "nothing official on the subject has reached me."

By the end of August, San Juan Island slipped into limbo. The soldiers labored to create a formal camp, while British sailors watched through spyglasses. The 10-man sapper team, under Lieutenant Robert, did its best to supervise the line infantry and artillery troops, who grudgingly sweated with pick and shovel on the redoubt. A few line noncommissioned officers threatened mutiny rather than take orders from lower ranks on Robert's sapper team. One William Moore, a British subject caught selling liquor to the enlisted men, also was dragooned into laboring on the redoubt. And "private property owners," the so-called squatters, whom Pickett had come to protect, already were agitating against the incursion of the federal government.[43]

During a lull in the redoubt work—on one of those San Juan evenings when the shorebirds cluster around herring balls in the strait, contending with Indian fishers—a visitor named Angus MacDonald, late of Scotland and now a resident of Victoria, happened upon an American sentry walking guard on the forming ramparts. The following conversation seemed to sum up all that had come to pass and still might possibly be.

> The Americans had only three unsheltered guns that could reach the frigates. As the troops started to parade, I went to look at the guns about a half mile from the parade. They were sentineled by one man. Curious to know how he felt and believing him to be an Irishman, I said a word or two in Gaelic, then said:

'You are an Irishman.'

'Yes I am.'

'Are they going to fight about this little island?'

'I do not know.'

'How would you like to fight against the flag of your own country?'

 The man with a quick lift of his rifle, and a more advanced lift of his foot, said:

'I would like to see old England catch a good drubbing anyhow.'

Leaving him loading his pipe and bidding him good day in the ancient Celtic of Scotland, I went my way thinking that there is some account between Erin and England that never was squared."[44]

The same could be said for the Anglo-American border. That would be remedied in Washington City, where word of the pig incident was soon to arrive.

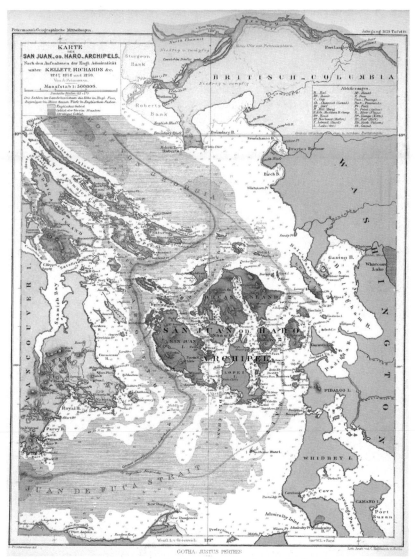

This c. 1859 German copy of a British map shows the San Juan (or Haro) Archipelago as it stood during the water boundary dispute. The legend notes that data was collected first in 1847 by Royal Navy Capt. Henry Kellett, then in 1858-59 by Capt. George Richards, also Royal Navy, during the joint boundary survey conducted by Great Britain and the United States. (WSU)

"WHAT? YOU YOUNG YANKEE-NOODLE, STRIKE YOUR
OWN FATHER!"

This political cartoon from the London newspaper, *Punch*,
underscores British attitudes toward the United States at mid-
nineteenth century. (SAJHA)

This is one of the earliest known photographs of Victoria, V.I., established in 1843. (LOC)

The Royal Navy had begun transferring its Pacific Station headquarters to Esquimalt Harbor, north of Victoria in 1858. (BCA)

President James Knox Polk (left) served only one term, but he brought much of the Far West under American control, realizing the dream of "Manifest Destiny." As Secretary of State, James Buchanan (right) discovered the flaw in the Treaty of Oregon language. As President he dealt with the unfinished business that resulted. (LOC)

This October, 1859 image shows Belle Vue Sheep Farm as it appeared in the height of the Pig War crisis. The two rows of tidy log houses, heavy-

As a governor of the Hudson's Bay Company, Alexander Grant Dallas (left) helped escalate the Pig War crisis. Montreal native Charles John Griffin (right) was assigned as agent for Belle Vue Sheep Farm in December 1853. It was he who recorded in his journal: "An American shot one of my pigs for trespassing!!!" (SAJHA)

duty fencing for sheep pens, and an English-style, double-bay barn in the background indicate a classic Hudson's Bay Co. facility. (BRBML)

Brig Gen. William Selby Harney (right) was within his rights to protect the interests of American settlers, but he exceeded his authority in baiting the British Empire by dispatching George Pickett (left) to San Juan Island, where he established his first camp on Griffin Bay (below). A longboat from HMS *Satellite* heads for shore with the British magistrate aboard. The painting is dated July 27, 1859, the day Pickett landed (LOC, NARA, & BRBML)

The U.S. Army's third camp (top) was relocated to the permanent site of the American Camp, just north of Belle Vue Sheep Farm. Soldiers of Battery D, Third Artillery (below) pose with a field gun, c. October 1859, at the campsite selected by Lt. Col. Silas Casey. (SAJHA)

Capt. Geoffrey Phipps Hornby (left) was the son of a former Pacific
Station commander and captain of the 31-gun steam frigate HMS *Tribune*
(below). His coolness in the crisis early on kept the peace until Rear Adm.
R. Lambert Baynes arrived. But he drew the wrath of Gov. James Douglas
(right), who was loathe to concede San Juan Island to the Americans and
did all he could do short of war to prevent it. (SAJHA)

When Rear Adm. R. Lambert Baynes (left) arrived on August 5 in Victoria Harbor aboard his flagship, HMS *Ganges* (below), he backed Hornby and quelled the Pig War crisis. Meanwhile, Capt. James Prevost (right), commander of the 21-gun steam corvette HMS *Satellite* and the British water boundary commissioner had a standoff of his own with the American commissioner Archibald Campbell. (SAJHA)

HMS *Satellite* (above and below left) was the newest and biggest steam corvette in her class when she entered service in the late 1850s. The ship was heavily involved in the Northwest Boundary Survey with her counterpart, the U.S. Coast Survey Steamer *Active* (below right), and stood sentinel in Griffin Bay during the Pig War crisis. (SAJHA & BRBML)

HMS *Satellite* (above) packed a wallop with her huge guns arranged 10 to a side with a chase gun in the bow. Here an officer takes his ease with a telescope in the crook of his arm. HMS *Plumper*, 12 guns, (below) stands off while shore survey crews take hydrographic readings along the coast of Vancouver Island. (BRBML & SAJHA)

The Royal Marines went to work shortly after landing on San Juan Island in March 1860 clearing foliage and constructing a fence to protect their vegetable garden from deer. The tents served both officers and enlisted men over the next several months. (DFC)

Garrison Bay is as still as a millpond in this pre-1865 view of English Camp. Note the sentry boxes at either end of the shoreline and the marines on the porch of the barracks. (DFC)

The Royal Marines brace at attention on the parade ground with the newly extended privates' mess room (with the section of new roof) in the background. Capt. George Bazalgette (inset), a China veteran, was camp commander from 1860 to 1867. (SAJHA)

HMS *Boxer* was shallow-draft gunboat that called weekly at the Royal Marine Camp with cargo, mail and passengers. The formal garden is at right, though Mrs. Delacombe referred to it as a "strawberry garden." (DFC)

The U.S. Army camp is complete in this view taken in 1868. The barracks/cookhouse complex is at far right. Officers' row is at far left with the two-story structure assigned to the commanding officer. (SAJHA)

This contemporary painting commissioned by the National Park Service captures the Fourth of July celebration held at American Camp in 1868. The two garrisons annually marched en masse to the respective camp to celebrate holidays. (SAJHA)

Camp life (clockwise from top left): The commanding officer's home at American Camp had two stories and a grand porch for entertaining; Officers wives and children rest in the shade of the big leaf maple at English Camp, c. 1870. In 2012, the tree was 340 years old; Capt. William A. Delacombe (far left) and his son, Willie (far right) and the family dogs entertain on Officers Hill at the English Camp; Captain Delacombe (second from left) poses with his family on the porch of the commodious home he had built overlooking the camp and Garrison Bay. (SAJHA & DFC)

British surveyor Capt. George Richards' drawing of San Juan Island was used to determine the best location of the Royal Marine Camp once the joint military occupation was decided upon. Note "Friday's Bay" (now Friday Harbor) named for a Hudson's Bay Company shepherd, Peter Friday. (SAJHA)

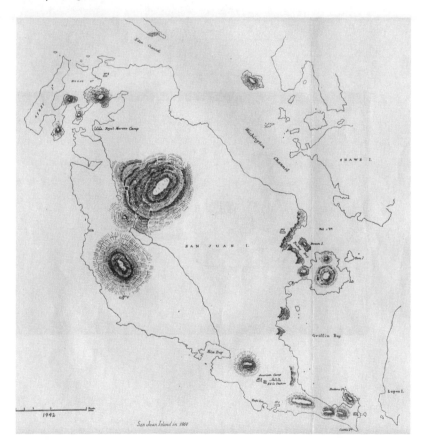

The same family group from under the big leaf maple (page 166), gather to watch the garrison on parade for the senior officer visiting from Esquimalt. Meanwhile, a group of Royal Marines beaches the camp longboat on Guss Island in Garrison Bay. Note the size of the commander's house looming at on the hill at far right. (DFC)

Period paintings often caught what cameras of the period could not: the motion of everyday life. The Royal Marine Camp (above) teems with activity as a ship is unloaded at the dock while a canoe skims on the bay. The folk-style painting of American Camp (below) shows troops drilling on the parade ground as a wagon negotiates the road from the camp to the Griffin Bay dock. (SAJHA)

Richard Bickerton Pemell Lyons, 1st Viscount Lyons (left), knew that General Harney had been acting on his own and thus made every effort to maintain the peace. He agreed that U.S. Army commander, Lt. Gen. Winfield Scott (right), was the best negotiator available to send on the long journey west. In painting (below), Royal Navy Lt. Edmund A. Porcher captured the Royal Marine Camp in later years as a young officer aboard HMS *Sparrowhawk*, seen here in the Garrison Bay. (LOC & BRBML)

Officers' Row at American Camp in 2012 (above) is shown after the building at right was moved back following 135 years in Friday Harbor. English Camp's formal garden was rebuilt in 1972 to commemorate the centennial of Kaiser Wilhelm I's decision awarding the San Juan Islands to the United States. Both camps and 2,064 surrounding acres compose San Juan Island National Historical Park (SAJHA)

AUCTION SALE ᴼᶠ PUBLIC BUILDINGS

OFFICE CHIEF QUARTERMASTER,
Department of the Columbia,
PORTLAND, OREGON, October 20, 1875.

There will be sold at Public Auction on **TUESDAY** and **WEDNESDAY**, the **23d** and **24th** days of November, the buildings comprising the late Camps occupied by the American and British forces on San Juan Island, Washington Territory.

THE SALE ON

TUESDAY, NOVEMBER 23, 1875.

At 11 A. M., will be at the Camp occupied by the U. S. Troops and comprises:

One BUILDING 69x20x8 with an Unfinished Addition 40x20x8.
One BUILDING $25x12x6^1{}_2$.
One BUILDING $20x12x7$.
One BUILDING with Kitchen 43x18x7.
Quartermaster and Commissary Store Houses, Blacksmith and Carpenter Shops, Hospital, &c.; in all about 25 buildings,

ON THE FOLLOWING DAY

WEDNESDAY, NOV. 24, 1875,

At 11 A. M., the Sale will be at the Camp formerly occupied by the British Troops, and comprises:

One BUILDING 41ᵧ29 with Wing $12^1{}_2x29$
and **KITCHEN** attached 12x20.
One BUILDING 32x13.　　　　One BUILDING 32x36.
Hospital, Store Houses, Carpenter and Blacksmith Shops, &c., in all about 15 buildings.

The buildings will be sold at each Camp, separately, and must be removed within 30 days after the Sale.

TERMS, CASH U. S. CURRENCY

R. N. BATCHELDER,
Major & Qr. Mr., U. S. A., Chief Qr. Mr.

In November, 1875 the United States government auctioned the buildings at both camps earning a little more than $1,900. Purchasers had 60 days to take them away. (SAJHA)

Chapter 13

WASHINGTON AND LONDON

While Harney and Douglas were squaring off, oblivious British and American officials in Washington City, were offering proposals and counterproposals for a water boundary. Such were the realities of transcontinental time and distance at mid-19th century. Violence could flare and pull the two nations into war without the knowledge of their respective governments.

The telegraph had been functioning regionally since Samuel Morse and others hatched the idea in the 1840s. But in 1859 it ran only as far west as Fort Leavenworth, Kansas, and as far east as Carson City, Nevada. Spanning the distance—which came to be known as the Central Overland Route—was a stagecoach, aptly described by Mark Twain in *Roughing It*. Theoretically the trip was three weeks each way, but six weeks was the rule, or, judging by human remains bleaching along the trail, it might take forever. Throughout the crisis both nations would dutifully send telegrams. Some made it under schedule, in just over two weeks. Others lagged by more than a month. It was still more reliable to send a courier aboard the steamer.

The Panama Railroad, founded by shipping magnate William Aspinwall, had been running since January 1855, carrying freight and passengers the 47 miles across the isthmus in just over three hours. Modern side-wheeler steamers with names such as *Northerner, Cortez, Constitution* and *Sonora* waited at either end with boilers fired to cut passengers' exposure to yellow fever or the *vomito*, as it was called then. Competition was hot and time was money. Depending on seas, a courier with a dispatch pouch could carry word from Victoria to New York City on the average of six weeks. [1]

That is almost exactly how long it took Harney's July 19 dispatch to reach Lt. Gen. Winfield Scott's New York City headquarters. The old general quickly relayed it to Washington City, where it arrived on September 3, 1859. But it still wasn't fast enough to beat newspaper reports that had miraculously made it first by telegraph via St. Louis.

So President James Buchanan experienced the timeless nightmare of all government officials—being the last to know. Buchanan already was familiar with the San Juan Islands. As the peacemaking secretary of state under Polk, he had helped complete the Treaty of Oregon. He also was one of the few to predict that issue of ownership of the islands might one-day cause trouble. Now the nation was boiling over as the sections looked ahead to the presidential race in 1860; a race the mild Buchanan had no wish to enter because the result, either way, was bound to result in civil war. Unbeknownst to the president or anyone in capital, a homicidal abolitionist named John Brown was planning to ignite a slave insurrection in the south. His troops would be armed with weapons he intended to steal from the federal arsenal at Harper's Ferry, Virginia (now West Virginia).

Buchanan was not unaware of the irony at work. As a career Democrat, he was acquainted with the shenanigans of William Selby Harney. He remembered Harney's ill-fated thrust into Mexico without orders early in the war. He remembered the rank insubordination to Winfield Scott and the messy charges and countercharges in its wake. He remembered counseling President Polk then to be firm with Harney, but Harney had been Andrew Jackson's pet... and Polk was known as "Young Hickory." Buchanan remembered it all. Now Harney was his problem.

The president could not have Harney stepping all over the British with the nation in such a vulnerable state. Despite the U.S. Navy's addition of several steam frigates starting in 1854, the Royal Navy could still blow anything the Americans had out of the water in any ocean. But Buchanan also was politically astute enough to know he could not now back away from the San Juan Islands like a kicked dog just because the British were angry—and they were going to be angry, that much was certain.

Acting Secretary of War William Drinkard drafted a reply to Harney that same day. Its tone left no doubt about Buchanan's feelings on the matter:

> The President was not prepared to learn that you had ordered military possession to be taken of the island of San Juan or Bellevue. Although he believes the Straits of Haro to be the true boundary between Great Britain and the United States, under the treaty of June 15, 1846, and that, consequently, this island belongs to us, yet he had not anticipated that so decided a step would have been resorted to without instructions.

Nevertheless,

> ...if you had good reason to believe that the colonial authorities of Great Britain were about to disturb the status, by taking possession of the island and assuming jurisdiction over it, you were right to anticipate their action. It has been too much the practice of the British Government to seize first and negotiate afterwards. [2]

Meanwhile in the British legation, the envoy, Lord Lyons, also read the morning papers. Only two weeks before he had been instructed by London that in any water boundary settlement he was to hold on to San Juan Island at all costs. He dashed off a note to

Secretary of State Lewis Cass that led with the standard questions:
Had it really happened? And, if so, had the U.S. Government
been aware of Harney's act? Lyons was "...extremely anxious that
this statement should not reach Her Majesty's Government without
such information respecting its truth or falsehood, and such
explanations concerning it as the Government of the United States
may be disposed to afford."[3]

The envoy also reminded Cass that as recently as May 12 he had
sent an official letter warning that if the water boundary was not
settled, and if the United States did not formally agree to restrain
its citizens on the island from acts of violence, a "local collision"
might occur, which would "embitter" any further discussion. For
more than three months, Her Majesty's Government had been
awaiting a response to this letter. Were the silence and Harney's
act connected? The two diplomats met two days later, whereupon
Cass assured Lyons that the U.S. Government already had written
Harney directing him to maintain joint occupation status on the
island. While the U.S. was not to assume jurisdiction over the
island, the troops were to remain on San Juan to protect American
citizens from northern Indians... or whatever.[4]

Lyons's renowned calm disintegrated two days later with
the arrival of the evening newspapers. More details and "full
intelligence" about Pickett's landing arrived with the day's mails,
the papers announced, including Forsyth's proclamation, which
was published verbatim. Lyons wrote Cass immediately, demanding
information and not double-talk. He wanted to relay a full account
of the incident to Lord John Russell, the British Foreign Secretary
in London, and the more details the better.

In light of the news, the 42 year-old Englishman also took
the opportunity to review Cass's comments of the fifth. Lyons was
particularly concerned by the word "status" which he thought meant
that soldiers would occupy the island, but not enforce the law; a fact
that he already had passed on to Russell.

"I am rendered particularly anxious upon this subject, by observing among the news inserted in the evening journals the following document purporting to be an order issued by Captain Pickett, commanding the party of United States troops which has landed on the island," Lyons wrote. The proclamation was attached along with a postscript assuring Cass that all communication with London was handled in code, so the information would remain confidential.[5]

Cass replied by begging the question. Instead of offering more information or explaining the proclamation, he tweaked Lyons for misinterpreting their conversation. How could more than 60 soldiers armed with rifled muskets occupy an island barely bigger than the city limits of Washington and not exercise some jurisdiction? Two more exchanges followed between the diplomats, whereupon Lyons wrote Russell with a correction, accompanied by a rather windy explanation.[6]

Although an attempt had been made in 1858 to lay an Atlantic cable, it had been unsuccessful, so instant communication between Great Britain and the United States was still seven years off. Telegrams to London went by wire to Halifax, Nova Scotia, thence by steam mail packet to Liverpool, where they were relayed by wire to London. The whole process, including deciphering, took about 10 days, weather permitting.

Russell learned of Pickett's landing when Lyon's telegram arrived on September 21. It was not the reply he had expected, especially after writing thousands of words on August 24 proposing, as had James Prevost, the Middle Channel (President's and San Juan channels) as an excellent compromise boundary through the islands. The Americans should, to Russell's mind, appreciate that they would have three islands—Shaw, Orcas and Lopez—to the British one, San Juan.[7]

He replied to Lyons the next day, in briefer fashion, stating that he too believed Harney had acted independently. But he also wanted an official reply to the May 12 note. Lyons was to request that instructions be sent to U.S. officers not to use military force on the disputed territory without direct authority from the president "...for if these acts are to take place by the sole direction of subordinate officers, and the president does not disavow them, the consequences must be as evil as if the president had authorized them from the beginning."[8]

While Russell was reading and dealing with these dispatches, more were on the way from Lyons. On September 12, Lyons relayed the contents of Drinkard's September 3 letter to Harney, which did not include the passage, *"...it has been too much the practice of the British Government to seize first and negotiate afterwards."* Even with note in hand, Lyons was growing more troubled, especially after receiving a direct report from Colonel Hawkins, who had arrived in Washington on the 13th from Vancouver Island, bearing newspapers and dispatches from Douglas. Hawkins's bundle of correspondence, combined with his firsthand observations, alarmed the British. Northern Indian raids apparently were only ancillary to Harney's true reasons for landing troops. Pickett's proclamation made it clear that the real intent was to make a grab for the island.[9]

This time Lyons did not bother writing. Instead, he marched into Cass's office, demanding an explanation. He could not believe a general in the United States Army could act on the most flimsy of pretexts, and he wanted to know if the U.S. Government really knew what was going on. Cass replied that he had heard nothing since Harney's first letter, but he assured Lyons that the presence of U.S. troops did not mean the U.S. would not leave the island if it was eventually declared British. Newspaper claims that U.S. guns on San Juan could reach the Victoria harbor were preposterous, he added.

Once pressing matters had been discussed, the diplomats returned to the by-now tiresome question of the boundary line. Lyons offered Russell's August 24 Middle Channel proposal, which would award San Juan Island to the British and leave the remainder of the islands to the Americans.

> The withdrawal by U.S. troops or an arrangement for joint occupation... would provide for the immediate difficulty... but the course most conducive to permanent friendship between the two countries would be the acceptance by the United States of the fair and equitable proposal contained in the dispatch from Lord Russell.

Cass responded by waving Campbell's proposal at Lyons, citing verbiage from Lord Aberdeen in 1846 that proposed the British would keep all of Vancouver Island and leave the rest south of the 49th parallel to the United States [10]

Russell pondered the dispatch covering this meeting and replied on September 26 that the current situation made it even more essential that the United States settle the boundary immediately with the Middle Channel as the line demarcation. San Juan Island must remain British, Russell wrote Lyons. Furthermore, Lyons was to press for immediate reply. [11]

If Buchanan was uncertain of his course, decisiveness came in a rush with Harney's August 7 dispatch declaring that Casey had landed with reinforcements. The president was especially alarmed by the passages, "...Any attempts at possession (of the islands) by them will be followed by a collision... " and that any rights the British had to the archipelago had been "...forfeited by the overbearing, insulting, and aggressive conduct of Her Majesty's officers." No wonder Cass decided to rely on time and distance to plead ignorance when asked by Lyons if there was more information from Harney.

Right then the president decided to turn to Lt. Gen. Winfield Scott. Three times in Buchanan's government experience the "Hero of Lundy's Lane" had been sent to border communities to

successfully defuse crises between local governments over national
boundaries. He would have to go to Washington Territory and
temporarily take command. It was true that Scott was 72 and so
corpulent he could barely walk and suffered from gout and dropsy.
On top of that he recently had been thrown from his horse. But at
this point half a Scott was better than a whole Harney.

Buchanan notified Scott by telegram on September 14 and
followed up with formal instructions through Acting Secretary of War
Drinkard on the 16th. The orders outlined the boundary dispute going
back to Francis Drake, but stressed that this was a swamp that Scott
should avoid. Instead, the general was to focus on making immediate
peace and leave the specifics of boundaries to the commissions under
whom both nations would have to build large fires. Scott was to ensure
that representatives from both nations could not "…exclude the other
by force, or exercise complete and exclusive sovereign rights within
the fairly disputed limits," as was stated by Marcy four years before.
This gave Scott complete latitude to settle the crisis, so long as he did
not back off from the claims of the United States.

The president had reason to be optimistic about Scott's mission.
He had learned, through Cass, that the British would be willing to
accept a joint military occupation as proposed to Pickett by Hornby
on August 3, thereby "correcting a wrong done by Pickett in not
permitting this course." This peaceful overture stood in bold
contrast to the vengeful screed emanating from Harney. Scott was
to do his best to implement Hornby's plan, reducing the American
force to Pickett's company and permitting the British to land an
equal number of Royal Marines. Scott also was to ensure that the
rights of U.S. citizens were on equal footing with those of British
subjects. However, if the crisis already had flared into armed
conflict, which, in Drinkard's words, "…would vastly complicate
the case," Scott was to instigate an immediate truce and arrange
for a temporary joint occupation until matters cooled. He then
stated the obvious: "It would be a shocking event if the two nations

should be precipitated into war respecting the possession of a small island." However: " If we must be forced into war by the violence of the British authorities, which is not anticipated, we shall abide the issue as best we may without apprehension as to the result."[12]

The general departed New York City on September 20 aboard the steamer *Star of the West*, accompanied by aids Lt. Col. George W. Lay and Lt. Col. Lorenzo Thomas and Assistant Surgeon Charles H. Crane. They were scheduled to arrive in Puget Sound on October 16.[13]

Lyons was called to Cass's office on the 14th, where he was "confidentially" told of Scott's mission, specifically that Scott "had been officially informed that the President considered that Captain Pickett had done wrong in not acceding to the proposal made by the British authorities for a joint occupation of the island." Although relieved the highly respected Scott was being sent to resolve the crisis, Lyons suspected the Americans knew more than they were letting on. Not only that, his superiors in London were still screaming for an "official" explanation of Harney's act, not to mention an "official" assurance that the U.S. abided by the spirit of his May 12 letter.[14]

> ...I await with some impatience a more formal and explicit communication from you... because I am persuaded that such a communication would be the most effectual means of displaying in their true light the just and friendly sentiments of the cabinet of Washington.[15]

While more inflammatory newspaper accounts trickled in by wire from New Orleans and St. Louis, Lord Russell in London had digested all that had crossed his desk thus far, plus examined a firsthand report from Hawkins. He wrote Lyons on October 6 that "...the more the irruption of the United States troops into the island of San Juan is examined, the worse the case appears." His research produced these conclusions: Campbell had probably been in cahoots with Harney; Baynes had attempted an amicable solution only to be insulted by Casey in Victoria Harbor; and Pickett had posted his proclamation in "defiance of the subsisting relations between the two countries." Therefore: U.S. troops should be withdrawn from the island, which meant U.S. laws could not be enforced; the troops could return only if an Indian emergency arose, and only then in a joint effort with the Royal Marines; and foremost, the U.S. should accept his Middle Channel proposal.

The steamer carrying Russell's missive had yet to dock when Cass finally sent an "official" response to Lyons on October 22. The secretary merely disgorged on paper all that had happened, then reiterated the United States' commitment to the Marcy letter of July 14, 1855. He also included a formal copy of Scott's instructions in which Scott had been directed to enforce the spirit of that letter. Meanwhile the U.S. still claimed the islands, but was anxious to realize its claim by peaceful purposes.[16]

The home governments had done all they could do to keep the peace. Neither wanted war, yet neither was willing to give up an island 16 miles long and six and half miles wide. National honor was at stake, a serious matter among nations in 1859 when the scramble for colonies had not yet abated. But business also was important. The British had invested millions of dollars by now in the American industrial infrastructure. A war would be crippling on both sides of the Atlantic. With the question still a long way from being decided—and after all, the Pacific Northwest was still the end of the world—a Band-Aid was required and that was going to be Winfield Scott, the one and only "Great Pacificator."

It all rested on him now.

Chapter 14

STAND DOWN

Winfield Scott loved New York.

This hardly places him in exclusive company. But it is significant in terms of how the U.S. Army functioned at mid-19th century. In 1859, army headquarters were in New York because Winfield Scott, the commanding general, wanted to live there. At that time, hard though it is to recall now, the United States was a nation with a profound mistrust of large standing armies. The regular army, with barely 16,000 men in uniform, was left to fend for itself, and that included the location of a headquarters. Scott liked the high-society parties, where he would hold forth like a big Buddha in a corner of the room. He liked going to the theater and eating in the best restaurants. He liked traveling up the Hudson to spend several weeks at his beloved West Point. But most of all he liked being as far as possible from Washington City, which, to his mind, had for too many years been overrun with Democrats.

Born and raised near Dinwiddie Courthouse, Virginia, Scott gave up a fledgling law practice in May 1808 to join an army that was expanding to contend with British aggression on the U.S. coastline during the Napoleonic Wars. A strapping six and half feet tall with a probing intellect and an abundance of courage, Scott made such a mark during the War of 1812 that he emerged a major general with a reputation in Europe as well as North America. His leadership at the Battle of Chippewa in 1814, when his brigade of regulars met British regulars on even terms and won, helped stave off secession talk among representatives of New England states.

Thirty-two years would pass before he was involved in another major war, but he did not disappoint. In what would amount to a second phase of the Mexican War, Scott emulated Cortez by cutting his lines of supply and marching his army over the Rio Frio Mountains into the Valley of Mexico. With a highly skilled officer corps—including George E. Pickett, Granville Haller, Silas Casey, and William Selby Harney—and a blend of regular army and volunteer soldiers, Scott took the city and ended the war in a matter of months.

Scott's career was not all success. He was recalled from Mexico to answer charges hurled at him by disloyal subordinates, mainly Democrats and especially Harney. This spurred him to assume leadership of the Whig party and run for president in 1852 only to be soundly thrashed by Franklin Pierce, who had served under him as a volunteer officer during the Mexican War. The latter blow resulted in the move to New York, where he slipped into the routine of arriving at work each morning in full dress uniform, full of spit and polish. Following an enormous lunch at Delmonico's he would spend the afternoon snoozing in his shirtsleeves. His diet and advancing age brought on a nasty case of gout, for which the treatment, then as now, was exercise and avoidance of rich food. He could not bear to give up the latter, so he opted for the former in the form of horseback riding. By then he was nearly as wide as he was tall, which did not make for a solid seat. He was thrown just before his trip to Washington Territory, and his injuries coupled with the undefeated gout meant he could barely move. He was literally stuffed into his carriage, and then hoisted in a basket aboard his Panama-bound steamer—a boarding procedure that would be repeated on each leg of his journey. But sending an infirm and immobile old man thousands of miles to stop a war was a gamble James Buchanan believed was worth the risk. Scott's prodigious skill and reputation as a warrior, combined with a lawyer's logic, had made him an ideal negotiator in crises that flared along the Canadian border between 1837 and 1839. Who better than a man whose magnanimous treatment of Mexican citizens resulted in him being cheered when he rode about the enemy city after the final assault at Chapultepec? Who better to calm the winds of war than a warrior respected on both sides of the line? Who better than the "Great Pacificator?"

Canadian-American border flare-ups were usually characterized by local citizens succumbing to nationalist passions, driven by an ever-constant lust for real estate or commodities such as fish or timber. The respective national governments were expected give nothing less than full support, especially the army and navy. Scott's principle peacemaking efforts came in 1837 in the Buffalo-Niagara Falls area, followed by a similar flare-up the very next year in Aroostook, Maine. In each case the general was summoned by Pres. Martin Van Buren to negotiate with his British opposites. Scott's object was not to attempt to negotiate a long-term peace. That was up to the diplomats in Washington and London. His goal in peacemaking missions was to restore calm and seek common ground among the antagonists. Despite the agitation of rabble-rousers, Scott succeeded in both instances, though not without displaying a little passion of his own. At Niagara Falls he confronted a mob, much as a Hollywood sheriff. "I tell you then, except it be over my very body, you shall not pass this line—you shall not embark," he shouted, after which this "revolution" died a slow, grumbling death.[1]

After a bracing voyage and smooth Isthmus crossing, Scott and party left San Francisco on October 17 aboard the *Northerner*, crossed the Columbia River bar, and arrived at Fort Vancouver on October 20. Scott did not go ashore. Instead, he ordered Harney to call on him the next day. It was in the *Northerner's* cabin that Scott first told

Harney that he was taking command of the department during his stay and then ordered him to accompany him to Portland.[2]

Their time together was strained, owing as much to the bad blood from the Mexican war and its political aftermath as to the recent deposal. How it must have pained Harney to witness the revision or outright cancellation of most, if not all, of his command decisions. To his mind he had operated well within his parameters as department commander, and he had correspondence to prove it. Among these were his blustery exchanges with Douglas, a September 14 dispatch to Scott, and an October 10 diatribe sent over Scott's head to Secretary of War John B. Floyd (an old political crony of Harney's later to become a mediocre Confederate general). Aside from any light they shed on Harney's competence in dealing with an international crisis, the letters gave Scott a revealing look at the workings of Harney's mind. It was clear by now that Harney knew his government was alarmed by his actions and that he was beginning to worry about the size of the political bite he had taken.

For example:

Harney continued to portray the Hudson's Bay Company as a paramilitary organization—with better cannon than U.S. Army forts, and steamers that could quickly be converted into potent warships—bent on dominating the Pacific Northwest. This charge was not entirely unwarranted, coming as it did in response to Douglas' disingenuous claim that the HBC did not exercise any power or authority on Vancouver's Island, and that its officers had no more pull with the government than any other citizen.[3]

He strayed into international boundary negotiations by justifying his acts based on Campbell's irritation with his British counterparts. Because everyone knew Prevost and Campbell were at an impasse, it must have seemed an ideal way to demonstrate the duplicity and aggressiveness of British colonial officials. Harney then stretched the truth when he wrote that Campbell, after reading

Pickett's orders, offered the captain assistance and approved of the landing. Campbell initially recorded alarm at Pickett's actions. It was only after Harney assured the commissioner that the army had no intention of taking possession of the island that Campbell responded more in relief than tacit approval.

In response to Drinkard's question as to whether he consulted boundary commissioner Campbell before occupying San Juan Island, Harney replied that he last saw Campbell on July 7 during his inspection tour of the territory's northwestern military posts. At that time neither man had an inkling that Douglas was assuming jurisdiction over the island. Harney was careful to raise the issue of "jurisdiction" in his orders to Pickett believing the government would condone rather than condemn his actions on that basis. The president had said as much in his September 3 letter through Acting Secretary of War Drinkard.[4]

A review of the correspondence and Harney's own words convinced Scott to dismiss Harney's perceptions and opinions about the San Juan situation. Additionally, he reversed the disciplinary measures Harney took against his recalcitrant officer corps, and then implored Harney to step down as commander of the Department of Oregon and take command of the Department of the West in St. Louis, Missouri. This was a face-saving overture by Scott as that command was considerably larger, nominally held sway over Harney's current position, but most importantly involved little contact with the British Empire.

Paranoia, duplicity, and intrigue were common among the officer corps of the old army. Scott could forgive or at the very least stand above that. What he could not abide was amateurism. This made him especially miffed at Harney and Pickett—the latter coincidentally at Fort Vancouver for court martial duty—for their lack of delicacy and precipitous actions over San Juan. Both men stood at attention together while being subjected to Scott's blistering remonstrance. The old general could expect such behavior from foolhardy volunteers and irate citizens from the north woods of Maine. But Harney and Pickett were professional officers who should have known better than to intrigue in areas best left to the civilian governments.

It was a mortified and much chastened Pickett—a fellow Virginian, from a good family no less—who finally reported that, thankfully, all had been quiet on San Juan when he left to head the court martial board convened to try one of Fort Vancouver's junior officers.

Scott re-crossed the Columbia River bar and by October 24 steamed around the peninsula and up Puget Sound to an anchorage about three miles north of Olympia. Again, he chose not to disembark and did not call on Gov. Richard Gholson as directed, likely because on previous peacemaking missions he found local officials to be a trial. Scott either wanted to avoid local frictions— Gholson was a fire-breathing Kentucky Democrat—or was physically unable to go ashore. The insulted Gholson, in a letter to Secretary Cass, complained that the general's ship never came to Olympia, nor did Scott share with him his instructions from the president.[5]

Gholson used Scott's slight to absolve himself of any responsibility for what might follow. This may have contributed to the civilian versus military discord that was to flare time and again throughout the crisis and the entire 12-year joint occupation to follow.

If Harney was displeased to see Scott, the British were delighted. The October 25 edition of the *London Times* informed its readers of Harney's actions but assured them, "England, with its armies and navies, is not likely to shrink before such a power as General Harney is likely to bring into action." President Buchanan restored reason by sending "…General Scott to take command, and the temper of this aged soldier [was] likely to be more under control than that of his predecessor."

The editor of the *Pioneer and Democrat* also lavished praise on Scott on his arrival, trusting the general to "uphold American rights" in the dispute. It was to be a trust misplaced, at least in the editor's eyes.

By October 26 Scott was in Port Townsend, where he decided to transfer his headquarters to the *Massachusetts*, his flagship during the siege of Veracruz in the Mexican War. A reporter from San Francisco's *Daily Alta California*, who accompanied Scott on the initial stage of his journey, recorded his impressions of conditions aboard the vessel, which changed considerably with a VIP aboard: "The *Massachusetts* proved a very comfortable and convenient conveyance. The general had fine and roomy quarters and a *glorious cuisine* [original italics]."

The general's larder was supplemented by deer, elk, duck, goose, and even a stray seal, all bagged by the ship's master, William Fauntleroy, and Scott's personal physician. En route to Bellingham Bay, soldiers standing guard on the growing redoubt on San Juan spotted Scott's ship and excitement rippled through the camp at the prospect of a visit from the great man. But it was not to be. The general again never left the ship, or his cabin for that matter, throughout his negotiations with Douglas.[6]

Scott directed the ship to ply the waters in question—from Port Townsend to Semiahmoo Spit—while dispatching the revenue cutters *Jefferson Davis* and *Joseph Lane* from all points with instructions for Colonel Lay, who had been sent to Victoria on the 26th to handle the negotiations with Douglas on his behalf. Unlike Casey, who had been snubbed aboard the *Shubrick*, Lay was visited aboard the *Davis* by Baynes himself, who then saluted the colonel on his departure. Furthermore, Douglas welcomed Lay to his home and opened his letter book to the American, allowing him to freely peruse correspondence between the British government and General Harney.

Once settled, Lay sent a message to Scott via the *Northerner*, which, on attempting to close with the *Massachusetts*, carried away the old steamer's flying jib boom and lost her own flagstaff with ensign.

The flag was retrieved before the ship got up steam to return to California.[7]

On the island, the Americans continued to dig in under the watchful eye of Hornby. Several eyewitness accounts exist of the fortification period, among them the *Daily Alta California* reporter, Peck's diary, and various accounts by island pioneers, such as Hubbs, written or dictated some 20 or even 40 years later.

Peck's diary offers some wonderful glimpses of the redoubt under construction. In addition to a daily weather report, in which he describes the torrents of rain that plunged the soldiers into gloom, he also reported the hordes of Indian prostitutes overrunning the camps, and the drunken misadventures of the Irish Sergeant McEneny. When Scott arrived off Port Townsend weeks of rain gave onto a gloriously sunny morning, a trend that continued until November 1. The first heavy frost appeared two days later. Peck also noted the latest camp rumors and expressed the soldiers' universal disappointment that General Scott had not called at the island.[8]

The *Daily Alta California* account offers a more objective but no less descriptive view. The reporter booked passage aboard a small sailing ship, the *Ebey*, in Port Townsend. The ship was bound for San Juan with a "deck load of heavy plank for gun platforms for the redoubt on the island" as well as provisions for the troops from the *Massachusetts*, which General Scott had requisitioned for his "migratory headquarters." The *Ebey* was caught in the tides that rip through the islands, and when the fog lifted the next morning the ship was in the Rosario Strait just off Bellingham Bay. It took another three hours to tack to Griffin Bay, where the reporter observed "Love Rock" (now called Harbor Rock, near the mouth of Fish Creek) serving as a target for *Satellite's* guns.

The *Massachusetts*, even with her armaments stripped, had worse luck with the fog. After leaving Bellingham Bay bound for Port Townsend on the 29th she became lost in the soup and ran aground on the spit that tails away from Smith Island. She remained "with her bows high out of the water for 24 hours."[9]

The reporter's descriptions of the prairie and forest on the Cattle Point peninsula could be taken from a later 20th-century travel guide, but not so the description of San Juan Village:

> ...the main street, which runs westwardly, consists of some twenty odd buildings and huts. Some of these were floated down from Whatcom, Bellingham Bay, and other localities, and give the embryo town quite a stable appearance. The town possesses a bakery, a butchery, three or four barrooms, one aristocratic "two-bit" house, a fruit stand, grocery etc., etc., all of which are liberally patronized.

The soldiers had taken over the Hudson's Bay dock, which meant that Paul K. Hubbs, Jr., could erect a tent nearby from which to harass British subjects. A road commenced from the town's only street to the top of the ridge, and thence to the Hudson's Bay farm and the camp, by now located just north of it. Preemption farms were "dotting the bay line of the shore," most of their owners continuing to dispute title in the town, while other more hearty souls were actually engaged in sowing winter crops. The soil is described as a "mixture of clay, sand and gravel and said to be great in the production of potatoes."

At the apex of the ridge was the redoubt, on which Lieutenant Robert and his troops continued to labor. The work, dubbed "Fort Harney" in Peck's diary, was:

> ...admirably located as to the Canal de Haro side; it presents a steep precipice, and its guns when mounted, will command the prairie slope to the bay, the view on the canal side, as well as the slopes from the high headlands, some mile and half distant. The work is just beginning its outline and a fair

portion is complete, only three gun platforms being planted. The work at the ditch is arduous, as the soil consisting of heavy gravel, intermixed with large granite boulders. A few days more and the redoubt will make a very formidable appearance."[10]

The *Massachusetts'* guns lined the road that ran about a quarter-mile from the redoubt to the entrance of Casey's new camp, which he noted was named for George Pickett. At least one gun had been mounted on October 14, according to Peck. The camp was nestled amidst tall trees that even then were under assault from the soldiers' axes.

There was a semblance of a parade ground, on which the command drilled for the pleasure of a Col. George Nauman, inspector of artillery for the Department of Oregon, visiting from Fort Vancouver. Silas Casey officiated mounted on a fine horse.[11] Observing the review were British sailors and marines, among them a Royal Navy lieutenant who had his own Daguerreotype camera and developing outfit. His images of the nascent camp nestled among the firs, taken on October 27, reveal a mix of simple wooden structures from Fort Bellingham and the conical Sibley tents that Casey had shipped from Fort Steilacoom. In one photo, several soldiers of the Third Artillery in full dress strike a pose next to a six-pound Napoleon cannon beneath the flagpole (stepped in the same spot as today's replica). Off to the side, a soldier in shirtsleeves and a battered forage cap tucks his hands in the waistband of his trousers. Another sits on a wagon tongue in the foreground, puffing on a corncob pipe. Behind them the parade ground slopes to the northwest, bordered by a thick tree line. The relaxed ambience of the photograph reveals that, even as the redoubt was going up, the British and Americans were continuing to fraternize.[12]

Crushing boredom, a powerful thirst, and lust inspired midnight expeditions to the gin mills and two-bit houses of San Juan Village caused consternation for officers on both sides. In some cases, the whores slipped by the guards into the encampments. The resulting jealousies, fueled by liquor, resulted in acts of "ruffianism" that were severely punished. The commanders were losing patience:

> If liquor selling interferes with the discipline of the army, martial law will be proclaimed — which will noticeably sap the progress of the town of San Juan. At present the vicinity is free from another social evil — gambling; but it is hard to tell how long the knights of the green cloth will permit the army to remain free of their presence.[13]

While officers attempted to hold their men in check, Scott was writing. His first letter proposing a reduction of forces followed by a joint military occupation arrived on Douglas' desk via Lay on October 26. At the same time Scott sent a hasty telegram with a copy of the proposal to Washington via steamer and the overland stage to the commanding officer at Fort Leavenworth, thence via telegraph to Washington. It took 28 days to get there, as did dispatches from Douglas and Baynes to their respective authorities, which underscored the necessity of having local officials who could make critical decisions.

Douglas had favored a joint military occupation in July and August, but was backing off from that proposal. On October 29 he suggested to Scott that armed forces be removed and the island returned to a joint civil occupation pending approval in any case from his higher-ups in London, which could take more than two months. While awaiting word from their governments, he hoped the general would reciprocate his peaceful intentions and withdraw all American troops on faith.[14]

As far as Harney was concerned, the British still could not be trusted. On October 28 he relayed a dispatch from Casey, who reported that Admiral Baynes had secretly been aboard the *Tribune*

when Casey arrived at Griffin Bay on August 10. His source was
Archibald Campbell. Casey cited this apparent duplicity as a valid
reason for insisting Baynes wait upon him aboard the *Shubrick* in
Esquimalt Harbor on August 11. Why Casey chose to raise this
unsubstantiated slight so long after the fact defies any explanation
other than with Scott making peace in the area, he wanted to pin
the entire blame on the British.

Harney robustly followed suit, adding a cover to Casey's letter.
He reminded Scott that he had mentioned the case of the hidden
Baynes during their interview in Portland, but now he wanted it
on the record to demonstrate the "duplicity and bad faith" of the
British on the San Juan island issue. And more:

> ...This statement exposes three high officials of
> Her Britannic Majesty's service, viz: the British
> commissioner, the admiral, the senior captain
> of the navy in these waters, to the imputation of
> having deliberately imposed a willful falsehood
> upon the authorities of a friendly nation to advance
> the sinister designs of the British Government in
> obtaining territory that rightfully belongs to the
> United States... Is it too much to suppose they would
> be guilty of like conduct should they be permitted
> to assume a position in which it would aid their
> purposes?[15]

Scott ignored the letter and continued to deal with the British
focusing on the realities at hand. As always, they seemed eager for
peace and business as usual.

On November 2, Scott replied to Douglas that he could
not accept the removal of all U.S. forces as a requirement to
settlement. Lord Lyons, the British envoy, had not expressed this
as a condition. If he had, Scott said he would never have left the
East Coast. Returning the islands to civil jurisdiction would restore

the ambiguities that started the trouble in the first place. The headlines and editorial content of the *Pioneer and Democrat* seemed to reflect a popular belief that the San Juans belonged to Washington Territory. And Governor Cholson already had shown he was "...not to be considered a fit person to be entrusted with matters affecting the peace of two great nations."[16]

Scott believed Americans on the island genuinely needed protection from Indians—marauding bands from Coast Salish as well as Northwest Coast groups. He cited as evidence the August 17 Nooksack raid on Whatcom, which had required the response of Haller's company while still aboard the *Massachusetts*.

The general attached a formal proposal to his letter that basically offered in detail the proposal outlined in his initial letter: Each nation would be permitted one company of light infantry (about 100 men), with each commander serving as magistrate to keep peace between the soldiers/marines and citizens of the respective nations.[17]

On reading Scott's reply, Douglas wrote Baynes, pointing out that Scott could not back down and stand-down all of his forces. National honor was at stake and the Americans on the mainland would be up in arms. Douglas believed the real calamity the islanders from both nations faced was not northern Indians, but each other. That is why he did not want to post military forces there without instructions from his government. His true desire, he said, was to return the island to the status quo, meaning the situation before Pickett landed. He assured Scott that American citizens would not be bothered.[18]

With the admiral's blessing, Douglas plunged ahead and wrote Scott that he could not accept Scott's proposal of a joint military occupation without his government's permission. Nevertheless, he offered to withdraw the naval force if Scott would withdraw Casey's troops. He then reassured Scott that, as per the Marcy agreement, he would not attempt to assume jurisdiction over the island. In view of the outrageous charges leveled by Harney at himself, the government, and the HBC, Douglas was particularly sensitive about Indian raids:

> ...Protection could not be afforded to persons, who, by wandering beyond the precincts of the settlements, and the jurisdiction of the Tribunals, voluntarily expose themselves to violence or treachery of Native tribes.[19]

The master of the *Joe Lane* himself rowed a longboat through the islands to bring Douglas' letter to Scott. Convinced of Douglas' sincerity, Scott moved quickly. On November 5, he demonstrated good faith by ordering withdrawal of all U.S. Army reinforcements and artillery from San Juan Island. Haller's company was to return to Fort Townsend; and Companies A and C of the Fourth Infantry, M and H of the Ninth to Fort Steilacoom; and the last of the Third Artillery companies to Fort Vancouver. Pickett's company would remain. Colonel Lay already had received a verbal agreement that the British naval forces would be reduced.[20]

On Monday November 7, the *Massachusetts* steamed into Griffin Bay where Colonels Thomas and Lay (Peck had them as "Johnson and Lee"—could he have mistaken Lay for Robert E. Lee?) were dispatched ashore with the orders. The pickets were immediately withdrawn, work stopped on the redoubt, and preparations were made to send the reinforcements home. Again, to the profound disappointment of those on the island—British and American alike—Scott chose not to disembark. The chill winds whipped up the bay, bringing on a bout of seasickness (or his "splendid" table did not agree with him). He hunkered down in his cabin. One can easily imagine him scanning the island with a spyglass and shaking his head in wonder at the folly of man. The redoubt fired a thirteen-gun salute in his honor—the only time guns were discharged from the work. Captain Prevost and his officers then visited Scott, while

Colonel Lay and several other U.S. Army officers visited Casey's encampment.

At the order to stop work on the redoubt, the soldiers who had been pressed into the digging and rock lugging details by the now despised engineers were joyful to a man. Peck recorded:

> There were great rejoicings at the order to suspend work on the fort. The tools were collected quicker than ever on a former occasion and brought to their proper repository, with many shouts and much confusion, and to us it is a sad disappointment, looking for considerable credit, as we did, for our services here.[21]

The stop-work couldn't have come at a better time. In November, northwest Washington and the San Juans are at the mercy of northeast winds that roar down the Fraser River Valley, glazing roads, knocking down trees, and freezing pipes. "The weather grows cold constantly since, and in our cotton houses (tents) we feel the change quite sensibly," Peck reported.

While the Americans were breaking camp the *Tribune*, larger of the two British warships, steamed out of the bay leaving the *Satellite* to observe the American exodus. In addition to the San Juan forces, Scott issued an order to all commanders in the territory, advising them that San Juan Island was still in dispute and that British subjects had equal rights with American citizens.

Specifics were relayed to Douglas by Lay, who wrote on behalf of Scott that the Americans would continue to occupy the lower portion of the new camp cleared by Casey just north of the HBC farm. Pickett and Company D would remain in the camp "further back—indeed out of sight—on ground cleared up by his company and with comfortable shelter for the winter erected with labor & expense, it is presumed there can be no local feeling even against his continuance there."[22]

Douglas was pleased with the result, and reminded the general that the military should not interfere with British subjects. Under private cover, he also attached a letter written by Vancouver Island Colonial Secretary William A. G. Young, asking that Pickett be removed. The governor, still rankled by Pickett's truculence and his proclamation, wanted no part of the Virginian on the island:

> ...You will smile at this and with no doubt with reason too, but the words stand recorded nevertheless, and have never been revoked by word, although undoubtedly by deed... his Excellency has been informed (but with what shadow of truth he cannot judge) that Captain Pickett is of somewhat hasty temperament and somewhat punctilious and exacting.

The governor was certain, Young wrote, that Scott would concur to a command that would "ensure a continuation of perfect harmony and tranquility, until the unfortunate question of title may be forever set at rest."[23]

Scott assured the governor on November 9 that no official from Washington territory would be permitted to interfere with any British subject. British subjects violating the law would be referred to the proper British authorities. In the matter of the change of station for Pickett, Lay responded that the deed was done. Pickett would return to Fort Bellingham, and Capt. Lewis Cass Hunt and Company C, Fourth Infantry would remain. An 1847 graduate of West Point—who did slightly better Pickett (the following year) by graduating 33rd of 38, the goat being Pickett's first cousin, Henry Heth—and a family friend of Secretary of State Lewis Cass, Hunt had excellent political connections. "You will find him a most agreeable and courteous gentleman," Lay wrote.

Hunt was especially agreeable to Scott. In a November 18 letter to a lady friend Hunt described the "disreputable performances of our silly stupid Commander Harney." He then boastfully noted that a note accompanied his instructions from General Scott in which the general expressed "...his entire confidence in the intelligence, discretion and *courtesy* required in the discharge of the delicate and important duties devolving upon me." Hunt believed Scott's use of italics to stress his confidence in Hunt's courtesy "...implied a want of that quality" in George Pickett. He went on to describe Harney as a "dull animal," Archibald Campbell as "weak" and Pickett as a man possessed of "poor judgment."[24]

Hunt was directed to bivouac his troops in "...that part of the camp near and within sight of the Hudson's Bay Company's buildings. The little clearing in the wood and behind the hill has had comfortable shelter erected upon it where one company will be stationed."

Baynes reviewed all the documents and wrote to Douglas on November 9 that he concurred with the agreement.

The "Great Pacificator" had done it again. The *Massachusetts* steamed to Port Townsend on November 8 to await the return of the *Northerner* for the return trip to San Francisco. After enduring another day of extreme weather, including four and half inches of snow, the *Northerner* arrived. But before taking Scott on board the ship was directed to serve as a dispatch boat hauling Lay and a flurry of letters and attached copies drafted by Scott for Harney, Gholson, and Douglas to Olympia and Victoria respectively.

The letter to Douglas contained further assurances that British subjects on the island would not be harassed and any miscreants would be remanded to British authorities. It also promised Douglas that the case of William Moore—the British subject arrested for selling liquor to soldiers on post and assigned to work on the redoubt as punishment—would be addressed by Colonel Casey.[25]

Harney was sent copies of Scott's correspondence with Douglas, the orders to withdraw reinforcements and replace Pickett with

Hunt, plus an admonition not to jeopardize what Scott and Douglas
had put in place:

> ...the general-in-chief wishes that it be remembered
> that the sovereignty of the island is still in dispute
> between the two governments, and, until definitely
> settled by them, that British subjects have equal
> rights with American citizens on the island.[26]

When informed of the agreement by Colonel Lay, Gholson was
enraged. He did not like being left out, nor did he appreciate being
warned to follow Scott's peaceful course. On November 13, the
governor ordered returned all fines collected from British subjects,
but he protested to Cass the decision to exclude the territorial
jurisdiction over British subjects in the islands. He was backed by
the legislature, which resolved against "military rule." Cass later
advised him that until the dispute was resolved, British subjects
were not to be disturbed.

When word of the settlement, with Gholson's interpretation,
reached the *Pioneer and Democrat*, the editor screamed, "...never has
anything occurred in the history of our Territory which has met
with so hearty a condemnation... as has the recent deserting of
our rights to the island of San Juan." Scott's settlement was viewed
as a sellout dictated by Douglas. The *Pioneer and Democrat* could only
conclude that Scott was a victim of old age and "...out of charity to
old age and an enervated body, let us... pardon this his first and
only great error—an error unpardonable in one in the enjoyment of
more youthful age or mental vigor."[27]

On November 11, the *Northerner* finally came alongside the
Massachusetts, by then leaking badly from running aground, and
the general transferred aboard. If Scott was anticipating relief on
a swifter and more commodious vessel he was not to find it. The
Northerner suffered a "defect in the boiler" and had to beat through a
furious storm under sail, which made most of the passengers "right

down sick." The ship needed to dock for repairs and take on more coal, so it "daringly" battled the Columbia River bar and tied up at St. Helens, Oregon. [28] During the respite, Scott again wrote Harney, urging that he resign his Department of Oregon command and move to the Department of the West in St. Louis as previously suggested. Harney had requested this command in the past to be near his home and Scott knew it. Had Scott left it at that Harney might have taken the bait. However, he had to add:

> Another motive has just occurred to me for renewing the subject. I have no doubt that one of the preliminary demands, which will be made by the British government upon ours, in connection with your occupation of the island of San Juan, will be your removal from your present command. In such an event it might be a great relief to the President to find you, by your own act, no longer in that command.

Scott further muddied his purpose by suggesting that he was ordering the transfer for "public considerations solely and have not received the slightest hint to that effect from Washington." He then gave Harney "leave to decline (the order)."

This Harney did with relish:

> In reply to this communication of the General-in-Chief, I desire to inform him that I am not disposed to comply with such an order. I do not believe the President of the United States will be embarrassed by any action of the British government in reference to San Juan Island; nor can I suppose the President would be pleased to see me relinquish this command in any manner that does not plainly indicate his intentions towards the public service.[30]

With the successful conclusion of negotiations, Douglas and Scott at once sent word by sea and land, realizing the diplomatic situation could have changed in the time it required to send word. Scott actually carried dispatches for both governments, but there also had been telegrams directed to Leavenworth via the overland stage. Everyone settled in to wait.

On Griffin Bay, Hunt organized his command, the British sailors continued with the monotony of port life, and the reinforcements broke camp. Squabbling broke out between Hunt and Pickett over the wooden buildings Pickett had shipped over from Fort Bellingham. While other companies shivered in tents, Pickett's men stayed relatively warm. In the old army, many of the buildings in frontier outposts were built with company funds, subtracted from each soldier's pay by the paymaster. Pickett was permitted to take what he wanted back to Bellingham Bay, but the Virginian left all to Hunt, which he was soon to regret. His second in command, Lieutenant Forsyth, and a junior officer from another company almost came to blows over livestock. It required Henry Martyn Robert, presumably the officer of the day, to stand between them and threaten arrest if they did not back off.

Once the redoubt work was squared away, the guns, ammunition, and other equipment were hauled from the edifice and lugged back down the prairie slope to South Beach. The equipment may have been gone, but the engineers had forever left their mark on the landscape of San Juan Island.

With nothing left to do, the soldiers watched sheets of rains whip down from sodden skies, day after day:

> These are really halcyon days of our soldiering, utterly idle, a thing unknown to an Engineer Soldier, but we are kept busy at nights in a vain effort to keep warm.[31]

The engineers were gone by November 30, the camp thinning as the various companies returned to points south. Pickett placed his company temporarily under the command of Lieutenant Forsyth while he sat on yet another court martial board at Fort Vancouver. [32] The company departed San Juan on November 28, taking only the bare essentials because of tight quarters aboard ship. These included rifles, knapsacks, 20 days worth of food, a few articles of equipage, and as Forsyth noted in his letter book, "a very small quantity of private baggage." Virtually all of the company property—cannon, stands of rifles, pistols, two months of provisions, brand-new uniforms, a large quantity of oats, and hospital stores—was left on the Hudson's Bay Company dock in the care of Captain Hunt. Hunt's men loaded the property aboard the schooner *General Harney* on the afternoon of December 3.

That's when another northeaster struck.

The ship had just got under sail when the wind caught her and with hurricane force drove her onto the rocks near San Juan Village, dragging two anchors. The ship rapidly filled with water while desperate soldiers and crew turned livestock overboard and salvaged as many stores as they could. They eventually gave up, waited for low tide and returned to their labors in the darkness. The storm raged for more than 24 hours. " The men suffered intensely from the cold, the captain's feet were frozen," Hunt wrote in a deposition justifying the loss of government property in his care. The little that remained that was not ruined was shipped to Fort Bellingham weeks later aboard the side-wheel steamer *Eliza Anderson*.[33]

Pickett returned to Fort Bellingham to find his men short of provisions and living in a barn in midwinter. He wrote Hunt demanding $300 for the buildings he left behind. Hunt forwarded the request to Vancouver Barracks, where Pickett's "best friend" quartermaster Capt. Rufus Ingalls cut the sum to $180 and advised Pickett to make do. Pickett must have cursed himself for being too generous or lazy or both.

It is discouraging to the men of the command to be moved from comfortable quarters into this empty barn and in addition, to accumulation of malfortune in losing the absolute necessaries for a winter campaign; however, there's no word of complaint— all work with a will. I am lamentably deficient in arms, cannot show more than forty effective rifles (for 74 men).[34]

So much for George Pickett's chance at glory on San Juan Island. Four months after their dramatic landing, the men of Company D had been run off the island like thieves and were living like pigs. It seemed a sorry end to such promise.

Chapter 15

PICKETT LANDS AGAIN

While George Pickett and his company were shivering in a barn on Bellingham Bay that winter of 1859-60, Capt. Lewis Cass Hunt was enjoying the table of and making a good impression on Capt. James Prevost aboard *Satellite* on Griffin Bay.

His swift boot back to Bellingham Bay confirmed for Pickett that he had stumbled onto the bad side of Winfield Scott. The general's official report on the matter was scathing. In an age when even bitter enemies maintained a veneer of decorum, Scott had condemned Pickett and Harney as idiots for nearly starting a war with the preeminent naval power in the world, not to mention the nation's number one foreign investor.

The stung Virginian soon after wrote a friend, wondering why he was being punished "...without even knowing what has been fault?" Scott had "...cast an implicit censure on me for *Obeying Orders* [his italics]." He also was irritated by stories circulating that he had exhibited "obnoxious behavior" in his dealings with British officials. The latter aspersion moved him to seek a letter of support from Hornby, who cordially damned him with faint praise, writing "...our intercourse had been of the most courteous nature, and aside from the official matters, of the most pleasant and agreeable kind."[1]

Pickett's sole comfort was a joint resolution issued by the

territorial legislature, with the still-peeved Governor Gholson's blessing, praising him (and Harney) for "the gallant and firm discharge of his duties under the most trying circumstances." Pickett later viewed the day he confronted Hornby as "one of the proudest of my life." Harney sent the resolution to his superiors in the War Department and another copy to Secretary of State Cass. The commanding general of the U.S. Army had rejected his policies and urged him to resign his command, yet Harney viewed the legislature's petition as an endorsement. And contrary to Scott's orders, he embraced Gholson's claim that the islands were sovereign U.S. territory and, as such, belonged under civil jurisdiction.[2]

Harney next turned north and cast a baleful eye at Lewis Cass Hunt. The captain confessed to one of his correspondents, a woman named Mrs. McBlair, that he was placing letters in the various newspapers of the region castigating that "reckless, stupid old goose" Harney for his fumbling at San Juan and other missteps as Department of Oregon commander.

> During the whole time I endeavored through several newspapers, to which I had access, to tone down public opinion. I published one or two squibs to throw ridicule upon the foolish affair ...and when Gen'l Scott arrived I endeavored thro' those papers to give a conservative turn to public opinion and prepare for those measures which I felt sure Gen'l Scott would take.

If that was his purpose, Hunt failed miserably. The territory, throughout the 12-year military joint occupation to come, would never accept what was essentially international martial law on San Juan Island. Scott was labeled a stooge to British and American commercial interests, and justifiably so, according to Hunt. In his view it was the "noble old fellow" Admiral Baynes who "...saved us from a war, a war in which the commercial interests of 50 millions of souls of the same race would have been destroyed, not to speak of the horrible consequences in other respects."

Hunt's letters resonate with disdain for government by the people: "All this wretched performance of Harney is the legitimate result of popular government. It was to please the dear people that Harney made his coup, and he did please the people, silly, blind fools that they are."[3]

Those "silly fools" were not so myopic to miss a sneer of contempt. But the reaction Hunt encountered from the American settlers on San Juan and the territorial officials on the mainland convinced him that his days on San Juan Island were numbered:

> I have a very difficult part to play here, inasmuch as
> I have the active hostility of General Harney... who
> is seeking a pretext to remove me, and send back
> Captain Pickett, his pet, displaced by General Scott.[4]

While Hunt was awaiting his dismissal, Scott arrived in New York on December 12, whereupon he cabled his report to Buchanan and sent on the dispatches from Douglas (dated November 9) to Lord Lyons.

In his letter to the colonial office, Douglas not only continued to press for a joint civil occupation, but also suggested as an alternative the abandonment by Europeans of the entire San Juan archipelago. He again stressed the economic infeasibility of stationing troops upon the island because it would attract more squatters (the old HBC bugaboo). Neither government should promise to protect settlers.[5]

Baynes concurred with Douglas at least on this point.

In a letter to the Admiralty, also dated November 9, Baynes also stumped for a joint civil occupation. He had been wary at first of Scott's offer because Scott had done nothing then to reduce his force on the island. "It was ridiculous to suppose that (the troops) had been placed there to protect a few American squatters from the hostile attack of northern Indians. They were evidently there as a menace to us, and until they were withdrawn, I thought it impossible to treat."

Only after Douglas' second dispatch to Massachusetts did Scott feel compelled to make an overture and withdrew Casey's forces. By contrast, Baynes held that the British landing forces would indicate that British subjects needed protection, which he believed they did not:

> Throughout this untoward affair we have been perfectly passive, exercising a degree of forbearance which their Lordships may not, perhaps, altogether approve, but called for, in my opinion, by the almost certainty of a collision at this distant point causing a rupture between the two nations; and I felt that as long as the dignity and honour of the British flag was in no way compromised, I should be best carrying out the views of Her Majesty's Government, and the interests of these colonies, by avoiding the risk of it... Acts of discourtesy on minor points were, on more than one occasion, shown by the authorities of the United States, though the military behaved with perfect propriety. This was all an irritating matter.[6]

But Douglas and Baynes had no influence in London where the decision for a joint military occupation already had been made, the British assured by American sincerity in sending Scott west. Again, the vast distances and the want of telegraph to the West Coast sowed confusion in everyone's mind, most especially Douglas'. Nevertheless, Douglas was unjustly praised for the restraint shown by Hornby.

> (Her majesty's Government) feel it to be cause of satisfaction that your original intention of sending

British troops to the island for the purpose of a joint occupation was not carried out. Such a measure might have led, at the moment, in question, to further disagreements, or even a collision.[7]

The British change of heart had not come without vinegar. Despite expressions of horror emanating from Washington, Russell wrote Lyons that he believed the American boundary commissioner, Archibald Campbell, must have been fully aware of and condoned Harney's actions. He also lambasted Pickett for his proclamation.

Two points rang clear: Exclusive U.S. jurisdiction could not be allowed; and if the U.S. insisted on keeping troops on the island, then a like number of marines should be landed.

With that, the joint military occupation was sealed.[8]

In January, Baynes reported that *Satellite* was still on station in Griffin Bay. Echoing Hunt's letters, Baynes noted the "most friendly feeling" existing between Hunt and Captain Prevost, as well as the rank and file. San Juan Village—"fourteen or fifteen shanties"—was nearly deserted while the preemption claims were still occupied by American settlers.

Douglas received Newcastle's joint occupation orders Jan. 16, 1860, and passed them on to Baynes. However, the admiral, believing Newcastle's letter "authorized but did not direct" the occupation, demurred until February, content with having a ship stationed on Griffin Bay. Once he received confirmation, he set plans in motion to place the marines on the island.

The problem was finding a suitable site. The admiral solicited from Captain Prevost a list of appropriate locations for a camp, while Douglas queried Lieutenant Colonel Moody on the mainland. Colonel Moody, the Royal Engineer commander, thought San Juan a poor choice, as it seemed to eliminate rest of the islands from consideration in the boundary dispute. Locating the two garrisons on the same island might also "...have the effect of dividing, even

in men's minds, the Island of San Juan between military forces in
occupation." Therefore he believed that Orcas Island was the logical
choice for the British garrison.

Prevost probably knew the San Juan Island shoreline better
than anyone, having been surveying it since the joint boundary
survey had commenced in 1857. He submitted a list of seven island
locations to Baynes, each marked on a tracing of San Juan Island
map. These included 1.) Rocky Point on the southeast end of the
island, 2.) Hubbs' claim, also on the southeast portion of the island
where the Cape San Juan development is located today, 3.) the
prairie just above Eagle Cove, 4.) a field just west of Belle Vue
Sheep Farm's home station, about 400 yards west of the American
encampment, 5.) the sheep station southeast of Little Mountain,
known today as San Juan Valley, 6.) the current site of English
Camp on Garrison Bay (apparently called Roche Harbour by the
British, though not to be confused with the site of today's Roche
Harbor Resort) and, 7.) the sheep station on the site of the future
town of Friday Harbor.[9]

Prevost was cool to the Cattle Point sites because of their
proximity to the U.S. encampment. He also wanted to avoid snarls
with American claimants such as Paul K. Hubbs, Jr., the U.S.
deputy collector of customs. Already residing on the Cape San Juan
site (No. 2), Hubbs had demonstrated during the Pig War crisis
that he was a personality to be avoided. Oddly enough, the Friday
Harbor site seemed perfect, but was considered too far away from
Griffin Bay to be effective.[10]

While the captain considered site No. 6 an ideal location for a
camp of any size, Baynes worried about the absence of fresh water.
This concern was dispelled on a subsequent trip when a *Satellite*
third officer, Lt. Richard Roche, wrote:

> About three quarters of a mile in a SSE direction
> there is a large patch of water, half lake, half swamp,

on the northern shore of which is a situation admirably adapted for an encampment. It slopes gently to the southwest, is well sheltered, has a good supply of water and grass, and is capable of affording maneuvering ground for any number of men that are likely to be required in that locality, there being a large extent of Prairie Land, interspersed with some very fine oak timber.[11]

Roche's site was enhanced by two streams of water, one running from a creek draining into the south end of the bay, the other being what is called today the "Roche Harbor watershed," emptying into Westcott Bay around Bell Point. The location also benefited from runoff from Young Hill, a 650-foot eminence rising east of the future parade ground. The marines eventually dug two cisterns on the edge of the parade to catch the runoff, which the park uses to this day to water the formal garden at the height of the dry season.

Garrison Bay indeed was a natural setting for a military encampment with a sheltered harbor and gently sloping beach front for landing of troops and supplies; a broad shell midden area, ideal for a parade ground, had already been cleared of large trees by the Indian inhabitants, while a progression of natural terraces would facilitate additional structures; and, finally, the bounty of fresh water, timber and stone provided natural resources critical to establishing and maintaining a military encampment.

Another Royal navy subaltern, Lt. Richard Mayne of HMS *Plumper,* believed spacing the camps so far apart was ludicrous:

I can't help thinking this a great mistake after we would not send troops there for the last 9 months, that it was not 'English' etc., etc. to do so to 'cave in' now, but I suppose it is ordered from home, and then sticking them on opposite sides of the island

as if they were to eat each other. I should like to see
how he (Hunt) will laugh at it.[12]

The Victoria *Gazette* reported that HMS *Satellite* had appeared at
the entrance to Victoria's inner harbor on Wednesday March 21 and
"received on board the company of Marines under Capt. Bazalgette,
destined for the occupation of San Juan. The Barracks adjoining
the Government Buildings are now quite deserted," the newspaper
reported. Missing on the voyage was Capt. R.M. Parsons of the
Royal Engineers, who had played a role in site selection and drafted
a plan of the camp that would be largely complete by the end of the
year. Governor Douglas believed the appearance of a sapper such as
Parsons in uniform would send a message to the Americans that the
site had been selected for tactical advantage, a perception he wished
to dispel.[13]

Baynes wrote a letter that same day as the landing advising
the Admiralty:

> ...I embarked the detachment as per margin,* on
> board the *Satellite* which ship proceeded with them
> on the 21st instant calling on the way at the United
> States' camp, for the purpose of delivering to captain
> Hunt, the officer commanding, a letter from me,
> a copy of which I enclose...* Captain Bazalgette,
> Lieutenant Sparshott, Lieutenant Cooper, 1 colour
> sergeant, 4 sergeants, 4 corporals, 1 bugler, 73
> privates and Mr. T.F. Mitchell, Assistant Surgeon.[14]

The marines landed on what became known as Garrison Bay
under the command of Capt. George Bazalgette, a 13-year veteran
who had served in the Crimean and China campaigns and shared a
cabin with Hornby on *Tribune*'s perilous Pacific crossing. The force
consisted of Bazalgette, two subalterns, a surgeon, and eighty-three
noncommissioned officers and men.

What they found was jotted down in the journal of Color Sergeant W. Joy:

> ...landed in a bay completely landlocked, our Camping Ground being on a shell bank—the accumulation of "Years", evidently, as it averaged ten feet high, from thirty-five to forty feet through, by 120 yards long, it was the work of Indians, as they live very much on a shellfish called "Clams", and of course deposit the shells just outside their Huts, hence the bank I mentioned, the brush wood grew quite down to the water's edge, in the rear the forest was growing in undisturbed tranquility...[15]

Baynes' instructions to Bazalgette were precise and mirrored the guidelines Winfield Scott had roughed out the previous November. The captain was advised foremost that he was not only to protect British interests on San Juan Island, but maintain a frank and free communication with his U.S. counterpart so as not to interfere with U.S. citizens, who had "equal rights on the island." Lawbreakers of U.S. citizenship were to be turned over to the U.S. commander for justice. The captain also was to safeguard the discipline and morale of his garrison by treating vigorously with bad influences, namely pimps and whisky sellers, and do his level best to "...prevent any of the detachment from straggling."[16]

As soon as the landing of the marines became a foregone conclusion, John de Courcy was relieved as magistrate effective March 20.

Hunt on March 27 dutifully reported to Harney the British landing, including Baynes' letter to Hunt and a copy of Baynes' instructions to Bazalgette, which Hunt observed were clearer than his own regarding jurisdiction. The British commander had been granted authority to eject miscreant British subjects from the island and full latitude to consult with the U.S. garrison commander about American violators. Hunt complained that since U.S. civil magistrate D.F. Newsome had resigned the rise of crime in San Juan Village was testing everyone's limits, particularly Hunt's.[17]

However, the captain had not allowed uncertainties concerning martial law to stand in his way. Earlier in the month he'd dispatched three soldiers to the town to ferret out stolen goods at a local whisky establishment, whereupon the soldiers were thrown into the mud—or as noted in the Port Townsend *Register*, "sent into the street on a 'double-quick Shanghai trot'"—by several burly inhabitants. Hunt reevaluated the situation and sought Henry Crosbie for advice. The former magistrate suggested taking the whisky peddlers to civil court, presumably in Port Townsend. Only two of three charged went to trial and they were acquitted.

Another, whom Hunt identified as a "German Jew whose establishment was the greatest nuisance of all," decided himself to get out while the getting was good. Unfortunately for Hunt, the other whisky sellers believed Hunt had run "the Jew" off the island. As a result, several saloon owners and their compatriots wrote Harney on March 7 complaining that Hunt had closed their saloons and evicted them from the island. In response, Harney through Pleasonton on the 21st ordered Hunt "not to interfere with the trade of our citizens" nor molest them in any way and to "forward to the headquarters, a full and complete account of all your actions effecting citizens."[18]

The order must have crossed Hunt's report of the British landing en route. Hunt reacted with fury. It seemed nothing less than a setup. A commanding general who was not familiar with the low quality of the plaintiffs and, most critically, had not even taken the time to hear Hunt's side of the story was censuring him. Hunt countered by sending Harney a description of the whisky sellers written by Crosbie, plus a petition from the "actual" citizens of the island extolling the merits of military over civil law. For good measure he added his own remarks pointing out that he had, in good faith, applied to civil authorities to enforce the law. This was:

> ...as salty an epistle as I dared write, conveying by
> implication and inference my opinion of the conduct
> of headquarters, and I am now awaiting with some
> little curiosity the sequel. With Harney all things
> are possible, and I should not be surprised if he gave
> his wrath full swing and removed me.[19]

This is precisely what happened.

On April 10, orders were issued. Forts Bellingham and Townsend were to again be abandoned. Pickett and Company D would return to San Juan and Hunt and Company C, as well as Haller and Company I at Fort Townsend, to Fort Steilacoom.

These were not simply perfunctory missives replacing a recalcitrant officer. Instead they served notice to the British that the Department of Oregon, once again under Harney's control, did not recognize the joint military occupation to which both governments had agreed. Moreover, George Pickett was to ensure that the British did not interfere with U.S. civilian magistrates, who would be enforcing the law, except in cases involving British subjects, which would be referred to Baynes before action was taken. In Harney's view, the islands were part of Whatcom County, Washington Territory and "the General Commanding is satisfied that any attempt to ignore this right of the Territory will be followed by deplorable results, out of his power to prevent or control."[20]

Meaning war.

Contemporaries and historians alike have concluded that Harney's second Pickett landing was ordered to defy Winfield Scott, who had shoved him aside and cleaned up the mess with the British. But Harney still believed that stationing Pickett on the island had been a logical and legitimate step considering Douglas' proprietary actions toward Americans in the San Juans. Acting Secretary of

War Drinkard had written as much. He also maintained that while he was aware of the interim arrangements made between Scott and Douglas—which did not prescribe a landing of Royal Marines—neither Scott nor the government had advised him that a formal joint military occupation had been approved.

What he had, in hand, was the support of the civil authorities of Washington Territory, who had issued a fine proclamation on his behalf—and his membership in the Democratic party. Harney had been sustained so many times by party patronage that he must have believed that James Buchanan, a Democratic president, would do what James Knox Polk had done during the Mexican War—namely chastise Scott and back Harney.

He as yet had no idea the world had passed him by.[21]

Despite his threat of "deplorable results," Harney ensured Pickett's orders included copies of correspondence between Douglas and Scott, Scott's instructions to Hunt, and copies of orders from Baynes to Bazalgette. Pickett was to relay his instructions to Baynes through Bazalgette.

While Pickett was making preparations to return to San Juan island, Hunt was writing over Harney's head to Scott, a violation of military protocol, but standard behavior in the highly political Old Army. Harney certainly was no stranger to it. The letter reads as a *mea culpa*, Hunt stating that he had done his best in a delicate situation, despite the "animus" shown to him by department headquarters. Still in all, he believed his removal had nothing to do with that. He believed the change had "long been contemplated." He closed on a homey note:

> The order comes at a most convenient time; gardens just planted; while four companies are sent to a post having accommodations for three only, and excellent quarters left vacant at Fort Townsend.[22]

Pickett landed on April 30 and immediately dispatched a messenger to Garrison Bay with a letter of greeting to Bazalgette with attachments.

Admiral Baynes' reaction to Harney's orders and Pickett's second landing was mild. After consulting with Douglas, he reported to the admiralty that neither of them intended to enter once again into fruitless correspondence with Harney. They would await developments from Washington, which they were certain would be swift and ultimately satisfactory. Even so, Baynes cancelled a scheduled cruise, opting to "remain in the neighborhood until matters wear a more promising aspect."[23]

Despite the tenor of Harney's letter, Pickett by then possessed a healthy appreciation for international diplomacy as well as the political winds at army headquarters. Following a welcome wagon visit to Camp Pickett by Bazalgette and his officers, the Virginian expressed to his counterpart "...every desire that cordial understanding, existing between you and Captain Hunt shall continue to be maintained between ourselves..."

Pickett's second stint on San Juan Island was a trial, however. Island residents were not paying taxes or customs duties, which attracted elements with little interest in establishing communities with farms, churches and schools. Indeed, on the American side, San Juan Village floated on a sea of bad whisky, prostitution and lawlessness. On May 21 he wrote:

> ...Matters are proving worse if possible. Whisky sellers without number are here and are still coming. Two-thirds of the Indians on this end of the island are drunk day and night... My hands are tied. I am to assist civil authorities. Where are they? Things cannot remain in this position...

And again on June 1:

Ever since knowledge of the joint occupancy, the desperadoes of all countries have fought hither. It has become a depot for murderers, robbers, whisky sellers – in a word all refugees from justice. Openly and boldly they've come and there's no civil law over them. All the Indian tribes in the neighborhood— Lummi, Swinomish, the Skagit and even the Cowichan and the Victoria Indians flock here in quantities to supply themselves with poisonous whiskey. As a result, this is a perfect bedlam day and night.[24]

Pickett grew more alarmed when a Haida Indian was shot dead in the street by "some rascal" and left in the mud, his family forming a cordon around his body and wailing in mourning rights for days on end. Having lived with a Northern woman with whom he had fathered a child, Pickett presumed that the Haida family would exact vengeance. Hoping to stave off a raid, he made an unsuccessful attempt to ferret out the murderers and in the end preserved the peace by issuing provisions to the widow. His proclivity for exaggerating his position arose again when, by the end of his dispatch, the dead Indian became a "chief." To underscore his concern he reminded his superiors that he had barely 40 men left in his company in contrast to his counterpart Bazalgette, who had a full complement of 84 marines.

As many as 4,000 Northerners, Pickett wrote, had been reported in the vicinity of Victoria. Many were expected to call at the fisheries located along the island's west coast. That had happened the previous fall during the height of the crisis and the Indian shore parties had been run off by Colonel Casey's men. Meanwhile Pickett had the Northern women to worry about. Boatloads were landed for "nefarious purposes" by white traders; one boat by some miracle, was overtaken and boarded by the *Massachusetts*, but most landed with impunity.

Other Northerners sought employment with the Hudson's Bay Company or American settlers; many of the latter recently discharged soldiers from Pickett's company. Pickett wrote in July that if Northerners were to be removed, it would have to apply to all equally. Otherwise he feared reprisal raids on isolated farms that were easy prey for the war canoes. The whisky sellers were still in full blast, too numerous and bellicose for the magistrate to handle. As with Hunt, the Justice asked Pickett for help, and Pickett with Hunt's firing fresh in his mind, at first strongly recommended, as per Harney's orders, that civilian matters rest with civilians. In the end, however, Pickett rendered assistance as had Hunt, such as in the case of a Northerner, whom Pickett arrested for robbery.

In one of the first tests of the joint military occupation, Pickett passed with flying colors. When approached by Griffin, who offered to pay the fine in return for the Northerner's release, Pickett refused, but only after consulting with his counterpart, George Bazalgette at English Camp. "I doubt if a northern Indian can be considered a British subject," Pickett sniffed.[25]

By mid-July the Indian scare had quieted, largely because on Vancouver Island James Douglas had ordered all Northerners disarmed before they entered the city's inner harbor. Thereafter, the only northern Indian problems involved petty theft, drunkenness and prostitution, enterprises primarily financed by whites. One purveyor was arrested for selling liquor at South Beach. His beached boat was found surrounded by canoes, "drunken Indians on board," by a squad of soldiers. Because he was a British subject, Pickett turned him over to his new friend and colleague Bazalgette. The two captains were spending so much time sorting out citizenship that Pickett requested better riding stock to negotiate the 13 miles of rough road that connected the camps.

While this international cooperation was going on, Winfield Scott was fuming as he read Hunt's letter detailing, with considerable embellishment, the change in command on San Juan Island. He had no way of knowing Pickett was steering clear of Harney and developing a positive relationship with Bazalgette.

In a May 14 letter to the Secretary of War, Scott made his case: Pickett had offended the British with his ridiculous proclamation and that was why he was replaced with Hunt. "Hunt (as our officers informed me) was remarkable for firmness, discretion and courtesy."

Scott railed at Harney again for recognizing Washington Territory's jurisdiction and predicted that if trouble did not ensue it would be because of the forbearance of the British rather than any restraint exercised by Americans,

> ...for I found both Brigadier General Harney and Captain Pickett proud of their conquest of the island, and quite jealous of any interference therewith on the part of higher authority.[26]

In his autobiography, Scott summarized the incident and Harney thusly:

> ...Brigadier General Harney, who commanded our forces in that quarter, was a great favorite with Five Democratic Presidents. Full of blinded admiration for his patrons, he had before in Florida hung several Indians, under the most doubtful circumstances, in imitation of a like act on the part of General Jackson in the same quarter, and now as that popular hero gained so much applause by wrenching Pensacola and all of Middle Florida from Spain in time of peace, Harney probably thought he might make himself president too, by cutting short all diplomacy and taking possession of the disputed island! Imitations on the part of certain people always begin by copying defects.

His next few words revealed the depth of his disdain: "It is not known that the protégé, Harney, was even reprimanded for his rashness. He certainly was not recalled although the measure was suggested by the writer."[27]

When Lord Lyons learned of the change in command, he wrote Cass on June 6. The situation was "deplorable," particularly Harney's threat of "deplorable results."[28]

But following a review of Scott's correspondence, not to mention the agreements struck by both governments, Lyons expressed confidence that the U.S. Government would correct the situation, particularly in the wake of a note he received from outgoing President Buchanan. In it the weary Buchanan lamented that he really didn't know "what to do" with the people of the West Coast, but was emboldened that Lyons, "by begging me to set my wits to work" was confident the president would find a mutually agreeable solution.

The mortified Cass and his boss, President Buchanan, once again claimed to be the last to know. However, Scott's letter to the War Department indicates that Cass had been aware of Harney's orders since May 14. No document trail exists on the matter between the War and State departments.

Was Cass feigning surprise while the matter was under investigation, hoping to have an answer before the Brits found out? Could it have been more Democratic patronage at work on Harney's behalf? Perhaps the War Department staff was on spring break. We'll never know. What we do know is that hard paper rescinding Harney's orders and ordering him back to Washington City, did not leave the capital until June 8.[29]

Finally, Harney had gone too far even for his fellow Democrats.

Col. George Wright, commander of the Ninth Infantry, was given the Department of Oregon. Wright recognized Scott's agreement but left Pickett in command. They were friends and

messmates dating back to the Mexican War, and it was Wright who
in 1855 had rescued Pickett from the tedium of Fort Gates, Texas,
to command a company in his new regiment.[30]

Several weeks later, when word of his firing finally reached
him, Harney grudgingly packed his things and by mid-July started
his journey east via the Cowlitz River landing, thence overland to
Olympia and down Sound. [31] His prospects were not all bad. As per
Scott's November offer, he was going to St. Louis and the Department
of the West, a command that extended from the Mississippi River
to the Continental Divide, from the Canadian to Mexican borders.
As Scott observed, Harney's "punishment" for the "San Juan
imbroglio," as it came to be called, was a slap on the wrist.

Harney stopped by Victoria on the Express Steamer on July 14.
Baynes noted:

> ...received no communication from him and
> consequently did not feel myself called upon
> to show him any attention after the coarse and
> unwarrantable language he made use of in his letter
> to the Adjutant General of October 29, 1859, with
> regard to myself, Captains Prevost and Hornby as
> well as Her Majesty's Government.[32]

Oddly enough, Wright wrote the War Department in late August
stating that he too had never been given any specific instructions
concerning the joint occupation of San Juan Island. Therefore,
he would fall back on Scott's instructions of November 5-9, which
were relayed to Harney by Colonel Thomas during Scott's West
Coast visit.

Pickett, meanwhile was throwing himself into the role of
peacemaker. On receiving from Wright his confirmation of
command and directions to abide by Scott's orders—of which he
states Bazalgette never received a copy—he wrote Bazalgette, closing
with this nugget:

> I do not for a moment imagine that anything would
> have happened to disturb the perfect understanding
> which has existed between us, both officially and
> personally since my arrival on the Island, but I
> think it due each other in the position we occupy
> to communicate at once any change of orders or
> instructions from our superiors in command.[33]

Those instructions were still taking shape. In January 1861, British officials were still wary of the mixed nature of authority on the island, particularly that the U.S. had on board a magistrate and collector of customs who were not subject to Pickett's orders. But Pickett was doing his best to strike a balance. Both bachelors, Pickett and Bazalgette got on famously not only in matters of jurisdiction, but on trips together to Victoria, where they were observed tipping glasses at the Colonial House.

Thus was the tone set for the spirit of mutual cooperation between the two camps throughout the joint occupation.

Chapter 16

JOINT OCCUPATION
AND SETTLEMENT

No one believed the joint military occupation would last 12 years. Even Douglas finally concluded that complete withdrawal of civil authority was the way to go, but he assumed like everyone else that with the crisis over the boundary commissions would finally settle the matter. He wrote as much to the Foreign Office on May 7, 1860. Therefore, on July 20, Russell wrote Lyons to request that the United States withdraw the civil authorities. The U.S. refused, which was to cause nothing but trouble.[1]

Acting Secretary of State William H. Trescot did urge the British and American commissioners to get on with it. The British government was prepared to be accommodating, even if it meant submitting the question to third party arbitration, much as Cutlar had suggested when he and Griffin first squabbled over the pig. Indeed, as early as 1858 Lord Stanley at the Colonial Office wrote that he believed that the matter should be settled by arbitration, while the Admiralty that same year urged an attempt to negotiate with the Americans on establishing the Middle Channel as the boundary. Failing that, the Admiralty believed the government should settle on Canal de Haro, which would cede the entire archipelago to the Americans.[2]

By December 1860, the British formally offered to submit the question to the kings of Norway and Sweden and the Federal

Council of Switzerland for binding arbitration. The settlement also would require the Americans to pay $500,000 to the Hudson's Bay Company and Puget Sound Agricultural Company for properties they had been forced to evacuate in the Cowlitz River Valley and Fort Vancouver as per the Treaty of Oregon. The claims of the companies were still outstanding.[3]

The United States grudgingly approved the arbiters, but balked at paying $500,000 for properties originally valued at $300,000 (although the HBC had reset the value of all properties to $650,000). The new Secretary of State, Jeremiah S. Black, told Lyons the issues would have to be settled separately. The settlement also would have to pass the Senate, and that body, anticipating a Republican administration and the prospect of secession by the Southern states, was hardly prepared to vote on it. A resolution written by Sen. James M. Mason of Virginia passed committee and was submitted to the whole body, but no action was taken.[4]

Unfortunately, not everyone was willing to wait on the diplomats. Fueled by wishful thinking and misinformation campaigns, citizens and elected officials living in Washington Territory still believed the San Juans belonged to the United States alone. That was one issue. The other was the American distaste for martial law in any form. As a result, the joint occupation would be subject to harassment from without and within, despite the efforts of Bazalgette and Pickett. Pickett spared no effort to be accommodating, which seemed a far cry from the man remembered for his belligerency more than anything else on San Juan Island.

The commanders took advantage of the HBC-built sheep run, improving it into a military road, which, before a telegraph was installed along its track in the mid-1860s, permitted rapid transit by horse and mule power. Each commander requisitioned animals for that purpose, and when they were not doing their own riding, messengers were dispatched with missives that dealt with the snarls of citizenship and jurisdiction – primarily over whisky sellers, who would continue to be the bane of both commands throughout the joint occupation. Little had changed when Capt. Lyman Bissell wrote in 1863, "When I assumed command of this camp in February 1862, I found the island infested with thieves and vagabonds of no particular nationality."

Whisky traffickers and crimes attendant to the trade dominate the official correspondence of both camps. For example, in September of 1860 one John Taylor was purveying whisky to soldiers, Indians and all comers from a boat on the beach. Pickett and a squad arrived at the scene to find several Indian canoes lashed to Taylor's craft filled with intoxicated Indians. The Indians maintained Taylor was a "Boston" (American), but Taylor said he was a British subject. This was a standard ploy among San Juan miscreants. If arrested by one side, the suspect claimed opposite citizenship. Pickett interrogated Taylor and believing him a British subject, sent him packing to Bazalgette with a note that closed, "I shall be ready at any time to give my affidavit to the above facts and if necessary that of Sergeant Patrick Keanan of my company can also be obtained."

The following year the Victoria *Colonist* reported that a Benjamin R. Spain was apprehended on the beach of the Victoria Indian reserve (presumably the Songhee settlement in the inner harbor) with a canoe-load of whisky destined for San Juan Island. Had it not been for high winds, the cargo would have been delivered, the constable claimed. The Victoria courts threw out the case for lack of evidence, but the newspaper account of the trial included a letter from the San Juan Village barber asking "Charely and Ben" to ship 40 gallons of alcohol, and if that wasn't possible then "twenty and two pounds" of brown sugar. The army responded by dispatching whisky patrols along the island's west coast (today's American Camp bluffs) "...three times a day and one at night." The troops were to order all Indian canoes away and if they refused to leave, officers were authorized to "fire at them."

San Juan Island in the 1860s was not a vacation paradise. Time hung heavy and what better way to fill it than with drink. According to one English traveler, over-imbibing was universal in America:

> I am sure the Americans can fix nothing without a drink...They drink because it is hot; they drink because it is cold...They begin to drink early in the morning, they leave off late at night; they commence early in life, and they continue it until they soon drop in the grave.[5]

Communications would be critically tested that winter when a Washington Territorial issue once again (and not for the last time) spilled into the Military Road correspondence. The Royal Marines in September quarried limestone and erected kilns on the site of today's Roche Harbor Resort for use in making whitewash. A sample of the product was sent to Victoria, where the Colonist reported viewing "...a splendid article of lime, white as chalk... now being made at San Juan island." The Americans were not unaware of this vast and lucrative resource, as two months later a Soloman Meyerbach (or Meyerback as it also appears), a baker residing on San Juan Island, and Paul K. Hubbs, Jr., were spotted there wielding pick and shovel. The two were undoubtedly inspired by the American-owned kilns established on the current site of Lime Kiln State Park on the west side of the island. They were apprehended by Royal Marine Lt. Edward C. Sparshott, in company with August Hoffmeister, the Royal Marine camp sutler. Sparshott told the Americans that the limestone deposits and kilns were within the boundary of the Royal Marine reservation. Anyone caught on the site in future would be thrown in the guardhouse by order of Captain Bazalgette. Meyerbach protested that if the British claim included Roche Harbor, it was far too large for a military reservation, being nearly 16 square miles or 64 quarter sections. Moreover, the quarry site was at least three miles away from the

English Camp parade ground, and "separated by an inlet of water at least a half a mile wide." An affidavit and petition for redress were sent to both commanders with copies filed in the Whatcom County Courthouse, and Pickett was urged by Meyerbach to "sustain" the rights of a U.S. citizen, (who is listed from Germany in the 1860 census). Bazalgette sought federal intervention from Pickett, who cautioned Americans on the island not to intrude on the British claim. He also advised his superior, Colonel Wright, to

> ...suggest to the officer commanding the British
> fleet the propriety of an equal reserve being laid off
> for each command... Should immediate action not
> be taken on the premises, I fear trouble will ensue.

The issue forced both nations to take steps to formally measure off their boundaries, and indeed the Roche Harbor lime deposits remained within the limits of the camp. Moreover, many of the documents in the public records pertaining to English Camp list the location of the camp proper as "Roche Harbour." Pickett took advantage of the issue to increase the size of the American reservation so that it encompassed nearly the entire Cattle Point peninsula, save for claims around San Juan Village and Hubbs's claim at Cattle Pass.[6]

As the months rolled by, the disparity in the care and feeding of the two military camps became painfully obvious to Pickett, who complained of the inattention given his post by the War Department. In a letter to Ninth Infantry deputy commander, Lt. Col. Silas Casey, he expressed envy at the efficiency of the British operation and alarm at the already growing neglect of his camp by department authorities. His men, he wrote, had not been paid in six months, while the British not only were paid each month, but earned additional "colonial or double pay." This difference in the pay and supply of the two forces would prevail until the end of the joint occupation.[7]

Matters of pay at a peculiar and remote frontier outpost must have seemed trivial following Abraham Lincoln's November election and the secession of seven Southern states. With every scrap of bleak news arriving by steamer or Pony Express, paranoia abounded in department headquarters. The primary focus was on rumored bands of secessionists ready to either turn the Pacific Slope to the South or create an independent "Republic of the Pacific".[8]

Suspicions also swept the Department of the Pacific's general staff, especially after Lincoln was sworn in on March 4, 1861. Two weeks later Winfield Scott relieved department commander, Brig. Gen. Albert Sidney Johnston, a proud Texan, *before* Johnston could resign. Unlike Brig Gen. David Twiggs, who shamefully turned the Department of Texas over to rebel forces, Johnston, who resigned April 9, vowed to remain at his post and honorably enforce U.S. government policies until relieved. Imagine his surprise not two weeks later when he learned Brig. Gen. Edwin Sumner was en route to replace him. A little more than a month later Scott ordered Johnston's arrest by land or sea after he didn't arrive in Washington as ordered.[9]

Sumner's first task after taking command April 25 was to divine the most effective use of the department's resources. He elected to close some posts and those troops not immediately dispatched east were marched hither and thither to reinforce one perceived weak point or another. This precipitated in June an intense round of juggling by Col. George Wright, whose reorganized District of Oregon encompassed Washington Territory and the state of Oregon. In addition to having already dispatched Capt. E.O.C. Ord to California with three companies of artillery, Wright was further ordered to part with seven companies of infantry, which would be sent east on the first available steamer.[10]

With only one company to man his headquarters at Vancouver Barracks, Wright complained vigorously and from his view with good reason. In 1861, Washington Territory (today including the states of Washington, Idaho and portions of Montana) remained a stronghold of Southern Democrats. Its first governor, and current delegate to Congress, was Isaac Stevens, a strong supporter of proslavery candidate John Breckinridge in the 1860 presidential election. This position nearly cost him a commission in the U.S. Army after Fort Sumter, when Stevens, a West Pointer, abandoned his conciliatory stance and urged the employment of deadly force to preserve the Union. Territorial citizens, many of whom hailed from southeastern states, eventually shared his sentiments by fiscally supporting the Union throughout the war ($7,755.33 the first year), but not the Republican Party. The one exception was Governor Gholson, who bitterly resigned his office after Lincoln's election and advocated secession of his home state.[11]

As with many Southern officers in the territory—among them future Confederate generals William "Dorsey" Pender, James J. Archer, Henry B. Davidson, Charles S. Winder and Robert Garnett—Pickett was conflicted over the coming storm. He was loath to abandon the Union and the army that had been his home for 19 years. His West Point appointment came not from his native Virginia, but Illinois where his maternal uncle had close connections with U.S. Rep. John Todd Stuart, a Whig and kinsman of Mary Lincoln. It was from this connection that Sally Pickett concocted the fiction that Lincoln had engineered Pickett's appointment in 1842. But Pickett also was angry with the Republican majority who he believed would not give Virginia and other border states such Kentucky, Maryland, Tennessee and Missouri a voice. In a February, 1861 letter to Maj. Benjamin Alvord, he wrote:

> The Republicans in their pride, flush of victory will not listen to terms proposed by the Conservative elements from those good & true states—when they ask but those rights and no more. No, they are ignominiously rejected. On the other hand, I do not like to be bullied nor argued out of the Union by the precipitating and indecent haste of South Carolina.[12]

Sectional tensions were apparent to Captain Bazalgette during a visit to the U.S. camp on February 1. He later told Colonial Anglican Bishop George Hills that the Americans expected dissolution of the union and were in "a great state of excitement... but know not what will become of them." Pickett and 1st. Lt. James Forsyth, his second in command and an Ohioan, had quarreled in Bazalgette's presence, then wisely re-channeled their anger over their inability to cash even Treasury bills to pay the men and run the camp. "Here am I of 18 years standing, having served my Country so long, to be cast adrift!" Pickett complained.[13]

The joint occupation seemed at an end when, in closing six posts to come up with seven infantry companies, Wright on June 11 ordered San Juan Island abandoned. Pickett and Company D were to embark on the first steamer available in preparation for transfer east. Adhering to the joint occupation agreement, Pickett advised Bazalgette of the movement. In late June, the Royal Navy commander in Victoria asked the Admiralty if the Royal Marine Camp should be shut down as well. Douglas and the home government were reluctant to abandon the island, no matter what was happening on the eastern seaboard of the United States.

But acting territorial governor, Henry M. McGill, protested the closure to Sumner, raising the specter of northern Indians falling upon helpless coastal settlements without the protection of a U.S. camp. Pickett himself, who was never shy about going over the head of an immediate superior, also wrote Sumner. The result was a June 22 letter to Wright from department headquarters, ordering the post reopened:

> The post (General Sumner) regards as having a
> national importance... he desires you reestablish it
> at once under the command of a captain.

Wright responded at once, claiming that he too had second thoughts, though not because of the U.S. claim to the island. More to the point was its "salient and commanding position on our northern frontier, admirably adapted to afford general protection to the settlements on the waters of Puget Sound." The captain he had in mind to command the post would be the same George Pickett.[14]

As usual, news of the potential closure reached England long after the issue had been settled. Rear Admiral Maitland, now in command of Pacific Station and ruminating over American troop movements, wrote the Admiralty on June 24 wondering if the Royal Marine Camp should not be shut down as well. If so, how should he dispose of the buildings, the value of which he estimated at between 1,500 and 2,000 pounds? The response from Douglas, not to mention the home government, was swift and vigorous. The camp would remain open whether the Americans remained or not![15]

Pickett relayed his fresh news to Bazalgette on June 25, though he neglected to mention that he had submitted his resignation from the U.S. Army the day before. Suddenly the very man who complained about closing his "salient commanding position" was now himself abandoning it with the barely veiled intent of joining the enemy.

Sumner wasted little time, ordering Pickett (and Company D) off the island, to be replaced by Capt. Thomas English and Co. H, Ninth Infantry. English was to proceed "without delay." Also that month Capt. James J. Archer was in a sense relieved of command of Fort Yamhill by 1st. Lt. Philip Sheridan, who refused to turn over command of the post when Archer arrived there as ordered from Fort Colville. As with Pickett, Archer, a Marylander, had tendered his resignation and was awaiting its approval. He left his post on July 17.

Pickett decided to remain on San Juan until relieved, so he was still on the island, wearing the uniform of a U.S. Army captain, on July 21 when the first Battle of Bull Run (or Manassas) was fought. The battle involved many of his West Point classmates, now colonels or higher, in both armies including his West Point classmate Thomas "Stonewall" Jackson.

Finally, on July 25, English with two officers (including Pickett's former second-in-command Forsyth) and 49 soldiers arrived. Pickett steamed up sound to Fort Steilacoom, where he left his company, signed over his stores and departed via horseback for Vancouver Barracks. He stopped in Olympia briefly to give his friend James Tilton $100 for the care of his son "Jimmy," still living with the Collins family in Grand Mound. Although the Collins homestead was on his way, he did not stop to see the boy and rode on out of his life.

Aside from Winfield Scott's specific arrest order on Albert S. Johnston, no written policy existed that addressed issues of treason attending the resignations of Southern officers. Some such as Robert Garnett—who was traveling in Europe when war broke out—simply did not return to their posts and were declared absent without leave. Others such as North Carolinian Dorsey Pender and Marylander Charles Winder resigned or took a leave of absence *before* the first shot was fired at Fort Sumter on April 12.

Sumner granted Pickett an "official leave of absence" pending acceptance of his resignation. However, with the war already four months along, Pickett took no chances and traveled east "incognito," even though he was accompanied by several Northern officers, including his second at Fort Bellingham, Capt. Hugh Fleming.[16]

By the time Pickett arrived in New York City in September his intentions were public and being an enemy alien he had to sneak through the city to launch his career in Confederate States Army and find an unwanted immortality at Gettysburg.[17]

Negotiations over the San Juan boundary proceeded during the Lincoln Administration, when in April 1861 the British forwarded an amended draft suggesting arbitration for the HBC claims as well as the water boundary. By then Fort Sumter had been fired upon, and the draft moved to the bottom of the mounting pile on Secretary of State William Seward's desk.

By November, relations between the U.S. and Great Britain nearly collapsed into the shooting war that Lyons, Cass, Scott, and Baynes had so deftly avoided. Former U.S. Senator Mason, now a Confederate envoy, and fellow traveler John Slidell were on their way to London to petition the Court of St. James for recognition when they were snatched from British steamer *Trent* on the high seas. Their captor was Capt. Charles Wilkes of the USS *San Jacinto*, the same Wilkes who 20 years earlier drafted the earliest U.S. charts of the San Juan group—charts used by American officials to justify their claims.

The incident prompted the British to place their forces on the eastern seaboard on full alert, precipitating another crisis. In response to news of the *Trent* affair, Douglas wrote the Duke of Newscastle of the Colonial Office that, in event of war between Great Britain and the United States, Royal Navy forces in the Victoria area could take back Washington Territory from the 49th parallel to the "...line of the Columbia River." With the U.S. having only two small revenue cutters and volunteer land forces available for defense, Douglas wrote:

> ...our only chance of success will be found in assuming the offensive and taking Puget Sound with Her Majesty's Ships...

He went on to state:

> ...with Puget Sound and line of the Columbia River in our hands, we should hold the only navigable outlets of the Country, command its trade and soon compel it to submit to Her Majesty's Rule.

But San Juan Island vanished on the diplomatic front, although boundary negotiations and the issue of reimbursement to the Hudson's Bay Company for lost revenues and properties continued even while the Lincoln Administration dealt with the war. Secretary of State William Seward and Lord Lyons actually concluded a treaty in 1863 that established a joint commission to review the claims of the Hudson's Bay Company for properties overrun by US settlers. But before the commission could get underway, the U.S. consul in Victoria, Lincoln appointee Allen Francis, claimed British documents existed that proved that the HBC never held legal deeds to their properties below the 49th parallel. When the US asked to view Company documents the British refused and all questions pertaining to the water boundary and compensation were tabled until 1869.

Throughout the war Francis sniffed a rebel privateer on every wharf and passed nearly every rumor he heard onto the secretary of state, who in turn passed them on to Lyons. After one too many false alarms, Francis's missives were not taken seriously. In justice to Francis, there *had* been one failed attempt to capture the steamer *Thames* and another story had circulated about the U.S. Lighthouse Tender *Shubrick* (Casey's "flagship") being converted into a Confederate commerce raider. As a result of these rumors known Southern sympathizers among the crew were fired by the collector of customs in Port Townsend.[18]

On San Juan Island the joint occupation proceeded peacefully, with English Camp especially providing an attraction and tourist destination for those eager to see the islands or seeking transportation from Victoria to the mainland. The marines seemed glad for the company. One frequent visitor from Victoria was Bishop Hills who on one occasion was given free passage on a commercial steamer. The trip took four hours and they reached the camp at the noon hour. He described the spot as "picturesque and serene." He was impressed by the "economy of arrangements" and most especially with the quality of the fruits and vegetables produced in the garden. The bishop would probably feel right at home on today's parade ground:

...deer can be had whenever wanted. Some of the post go out to shoot them, or Indians bring them." Wild fowl is abundant. There were hanging up in the larder of the kitchen geese, ducks, the common wild duck & canvas back, teal & wild muscovy. A fine wild goose can be had for a half a dollar if you buy one, later they will be made much cheaper.

After lunch Hills and Lieutenant Sparshott went horseback riding, presumably to the top of Young Hill where the bishop was given a panorama of the island and views of Mount Baker and Mount Rainier. They then must have continued along today's Cady Mountain where Hills claimed to see "...large flocks of sheep & settlers houses. The American Camp lay also at a distance before me some twelve miles..."

On his return the bishop found the storehouse cleared and swept, and men prepared for services, which he conducted by candlelight before returning to Victoria.[19]

Members of the American garrison were welcome as well. In fact, the two camps regularly exchanged visits on special occasions – usually the Fourth of July at American Camp, and Queen Victoria's birthday, May 24, at English Camp—a tradition begun by Pickett and Bazalgette the very first year. Newspapers of the period reported horse races on the prairie at American Camp, with Bazalgette winning the 1861 race aboard "Jerry," while Pickett's horse bolted for the spring near South Beach. Pickett's men cheered, according to one reporter.

The soldiers and marines, as well as 180 "excursionists," who reached "the beautiful and sequestered little spot" in about two hours, celebrated Queen Victoria's birthday in 1866. As Bazalgette was in Victoria attending the Governor's Ball, Lieutenant Sparshott served as host. Evidently it required more than a half an hour for the passengers to disembark and thereafter began the celebration replete with refreshments and athletic contests of ever stripe, which were open to all comers, including the excursionists, Sparshott and the post surgeon.

> The wheel-barrow race blindfolded evoked intense amusement, the men rushed about in all directions and several of them disappeared, barrow and all, over the embankment... As the steamer was about to get under weigh the last game which consisted of walking a greasy pole extending 15 feet from the end of the wharf at the extremity of which was a stick three feet high with a bunch of evergreens, worth $3 to the person who could reach it came off... From the deck of the vessel the excursionists witnessed several men who attempted the perilous journey take an involuntary header into the briny deep...

At the end of the day, the group gathered "beneath the shade of a large tree" to sing "God Save the Queen" whereupon a Mr. W.K. Bull gave a speech which "...went to the hearts of the men of the garrison, who gave him three cheers."[20]

Most of the friction that occurred during the joint occupation continued to be on the southern end of San Juan, where the growing numbers of American settlers, eager to snap up land claims, sell illegal whisky and purvey prostitutes in the disputed islands, could not abide martial law. Complicating matters, the Territorial government on the mainland often sided with the settlers against the local military. No such fractiousness existed between San Juan's Royal Marines and the British provincial government, especially when disputes arose with the Americans, but neither were British officials free from controversy.

As civil jurisdiction on both sides had been suspended maintaining law and order had to be continually redefined for each commanding officer. For example, early in 1863 American

Camp commander Capt. Lyman Bissell stopped Whatcom County Justice of the Peace E.T. Hamblett from ejecting a British subject from a claim on the island. Bissell then suspended Hamblett "as a functionary of Washington Territory." On reading Bissell's report, Department of the Pacific commander Maj. Gen. George Wright approved Bissell actions, citing Winfield Scott's original orders that territorial officials were not to interfere with British subjects. To void future conflicts, however, Bissell was directed to confine jurisdiction of American civil authorities to the southern end of the island. The northern end should be under British law.

But then Bazalgette expelled William Andrews, a U.S. citizen, whom Bazalgette claimed had killed an Indian in the vicinity of the Royal Marine camp and another Indian at San Juan Village in 1860. In each case, the incumbent U.S. justice had failed to act, therefore Bazalgette pleaded with his U.S. counterpart to intervene. In the spirit of the joint occupation, a bi-national patrol, led by Bissell and Royal Marine Lt. Henry Cooper, went to the Indian camp and learned from the headman that three of his people could identify a certain "Bill" as Andrews. The three accompanied the officers to the San Juan Lime Company at Lime Kiln Point, where they identified Andrews, who was in company with Augustus Hibbard, the owner. Bissell expelled Andrews and posted a list of other Yankee troublemakers, giving them 24 hours to leave the island. One of them was Hibbard, who not only owned the lime works, but also sold liquor on the premises and elsewhere on the island. The previous fall, Bissell wrote his superiors that Hibbard had "...tried to create a disturbance between the officers of the two camps by writing a dictatorial letter to Captain Bazalgette, because Captain Bazalgette ordered [Hibbard's] men out of his camp that went there for the purpose of selling liquor to his men."

The suspended Hamblett responded by organizing a meeting of fellow U.S. citizens to draft petitions insisting on civil rather than military control over the American portion of the island.

Hamblett's resolution and its outfall further confounded U.S. military authorities, spurring General Wright to direct that territorial authorities be permitted to enforce civil law. However, the joint occupation arrangements with Great Britain would be rigidly maintained and U.S. settlers seeking army protection "must settle and remain within the portion of the Island within our jurisdiction."

By 1864, Wright's replacement, Maj. Gen. Irvin McDowell (the loser of the First Battle of Bull Run), saw it differently after visiting San Juan Island in September 1864. Americans and British were scattered throughout the island, thus making geographical boundaries moot and impractical, he wrote Alvord. From here on out, McDowell ordered, civilians would submit to civil authority only if they chose to do so and joint military rule should continue.[21]

Washington Territory next petitioned Secretary of State William Seward to grant civil jurisdiction in 1866, the territory believing the rule of a single military officer arbitrary and unacceptable. Officers had been urged only to advise in squabbles, but some in sheer desperation had acted and this caused trouble.

Such was the case in September 1866 when a complaint was filed against post commandant Capt. Thomas Grey and his deputy 1st. Lt. William Preston Graves, both Second Artillery, by Deputy U.S. Marshall Jared C. Brown.

Grey and Graves tore down 150 feet of paling fence that had been erected by Isaac Higgins, whose San Juan Island history predated Pickett's landing. His fence blocked the road from the military post to the old Hudson's Bay Company dock on Griffin Bay. Higgins had been warned to remove the fence but responded with threats and verbal abuse, according to Grey, who was no slouch about dishing it out himself as the British would soon learn. When he refused to remove the barrier, Grey ordered Higgins expelled from the island, advising headquarters that Higgins was "one of the most disreputable vagabonds in Washington Territory."

Grey's action gave the territory the excuse it needed to enforce its claim to jurisdiction, citing a clear case of abuse of power by federal officers. Higgins lodged a grievance complaint and an indictment for "malicious trespass" was filed on September 7, 1866, against the officers in United States District Court, Third Judicial District at Port Townsend. A warrant was issued, but efforts to arrest the officers were unsuccessful. Consequently, another indictment was filed for obstruction of legal process, and yet another for assault and battery, which also named four enlisted soldiers.

Warrants were issued again in March and April 1868. Higgins also sued Grey for $10,300 for arrest, confinement and expulsion from his property. Grey again refused to appear, but it mattered little. The court ordered Grey to pay Higgins $5,000 on Sept. 12, 1866, after which the two officers finally hired a Steilacoom attorney. A Pierce County judge threw out the case while the territory's trespass indictment also was cancelled in 1868.

The Grey-Higgins incident prompted Maj. Gen. Henry W. Halleck, Department of the Pacific commander by November 1867, to advise the War Department that the only way to end the tension between military and civil authorities on San Juan Island was to take decisive action one way or another. His suggestions included placing the entire territory under martial law or changing the boundaries of the territory to exclude the San Juan Islands. He then took a page from William Selby Harney's book and questioned whether the British had the wherewithal to colonize British Columbia, calling them a "flaccid" race. The U.S. should put a stop to the mess, force a treaty with the British and take over the whole thing, he wrote, further endearing himself to the State Department.[22]

Halleck's warped views on national will aside, the British remained determined to keep the peace on San Juan even if it meant sacking Captain Bazalgette. On Dec. 26, 1866, presumably after a Christmas party at American Camp, he wrote to his U.S. counterpart, Captain Grey, requesting the immediate return of a Royal Marine deserter who had been spotted in the American cantonment. Bugler George Hughes had not answered roll call at English Camp on May 22, 1861 and now he was apparently performing the same function as a U.S. soldier in Grey's company. Desertions were not all that unusual on the frontier, and men on both sides had taken "French leave" from both camps over the years lured by gold on the mainland or fed up with the isolation. Often they returned when they grew hungry enough. That Hughes would turn up in the uniform of the contending nation was so bizarre that it kicked off an international incident that went all the way to the desk of the Lord President of the Privy Council.

George Hughes was carried on the British mustering rolls as a bugler. The Devon native was part of the China battalions and an original member of the garrison who did indeed disappear from the rolls in May 1861.

On his return to the Royal Marine Camp, Bazalgette agonized over what he should do in a letter to his superior, Captain Radulphus Bryce Oldfield, RN, senior naval officer at Esquimalt. How should he go about seeking the return of Hughes without threatening the cordial atmosphere that had existed between the two camps? Oldfield responded by assuring Bazalgette that he was well within his rights to seek the deserter's return, however he should ask politely.

Unfortunately for Bazalgette, Grey, running true to form, not only declined to return Hughes, but was taken aback by the request.

> Not recognizing that you have any legitimate grounds
> for requesting this soldier to be turned over to you as
> a Deserter, I therefore decline to comply with your
> request. I am not aware of your having returned to
> this command a deserter, therefore no one would

regret the interruption of the "good understanding
which has always existed between the two camps"
more than I should and I cannot but express my
surprise at your anticipating in the case of Hughes
any such result.

Grey acknowledged that a bugler named George Hughes was in
his command, but that the man had an extensive military history,
albeit one that he claimed began in 1862 with the First Washington
Territory Infantry. In fact, he had joined the U.S. Army in January
1866 and arrived on San Juan Island in June. But despite his
irritation over Bazalgette's demands, Grey continued to abide by the
spirit of the joint occupation agreement by writing another letter
that same day thanking the Englishman for seeking his opinion on
another matter of a British whisky seller.[23]

The Hughes correspondence was forwarded through channels
by both commands. And the response again illustrates the
importance each nation placed on maintaining the peace on San
Juan, especially in view of rising tensions in the post-war period
over the "*Alabama* Claims," and other issues. In a January 21 letter
to Oldfield, General Halleck promised that the case would be
examined as soon as Maj. Gen. Frederick Steele, commander of the
District of the Columbia, returned. Meanwhile, Grey was not to
enlist anyone on San Juan Island, nor was he to allow into his camp
any deserter from the Royal Marines.

Two months later the source of the irritant was removed when
Musician Hughes was ordered by telegraph to Fort Steilacoom.
While the bugler was packing his bags, Richard Temple-Grenville,
the Duke of Buckingham and Chandos and Lord President of the
Privy Council wrote:

On this allegation, without rendering any proof of
the identity or of the desertion Captain Bazalgette
demanded not enquiry or investigation, which

would have enabled him to send home a full report for consideration by Her Majesty's Government, but the surrender of an enlisted soldier of the United States Army... His Grace considers it necessary therefore to draw the serious attention of their Lords Commissioners of the Admiralty to the case in order that they may direct such instructions to be sent to Captain Bazalgette as they may deem fit to prevent reoccurrence of any similar proceedings.[24]

The above was written March 22. On April 1, Captain W. A. Delacombe, RM, and 1st Lieutenant A.A. Beadon were ordered to replace Bazalgette and Sparshott, "who have both been absent from headquarters since 1851." Delacombe and Beadon and their "military attendants" were travel to Vancouver via Panama by the Mail packet by April 17.[25]

Delacombe followed Bazalgette's precedent by handling the garrison and the joint occupation in a judicious manner. He took immediate steps to improve the daily lives of the garrison with a building program that included expanded quarters for the enlisted men, a library and a commodious commander's house, which was soon occupied by his wife and family. The camp had become a showplace on the island. Mountaineer Edmund T. Coleman stopped by in 1868 on his way to making the first Euro-American ascent of Mount Baker.

In passing along we noticed the camp of the English garrison on San Juan Island, and we were struck by the singular beauty of the scenery around it. In the foreground is the level greensward with a noble tree rising from its center, and fringed with spreading maples. Up through these are the winding walks to the officers' quarters, and beyond, a lofty hill on which a summerhouse has been erected, where the

surrounding shores are seen to advantage. Between
this and the American Camp, seven miles off, lie
farms in a high state of cultivation.

But not all was not sweetness and light, especially for the
Hudson's Bay Company whose once thriving plantation was
squeezed by circumstances attendant to the joint occupation. With
the coming of the soldiers and marines also came more settlers,
many of whom squatted on HBC property and diminished sheep
grazing areas. Moreover smugglers, whisky sellers and prostitutes
beset the island, who Griffin claimed were "demoralizing" his
employees. The company's London headquarters, acting on advice
from Alexander Grant Dallas, an HBC director in Victoria, ordered
on Feb. 9, 1861 that Belle Vue Sheep Farm should be closed "as soon
as circumstances would permit." Charles Griffin left exactly one
year later and was replaced by Robert Firth, a shepherd, who later
leased the farm from spring of 1864 until 1873, when he became
owner of the land.

Three years following issuance the Firth lease, William Tolmie,
the director of Company's subsidiary Puget Sound Agricultural
Co., fired off a letter to HBC headquarters itemizing the Company's
losses at San Juan to the tune of £5,395. The U.S. federal and
territorial governments were largely to blame and restitution
should be sought. (see Addendum IV).

Still another agricultural dispute in 1870 entangled Delacombe
in a struggle with a British subject very similar to Thomas Grey's
tiff with Higgins. One of the farms Coleman described, elegantly
dubbed the "Hermitage," was to test the joint occupation agreement
one more time. The place was located at the current intersection of
Boyce and San Juan Valley roads and was being worked by Alexander
McKenzie, a British subject whose naturalized American brother,
Murdoch, owned adjoining acreage.

But the Hermitage was, in fact, the claim of Edward Warbass,
a U.S. citizen and the former U.S. Army sutler, who was away from

the island at the time. Warbass had left his claim and the cabin erected upon it under the care of Angus McDonald, a former Hudson's Bay employee, who in 1867 "made an agreement" with McKenzie to crop the land until Warbass returned. McDonald died in 1868, but McKenzie stayed on, made improvements, planted and harvested crops and set up housekeeping. This happy idyll continued until April of 1870 when McKenzie was approached by August Hoffmeister, the English Camp sutler, who, acting as agent for Warbass, told McKenzie he could have the farm for $600. McKenzie refused to acknowledge Hoffmeister as agent, and Warbass as owner, whereupon Hoffmeister returned a few days later, accompanied by an officer from the U.S. camp, who ordered McKenzie off the premises. McKenzie refused to leave, claiming British citizenship, which meant an appeal would have to be made through Delecombe.

The U.S. commander, Capt. Joseph Haskell, wrote Delecombe on April 21 stating that Warbass, through Hoffmeister, had claimed American protection. He asked Delacombe to order McKenzie, who was in the process of sowing another crop, to "stop plowing" and leave the property. Haskell explained that while he disapproved of "looking after special interests," it was his duty to "look out for Creditors as well as the owner of the property."

Delacombe responded two days later, pointing out that the McKenzie brothers (there was a third in addition to Murdoch and Alexander) were good citizens and that he knew Alexander had been in uninterrupted possession of the property for three years, "making improvements and putting up and repairing fencing and that he was in the habit of getting his brothers to help him." Nevertheless, Delacombe agreed to order McKenzie off the property until Haskell could decide the question.

Frustrated with Delacombe, McKenzie next hired a lawyer in Victoria to take legal action against the Royal Navy for interfering with his business, which prompted Pacific Station commander Rear

Admiral A. Farquhar to ask Delecombe to explain himself. The
captain, while admitting McKenzie had a legitimate claim and that
the brothers were "honest settlers," was miffed that McKenzie had
gone around him and hired a lawyer.

> ...instead of my dealing harshly with them I have
> gone out of my way to endeavor to prove in a measure
> of the truth of their statement which my letter to
> Captain Haskell shows, and therefore consider
> the course they have taken in getting some lawyer
> in Victoria to draw up a letter to you, after finding
> they could get no satisfaction from the American
> Authority, is most ungrateful.

On June 8, Delacombe met with McKenzie, advising him
that he would write Haskell for permission for McKenzie to take
in his crop, but that he would still have to vacate the premises.
McKenzie refused to leave, pointing out that his brother Murdoch,
an American citizen, had now claimed the farm and was under
U.S. protection the same as Warbass. Delacombe probably heaved a
mighty sigh and rode the few miles more to the U.S. camp to verify
this new information. Haskell remained adamant: He wanted
McKenzie off the property. Delecombe returned to the Hermitage
to find McKenzie had taken possession of the house and in a fit
of pique had "turned what things it contained outside." He also
informed a marine lieutenant that he would have to be removed
"by force." The game was turning serious in Delacombe's mind. He
wrote Farquhar:

> I consider this man has no claim and is pitting
> the authority of the United States and also mine at
> defiance, I therefore respectfully beg you will be
> pleased to give me an order for his eviction from
> the island.

Farquhar's reply, in so many words was: "You handle it."

Two weeks later, Delacombe dispatched an armed escort to the Hermitage. The sergeant was directed to once more order McKenzie off the property and if he did not leave, then to bring him to Garrison Bay, where Delacombe would once more try to reason with him. McKenzie came along of his own accord, Delacombe reported, and was warned that he would be evicted from the island if he persisted. When McKenzie said he did not care, Delacombe found him quarters for the night in the blockhouse. The now ex-farmer was then offered passage on the next day's boat to Victoria "of which he took advantage."

In a letter to the Admiralty, submitted two years later, McKenzie saw it differently:

> Captain Delacombe sent a Marine to me to tell me that Admiral Farquhar was at the camp to hear my case. I accompanied the man to the camp, but instead of seeing the admiral I was put into the Guard House and kept a prisoner until a boat could be procured to carry me to Victoria. Captain Delacombe told me never again to set foot on the island. My firm conviction is that Captain Delacombe expelled me from San Juan Island in order that he and Hoffmeister might appropriate the land for their own use and benefit. What I would earnestly solicit is a fair unbiased hearing.

The Admiralty was as unmoved by McKenzie as Farquhar, the issue faded away and the joint occupation proceeded unfettered. [26]

While local issues were sorted, the government of Washington Territory continued agitate over what it perceived as martial law on San Juan Island and redcoats quartered south of the 49th parallel. On Jan. 9 and 15, 1868, the legislature passed another memorial to the U.S. Congress to end the military occupation of the island, listing all previous grievances. The climate had seemed right for the move because the U.S. Senate recently questioned whether the occupation was feasible. But the Johnson and Grant administrations held firm to the end—much to the relief of the British, not to mention the Canadians, who had achieved independence in 1867 under the umbrella of British foreign policy.

Pres. Ulysses S. Grant's envoy to Court of St. James, Reverdy Johnson, concluded an agreement with Britain in 1869 that would submit to a third-party commission the San Juan water boundary, as well as several other pressing issues including a major disagreement over the issue of Confederate commerce raiders during the late war.

The C.S.S. *Alabama*, *Shenandoah* and other Confederate raiders had devastated the U.S. whaling and merchant fleets during the Civil War. What was not sunk was either sold off or transferred to foreign registry, which sent insurance rates skyrocketing and tax revenues plummeting in the United States. That the British government never formally recognized the Confederacy as an independent nation—and considered the commerce raiders with their Southern officers and British crews scarcely more than pirates—did not matter. British shipyards had designed and built vessels such as the *Alabama*, or sold ships on hand such as the powerful *Shenandoah* under contract with the Confederate government. Moreover, Britain recognized the South as a belligerent, remained neutral and colonial ports had given succor to the commerce raiders throughout the war. U.S. shipping magnates had lost money and someone had to pay.

This made it all the more intriguing when that same year Massachusetts Sen. Charles Sumner rose from his seat and thundered that if the British did not pay restitution for the shipping sunk by the *Alabama*, then she should cede Canada to the United States. The issue became known as the "*Alabama* Claims" and would add years to the delay in settlement of the San Juan boundary question, as Grant was still bitter over the tons of British weapons shipped to the Confederacy and firmly believed the commerce raiders contributed to prolonging the war. Grant was no friend of Sumner, but backed the bombastic senator even to the point of endorsing the acquisition of Canada. War fever fulminated in the popular press but not on Wall Street where conventional wisdom had it that war with Britain would bring economic collapse. Not only had British capital fueled American industry from the start, but also British loans were settling the war debt and reestablishing the nation on a peacetime footing.[27]

Someone finally explained these facts to Grant. Soon negotiations over the *Alabama* Claims, Grand Banks fishing rights, Fenian raids in Canada and, yes, even the San Juan Boundary Dispute, once more took a peaceful course toward arbitration.

On May 8, 1871, the Treaty of Washington was signed by the British and Americans and ratified by Congress the following month. Kaiser Wilhelm (Emperor William) I of the newly constituted German Empire was named arbiter largely because of the influence of George Bancroft, the U.S. ambassador in Berlin. The Kaiser selected a three-man commission, which was directed to meet in Geneva to review evidence from both nations as to whether the boundary should be the Haro or Rosario straits. Three men. How ironic. That is precisely the number of men Lyman Cutlar suggested review the true value of the pig all those years ago.[28]

The commissioners—Professor Heinrich Kiepert, a geography teacher at the University of Berlin, Councilor Levin Goldschmidt of the Imperial High Court of Commerce and Dr. Ferdinand Grimm, vice president of the High Court—deliberated for more than a year and had their share of disagreements. Dr. Goldschmidt in particular was dismayed at the choice of channels from which they were to make their selection. He believed the obvious choice was missing from the table: the Middle Channel (President's and

San Juan channels) that runs between San Juan, Orcas and Shaw islands. He felt so strongly about it that he had suggested amending the treaty.[29]

The British were at first receptive to Dr. Goldschmidt's opinion as Capt. James Prevost—who as a rear admiral presented the British arguments in Berlin—had suggested the Middle Channel in 1859. But U.S. Secretary of State Hamilton Fish wasn't having any of it. The New Yorker never wavered from Archibald Campbell's conclusion: If one traced the boundary to the middle of the Strait of Georgia, then took a straight edge and drew another line directly south, the line would run through the Haro Strait. As far as he was concerned the question was moot. No objective commission could possibly rule otherwise. Either the commission adhered to the letter of the treaty and chose between the Haro and Rosario straits or the U.S. would back out.

After nearly a year, the commission finally voted two to one to award the islands to the United States, with Goldschmidt writing a lengthy dissenting opinion. The Haro Strait had to be the "southerly" channel dividing Vancouver Island from the mainland cited in the Treaty of 1846. As Dr. Grimm opined, the Haro Strait touches Vancouver Island. The Rosario Strait does not. Also, the Haro Strait is deeper, wider and more amenable to international shipping. It was truly "…most in accordance with the true interpretation of the Treaty concluded."[30]

The judgment was endorsed by the emperor and a ruling was issued on October 21, 1872, beginning with the royal, "We, William, by the grace of God, German Emperor…" of course.

Messages were sent to both posts via telegraph and Captain Delacombe was ordered to close the camp and immediately began making preparations for departure. On Monday, November 18, HMS *Scout*, under the command of the senior naval officer, Capt. R.P. Cator, arrived in Garrison Bay (which he called Roche

Harbour) to withdraw the garrison and its stores, "naval and colonial." His first business at hand was to inform Delacombe that he was to remain on the island for a few days with several "unarmed marines" and boats to certify the lands of British subjects residing there and advise his counterpart Ist. Lt. James Haughey. The loading required nearly three days. On Thursday the 21st the Royal Marines, sailors from the *Scout*, as well as Lieutenant Haughey and several of his officers and men, stood at attention while the British colors were lowered. Department of the Pacific commander, Brig. Gen. Edward Canby, sent his regrets at being unable to attend and also that a U.S. warship could not be on hand to render the appropriate salute. No cannon were available on shore because they were forbidden as part of the joint occupation agreement. U.S. officers exchanged worried missives over the matter, and then let it drop. A simple good-bye with kind letters would suffice.

The following day, the Royal Marines packed up their gear and left. Haughey's men brought a large U.S. flag from the American camp to run up the pole soon after the Union Jack came down. But to their surprise the pole had been chopped down. Evidently it was to be used to replace a spar lost by a British ship on a rough Pacific crossing. Old Glory instead went up the telegraph pole.

That night Cator received a telegram from the Admiralty now directing that Delacombe also be withdrawn, but offering no instructions on how to dispose of the tidy installation that included 27 structures, gardens and a terraced hill. Cator was in a quandary, especially after being informed that "parties of American citizens" were on their way to claim the buildings and grounds. He decided on his own to continue with the plan of leaving Delacombe behind with a few marines and wired the Admiralty accordingly the next morning. By 1872, it required hours rather than weeks to communicate with London, therefore when three days passed with no answer, and presuming the telegraph was down, Cator decided to turn over the camp to the Lieutenant Haughey "on behalf of the government." Delacombe saw to the details and at 2 p.m. on the 25th, the last Royal Marines boarded the steamer HMS *Peterel* and left "Roche Harbour" for Esquimalt.

The San Juan Boundary Dispute—The Pig War—was finally over.

As with all stories of near misses, "ifs" abound. If James Douglas had not placed the Hudson's Bay Company on the island, the Americans might not have responded with customs collectors and county sheriffs. If Lyman Cutlar and Charles Griffin had not both exploded with rage that June morning and settled their differences, A.G. Dallas, William Selby Harney and George E. Pickett might never have been involved. Conversely, if the Royal Navy officers had followed Douglas' orders and forced the issue with Pickett, the Pacific Northwest might be shaped differently today.

History ultimately turns on individual choices. Despite the blunders, the right choices were made in the end. Two powerful nations nearly went to war, spent thousands of dollars and pounds and exchanged tons of paper over ownership of an island 16 1/2 miles long and six miles wide. But honor had been served and the peace kept, the pig being the only casualty.

Some war. Some pig.

NOTES

ABBREVIATIONS FOR NOTES AND PHOTOGRAPHS:

ADM.......British Admiralty, National Archives of Great Britain (NAGB), Kew, England

BC ....Buswell Collection, Center for Pacific Northwest Studies, Western Washington University, Bellingham, WA

BCA ....British Columbia Archives

BRBML .. Yale University Collection of Western Americana, Bienecke Rare Book and Manuscript Library

DFC ....Delacombe family collection, United Kingdom

FO ....British Foreign Office, NAGB, Kew, England.

LOC ....Library of Congress

NA ....National Archives and Records Administration, United States of America

NAC ....National Archives of Canada

NAGB .....National Archives of Great Britain, Kew Gardens, London, England.

OR ....*The War of the Rebellion: A Compilation of the Official Records of the Union and Confederate Armies* / Series 1 - Volume 50 (Part I), Series I, Vol 50, Part 1

ORN ....*Official records of the Union and Confederate Navies in the War of the Rebellion* / Series I - Volume 4: *Operations on the Atlantic Coast* (January 1, 1861 - May 13, 1861).

SAJHA ....San Juan National Historical Park Archives

UWSC......University of Washington Library, Special Collections. Granville O. Haller Papers, 1842-1993.

WASA .....Washington State Archives

WSU ....Manuscripts, Archives, and Special Collections, Washington State University Libraries, Pullman, WA

Note on end notes: Subject matter in note text is presented in order of citations.

CHAPTER 2 – THE QUEST FOR WEALTH: SOURCES OF TROUBLE

In writing this brief survey of explorations that resulted in claims and counterclaims to the Oregon Country, I found the following revealing and insightful: David Lavender's *Land of Giants: The Drive to the Pacific Northwest, 1750-1950* (1958); William Goetzmann's *New Lands, New Men America and the Second Great Age of Discovery* (1986) or his *The Atlas of North American Exploration From the Norse Voyages to the Race to the Pole* (1992) written with Glyndwr Williams; Enlightenment values and exploration also are probed in *Enlightenment and Exploration in the North Pacific 1741-1805* (1997), edited by Stephen Haycox, James K. Barnett, and Caedmon A. Liburd (1997); Richard J. Nokes' *Columbia's River The Voyages of Robert Gray, 1787-179* (1991) and *Almost a Hero: The Voyages of John Meares, R.N., to China, Hawaii and the Northwest Coast* (1998); Donald Cutter's "The Malaspina Expedition and Its Place in the History of the Pacific Northwest" in *Spain and the North Pacific Coast: Essays in Recognition of the Bicentennial of the Malaspina Expedition, 1791-1792.* (1992); Felipe Fernandez-Armesto's *Pathfinders: A Global History of Exploration* (2006); Alan Frost's essay, "Nootka Sound and the Beginnings of Britain's Imperialism of Free Trade" in *From Maps to Metaphors: The Pacific World of George Vancouver* (1993); James Gibson's *Otter Skins, Boston Ships and China Goods: The Maritime Fur Trade of the Northwest Coast, 1785-1841*(1992.); Barry Gough's *Fortune's A River: The Collision of Empires in Northwest America* (2007); Samuel Eliot Morison's *The European Discovery of America: The Southern Voyages, A.D. 1492-1616* (1974); Richard Nokes's; and finally Walter A. McDougall's daring *Let The Sea Make A Noise: A History of the North Pacific from Magellan to MacArthur* (1993) takes a step beyond academia and allows the principles to speak for themselves.

Specific references are:

1   Cutter, *Spain and the Pacific North Coast*, pp 1, Morison, *Southern Voyages*, p. 203, Fernandez-Amesto, *Pathfinders*, p. 196

2   Nokes. *Columbia's River*, pp. 72-74

3   Frost, *Metaphors*, p. 107

4   Ibid., p. 109

5   Scott and DeLorme, *Atlas of Washington State History*, Map. 15

6   Nokes, Columbia's River, p. 140

7   Ibid., pp 186-189

8   The name Orcas Island was given by British cartographer, Capt. Henry Kellett, during his survey of the island group in 1847.

CHAPTER 3 - MANIFEST DESTINY AND JOINT OCCUPATION

1   Black was said to have remarked when he saw the Union flag over Fort Astoria, "Damn me, damn me, I could have knocked down those walls with a four pounder." On claiming his prize of war, Black christened the flagpole with a bottle of Madeira.

2   Mackie, *Trading Beyond the Mountains*, pp. 44-68.

3   Billington, *Westward Expansion*, p. 383, 532-533. Billington's thesis of the westward expansion remains the seminal work on the subject in the historiography of the American West. His view that the passage of Walker Tariff and the repeal of the Corn Laws sped the signing of the Treaty of Oregon is further underscored by fiscal realities. The British then (as now) were the largest foreign investors in the fledgling United States—a fact that would overwhelm political jingoism throughout the 19th century (See Chapter 16, n. 12.)

4   Ibid.

5   Ibid.

6   FO, Abstract.

CHAPTER 4 - THE TREATY OF OREGON: A TABLE SET FOR TROUBLE

1   As quoted in Foreman, *A World On Fire*, p. 19; Wilkes, *Narrative*, p. 296

2   FO, *Abstract*, pp. 50-51.

3   Nokes, *Columbia's River*, p. 66

4   FO, *Abstract*, "Treaty of Oregon, 1846, Article I"

Note: The United States and the United Kingdom did not establish official embassies until 1893. Since 1791 (1815 for the United States), the respective missions were known as legations, their heads entitled *envoy extraordinary and minister plenipotentiary*.

5   Ibid., p. 108

6   Goetzmann, Army Exploration, pp. 105-107; FO Abstract, pp. 118-199. The map cited by the British—*Geographical Memoir Upon Upper California in Illustrations of His Map of Oregon and California*, 30ᵗʰ Congress, 1ˢᵗ Sess., Sen. Misc. Doc. 148, 1848—was drawn in 1848 by Charles Preuss as a follow-up to his 1846 Fremont version that traced the Oregon Trail from the mouth of the Kansas River to where the Walla Walla joins the Columbia. Preuss was a German immigrant from St. Louis. This was a map of the entire West and was considered a breakthrough for the times in that it revealed all of the mountains, rivers and basins. However, according to Goetzmann, it lacks accuracy, showing mountains where none exist and, of course, providing the British an excellent reference for their claim of Rosario Strait. As with any good cartographer, Preuss combined research with firsthand observation and, unfortunately for U.S. diplomats, this included Vancouver's charts, but not those of Charles Wilkes, which in all fairness would have been relatively recent and perhaps unavailable to Preuss at the time. Wilkes's charts, incidentally, quite clearly show the San

Juan Islands situated in the Strait of Georgia. The Haro Strait is labeled "Canal de Haro while Rosario Strait is labeled "Ringgold" Strait.

7   FO, Abstract, pp 108-109

8   Wood, *San Juan Place Names*, pp 46-47

CHAPTER 5 - THE SAN JUAN SHEEP WAR

1   James Charles Prevost (1810-1891) was the ideal choice to command *Satellite* and serve as water boundary commissioner. He was the son of Admiral Thomas James Prevost and the son-in-law of Rear Admiral Sir Fairfax Moresby, Pacific Station commander, 1850-53. It was under Moresby's command here that Prevost, as captain of the HMS *Virago*, dealt with American miners and squatters during the brief, but intense Queen Charlotte Islands gold rush. His great granddaughter resides in the San Juan Islands.

2   As quoted in Miller, *San Juan Archipelago*, pp. 15-16.

3   Report of Captain Alden to Prof. A.D. Bache, Superintendent United States Coast Survey, Oct. 31, 1853, 36th Congress, p. 87. James Alden, Jr., a direct descendent of John Alden and Priscilla Mullins of *Mayflower* fame, was a passed midshipman on the USS *Vincennes* under Capt. Charles Wilkes. The U.S. Exploring Expedition was the nautical counterpart to Lewis and Clark, exploring the entire Pacific basin, nearly pole to pole, making observations and creating charts that have barely been surpassed by modern technology. Alden was assigned as a naval assistant to the West Coast survey in May 1851 and given command of the newly acquired U.S. C. S. Steamer *Active*, a side-wheeler that had been brought around the horn (as the *Gold Hunter*) to serve as a merchant/passenger ship. Initially based in San Francisco, the

Active moved to the newly established Mare Island Naval Shipyard in 1854. It was there that Alden served and established a friendship with Capt. David G. Farragut, the yard commander. Alden became familiar with nearly every feature of the Pacific Coast, which included the inland waterways of Puget Sound. Alden's nephew, James Madison Alden, was an artist for the Coast Survey and later the Northwest Boundary Survey. The younger Alden went on to become a noted landscape painter whose subject included Yosemite.

4 Ibid.

5 Most of the HBC farming operations were run under the aegis of the Puget Sound Agricultural Company, a subsidiary headed then by Dr. John Tolmie, based at Fort Nisqually on Puget Sound. But Company records indicate that Belle Vue Sheep Farm was a direct satellite of the HBC at Fort Victoria. This may further underscore that in addition to the island's agricultural potential, the establishment of the farm was a politically expedient.

6 Belle Vue Sheep Farm Journals, May 3, 1854. Griffin's cabin was one of "seven small houses" in the Belle Vue Sheep Farm establishment, just up from Grandma's Cove. Griffin's headquarters also consisted of an outhouse and barn and six acres under cultivation adjoining the dwellings. Another 40 acres were planted just north of Eagle Cove. The Hudson's Bay Company imported a variety of breeds into the Pacific Northwest starting with the more numerous California varieties in the 1830s-40s. The California sheep probably included the Churro, which was descended from the Spanish Churra brought to the Americas shortly after the conquest. The breed continues today in the Navajo Churro. In the late 1830s, at the behest of James Douglas, Merino, Leicester, Cheviot and Saxony breeds were imported from Europe to improve the quality of wool. See *Cultural Landscape Report, Vol. II, Fort Vancouver NHS*, Vancouver, WA.

Isaac Neff Ebey came West in 1848, leaving his family behind in
Missouri and crossing the Plains to find a home in the Oregon
Country. The discovery of gold at Sutter's Mill side-tracked him
for a spell to California along with just about every other home-
builder looking for a shortcut to prosperity. There he purchased
a share of one of the legion of rotting square-riggers in San Francisco Bay and returned in 1850 to stake his claim on the good
life the frigid waters, the dark forests, the back bays and wind-
swept islands of Puget Sound might bring... and sealing his fate
in the bargain. An educated man, brave and affable—U.S. Navy
Lt. Philllip C. Johnson of the Coast Survey Steamer *Active* once
referred to Isaac Stevens as "the dirtiest man I've ever seen, except for Isaac Ebey"—Ebey became a community leader from the
start, serving in turn as a district attorney, collector of customs
for the Puget Sound district, delegate to the Oregon territorial
legislature, a captain of the Territorial Volunteers and, briefly, as
adjutant general for Washington Territory and probate judge for
Island County. He moved to Whidbey Island in the fall of 1850,
claimed a tract of prairie land between Penn Cove and the Sound
and filed under the Oregon Provisional Government Land Act
of 1844. He built two structures, which he called "The Cabins,"
then sent for his wife and children in Missouri. On Aug, 11, 1857
Ebey was murdered and decapitated in his front yard by a Tlingit
raiding party in revenge for an American victory over a northern
raiding party at Port Gamble the year before, The murder created a sensation among Euro-American settlers and Coast Salish
groups living in the Northern Straits region. Gov. James Douglas
himself sent out HBC steamers to try and track down Ebey's head
and bring the raiders to justice.

7   FO, Abstract, p.124-127. Thomas Holland drowned in the
Haro Strait with several other employees that July when returning by canoe from Fort Victoria. Charles Griffin suspected that
they were drunk. Holland was a handy man around the farm and

had been a major contributor in building the Cowichan Road. One bridge on the track bore his name for several years.

8   Belle Vue Sheep Farm Journals, May 6, 1854. "Rum" is an archaic English expression with multiple meanings, but meaning here is lawbreaking or disreputable behavior.

9   As quoted in Miller, San Juan Archipelago, p. 28

10 Gough, *The Royal Navy and the Northwest Coast*, p. 90. The policy of swift reprisals that included mass destruction of property did not sit well with Douglas, who feared a massive Indian uprising. Once he succeeded Blanshard, the Indians on the lower end of Vancouver Island were handled with restraint. However, in dealing with the Northerners the Royal Navy returned to draconian measures.

11 RG76, NA. *Geographical Memoir*, p. 29. If tides were optimum through San Juan Channel between the tip of San Juan Island and Lopez Island, the "beach" may have been Grandma's Cove, situated just below Belle Vue Sheep Farm headquarters. The cove is sheltered, the beach sandy and a trail leads to the top of the bluff. When the Cullen/Barnes party moved off to another beach, it could have been one of several coves located along the island's southern coast, or anywhere along South Beach. The Americans also could have driven the rams over the hill to Griffin Bay to a spot near the Hudson's Bay Company dock. But the commandeered canoe was likely beached below the Indian village, which was located between Belle Vue Sheep Farm and Grandma's Cove. The author's guess is that the auction site was the large cove directly down the prairie from the redoubt. The American account has the incident taking place at a sheep station on the island's northern end, which seems far-fetched considering the time and distances involved. George Gibbs, a geologist with the U.S. Northwest Boundary Survey, in March 1859, described four

other sheep stations on the island, each with a "corral" and a cabin. (See note 12.)

12 As quoted in Thompson, p. 10. A healthy ram can weigh from 175 to 200-plus pounds apiece, which underscores that it was no easy task loading the animals into the canoes. No wonder the Americans pulled firearms when Griffin ordered them to release the animals.

13 Roth, *History of Whatcom County*, pp. 77-78 and Edson, *The Fourth Corner*, p.98. Kanakas with knives charging down the hill probably spiced up the account with visions of Captain Cook's demise on a Hawaii beach in the 1770s. If Griffin's Kanakas rowed across the channel to Victoria and the Americans saw the *Beaver* emerge before they could launch their boats, the incident had to have taken place near Belle Vue Sheep Farm and the island's southern end. Douglas later wrote that the *Beaver* went after the Americans with an armed posse on board, but was about two hours behind. Native Hawaiians crossed the Pacific to work in the Pacific Northwest starting with the Astorians in 1810 and continuing with the North West and Hudson's Bay companies. Many married into Northwest Coast Indian groups, which created excellent links for trade and enhanced the labor pool. Several families among the Lummi Nation, located north of Bellingham, claim Kanaka ancestors.

Blucher and the Prussian Army arrived on the field of Waterloo in time to save Wellington's army from Napoleon's Imperial Guard.

14 Miller, *San Juan Archipelago*, pp. 29-31. This came to about $15,000 in American dollars at mid-19th century.

15 Ibid., p. 31

16 The National Guard, State of Washington, *Collection of Official Documents*, p. 2.

17 Ibid., p. 2.

18 FO, *Abstract*, pp. 130-133.

19 As quoted in Miller, *San Juan Archipelago*, p. 46.

20 FO, *Abstract*, pp. 145-146; and RG76, NA, *Geographical Memoir*, p. 29. U.S. geologist Gibbs, again in March 1859, conversed with Griffin as well as C.L. Denman. Denman told him that he had been engaged to lay out claims by a lawyer named Sabatt "in strength of advices and secured from Washington." Twenty-six claims of a quarter section each (160 acres) were staked, with 27 quarter sections (or 4,000 acres) left to the Hudson's Bay Company. Gibbs observed that only two of the claims had been settled by then (one by a Scotsman, the other by two Kanakas), which seemed to confirm that "the whole seemed to be a matter of bare speculation."

21 Lyons to Cass, April 27, 1859, *40th Congress*, p. 218.

CHAPTER 6 - THE PIG INCIDENT

1 *Bellingham Bay Mail*, Whatcom, WT, May 2, 1874. Under the heading "Deaths," an L.A. Cutler, "aged 40 years" died at home in Samish (now Samish Island). Cutlar was received his mail there.

Griffin to Douglas, June 15, 1859, San Juan Island NHP Archive, hereafter SAJHA (copy from BC Archives); and RG76, NA, *Geographical Memoir*, p. 31. One other interesting comment Gibbs makes is that Charles Griffin, who was "very open and unreserved," told him that in his opinion the islands had always belonged to the U.S., and that Prevost had blown the issue by offering the "Middle Channel" as a compromise boundary. Judging by this fuming letter to Douglas, Griffin was paying lip service to Gibbs. Tabulations vary on the number of Americans on the island at the time of the incident. Twenty-two men signed the petition submitted to Harney, but not all were residents as evidenced by the signature of Paul K. Hubbs, Sr., a resident of Port Townsend. Including families, there may have been 25 to 29 Yanks on the island as opposed to seven British subjects.

2   Ibid.

3   *Belle Vue Sheep Farm Journal*, June 15, 1859. The three exclamation points are Griffin's.

4   Ibid.

5   *40th Congress*, pp. 183-184 and Miller, *San Juan Archipelago*, pp. 54-55. The courthouse is the oldest brick building in Washington State, having been hauled around the horn from Philadelphia in 1858 by brothers Thomas G. and Charles E. Richards at a cost of US $8,000. They had hoped to make a fortune selling grubstakes to miners bound for the Fraser River Gold Rush. Unfortunately for them, James Douglas issued a decree that all miners had to report to Victoria before traveling up the Fraser to the diggings. That made Whatcom a ghost town overnight and the brick store soon became public property. It still stands at E and Holly streets in downtown Bellingham, Washington.

6   Jacob was discharged by Griffin on June 28 for "having been beastly drunk all yesterday, & having connived with Clallam 'Joe' in stealing liquor." *Belle Vue Sheep Farm Journal*, June 28, 1859.

7   The Washington State Historical Society in Tacoma has a double-barrel *shotgun* in the collection donated by the Thomas family. It is complete with pedigree and was included as the weapon of record in the exhibition, "George Pickett and the Frontier Army Experience," which ran at the Whatcom Museum of History and Art in Bellingham from December 1994 to April

1995. The San Juan County Historical Museum has in its collection an 1854-pattern Harper's Ferry percussion cap, muzzle-
loading rifle, a military-issue weapon, which was donated by
a local family. The family claims Cutlar gave the rifle to an
ancestor. No paper trail exists for the rifle, which makes it suspect. However, Cutlar used the word "rifle," not "shotgun," in
his affidavit. Where does the truth lie? And does it really matter? We do know that the gun was loaded.

8   *40ᵗʰ Congress*, pp. 260-261

9   Dallas, Tolmie and Fraser have streets named for them in Victoria. Mt. Dallas on San Juan Island also is named for Dallas. Dallas
stressed his travel aboard the *Beaver* in response to Harney's charge
that they came aboard the warship, the HMS *Satellite*. See Chapter 15.

10 *40ᵗʰ Congress*, pp. 260-261

11 Hubbs, Jr., "Pickett's Landing on San Juan and the Cutler
Incident," *San Juan Islander*, Oct. 22, 1909. This piece also was included in Hubbs's obituary in the same newspaper on Feb. 17,
1910. Hubbs' brush with history ended with the boundary dispute. He remained in the islands for most of his life, working occasionally, living off nature and telling the Pig War story to those
willing to listen.

12 Hubbs, Jr., *Seattle Post-Intelligencer*, June 4, 1892.

13 Pickett's second in command was 2ⁿᵈ Lt. James W. Forsyth, an
able officer who made up for Pickett's poor engineering skills. The
Maumee, Ohio native was often left in charge by Pickett and not
always in the most ideal conditions (See Notes, Chapter 8, 15.).

14 McKay, Charles, "History of San Juan Island," *Washington
Historical Quarterly*, 2:4, 1908, pp. 290-294. Nova Scotia native
Charles McKay died at 86, or 90 years, two months, and 11 days,
depending on the census year and conflicting newspaper accounts.

McKay lived long enough to watch San Juan Island develop from a frontier wilderness with a scattering of Indian and European settlements to a vibrant agricultural /industrial community. He arrived in June 1859 after trials in the gold fields of California and British Columbia, and was just in time to participate in the Pig War crisis. McKay was a member of the first San Juan County board of commissioners and also represented the new county in the state legislature. His descendents still reside on San Juan Island.

15 Miller, *San Juan Archipelago*, pp. 57-58. The historian David Hunter Miller spent a large portion of his time in the 1930s and 1940s exploring this incident and then assembled a research trail historians tread to this day. *San Juan Archipelago* was actually one chapter in a greater diplomatic history. The paperback-bound volume is primarily a regurgitation of primary sources linked by a spare narrative that includes several lucid conclusions, among them the perception about Dallas's behavior. See Chapter 15 for a passage from his August 5 letter to Douglas.

CHAPTER 7 - WILLIAM SELBY HARNEY

1   This included the famous march into Florida in 1818. See Chapter 8.

2   Ness, *The Regular Army on the Eve of the Civil War*, p. 27.

3   Clow, "William S. Harney," *Soldier's West*, p. 43.

4   Ibid., p.45. Greyhounds are known for a tight cranial cavity. Kearny had no use for flamboyant officers and did not suffer fools. Following the U.S. conquest of California, he arrested the posturing John C. Fremont and marched him back across the plains in rear of his formation, shackled in irons.

5   Murray, *The Pig War*, p. 16. Harney eventually replaced Wool as commander in the Pacific Northwest.

6   Polk, *Diary of a President*, pp. 197-198. Ironically Secretary of State James Buchanan, who would one day fire Harney for displaying similar zeal, urged clemency by the court martial board.

7   It is not known if Pickett was aware of Harney's gallows humor, but he employed his own variant of the act on 22 North Carolinians during the Civil War, which almost resulted in his own hanging as a war criminal by U.S. authorities.

8   In another little twist of Pig War lore, Fleming was fired and reassigned as Pickett's second in command at Fort Bellingham. He was reassigned before the Pig War crisis, but in 1861, took the same steamer with Pickett back to the East Coast.

9   This included the famous march into Florida in 1818. See Chapter 8.

CHAPTER 8 - THE PETITION

1   Navy Department. *Dictionary of American Naval Fighting Ships*, Vol. IV, p. 263. The slow-moving warship *USS Massachusetts* was 161 feet long and 31 feet abeam, and was listed as anywhere from 749 to 779 tons. The Samuel Hall shipyard in Boston built her in 1845. The ship plied the Liverpool to New York route as an auxiliary steamer until it was purchased by the War Department for the Mexican War, during which she served as Lt. Gen. Winfield Scott's flagship in the harbor of Veracruz. The *Massachusetts* steamed on Puget Sound from 1856-57, then again from May 1859 to the outbreak of the Civil War, operated alternately by the navy and army. While on the sound, she carried from four to eight 32-pound guns and a company of soldiers or marines. During the Pig War incident she was under lease to the army's Quartermaster Corps. The *Massachusetts* was one of the first combination sail/steam-powered vessels in the inventory and as such, featured a screw propeller that could be raised with the ship un-

der sail. The screw eventually was left permanently in place, but the ship was so slow under steam, and required so much fuel, that Capt. Alfred Pleasonton, Harney's acting adjutant, advised Lt. Col. Silas Casey to operate the vessel under sail if at all possible. The navy removed the ship's engines in 1861 and converted her into a brigantine and renamed her *Farallones*.

2   Richards, *Isaac I. Stevens*, pp. 326-327.Harney's harassment of the HBC was well known to Company employees at Fort Vancouver. He'd requisitioned Company property without compensation. He also referred to Northerners as "British Indians" even to the extent of charging that their raids were "instigated by the Hudson's Bay Company, in order to drive the Americans from the lands which this immense establishment covet for their own purposes."

3   *Belle Vue Sheep Farm Journal*, July 9, 1859.

4   McKay, "History of San Juan Island," *Washington Historical Quarterly*, 2:4, 1908, p. 291.

5   *Belle Vue Sheep Farm Journal*, July 9, 1859. Perhaps it was here that the "warship" misunderstanding arose and the Americans may have not been telling tall stories. The *Beaver* had once been the only steamer in northern waters, and *often* had been chartered by the government as a gunboat to deal with marauding Indians and county sheriffs absconding with sheep. Most American citizens in the area were aware of this fact. Perhaps Hubbs decided to stretch the truth just a bit, one ship with guns being as good as another. Or maybe Hubbs did not mention the *Satellite* at all. Maybe he said "gunboat," and Harney, who probably saw the *Satellite* when in Victoria, assumed that was the "warship." McKay wrote: "They (the HBC) had sent a gunboat to take one of our men to Victoria..." Ironically, attorney Paul K. Hubbs, Sr., had the sequence of events and the identity of the ships involved nearly spot-on—except that he identified the humble survey ship *Plumper*

as a "frigate"—in his September 3 letter in support of Harney to Pres. James Buchanan. Presumably this information came from his son. A.G. Dallas vigorously disputed the letter, referring to it as "unintelligible."

HMS *Satellite* was a 21-gun screw corvette, the largest in her class in the Royal Navy. Corvettes were flushed decked (meaning no poop or quarterdeck astern) with a single tier of guns on the upper deck. At 200 feet in length, the *Satellite* was eight feet longer than the HMS *Tribune*, a frigate and traditionally a larger class of vessel. Twenty, eight-inch guns were mounted broadside, with a 10-inch chase gun on a circular emplacement at the bow. Swift and powerful, she personified the transition period between auxiliary steamers, which still relied on sail in the open sea, and warships that relied solely on steam power. Vessels of the *Satellite's* class were ideal for enforcing British policies on inland waterways such as the Strait of Georgia, and the Fraser River delta in British Columbia. Auxiliary steamers made the difference by steaming up the maze of delta waterways of the Pieho River during the assault on Canton during the Second Opium War.

6   Crosbie to Cass, April, 1860, *36ᵗʰ Congress*, pp. 1-4; and Bancroft, *British Columbia*, p. 617. U.S. Magistrate Henry Crosbie is generally considered a dispassionate and reliable source on the Pig War. He also pointed out that northern Indian raids were the main reason the British preceded the Americans in settling on San Juan.

7   Hubbs, Jr., *Seattle Post Intelligencer*, June 4, 1892.

8   Harney to Scott, July 19, 1859, *40ᵗʰ Congress*, pp. 147-148. As stated in the narrative, the petition, which Harney attached to his letter, never mentions the Hudson's Bay Company by name. But Americans often looked upon the HBC and British government as one and the same, and actually under Douglas it was generally

true. The conflicts between the home government and the HBC—
licensing in the gold fields, the secretiveness over the Belle Vue
Sheep Farm, and the anti-colonial attitudes of many in the British parliament—were unknown to most Americans.

9 Ibid., pp. 147-148. Harney viewed the existence of the Vancouver Island colony and New Caledonia (soon to be British Columbia) as temporary, as not enough British colonists existed to
make them viable political entities. Harney undoubtedly read reports of the topological survey in 1854 (Whiting and others) that
stressed the military significance of the San Juan Islands.

10 Ibid., pp. 147-148.

11 Miller, *San Juan Archipelago*, p. 64. *Dartmoor* was an infamous
British prison in Devon where from the spring of 1813 until
March 1815 about 6,500 American sailors were imprisoned.

The War of 1812 was still in the nation's living memory during
the Pig War crisis.

12 Ibid., p. 147-148 and Miller, *San Juan Archipelago*, p. 63.

13 Utley, *Frontiersmen in Blue*, p. 188. Haller and two companies of
infantry were ambushed and barely escaped massacre by more
than 500 Yakamas. Haller lost five killed and 17 wounded after
being besieged for two days on a hilltop, followed by a two-day
running retreat that cost him his howitzer and pack train. However, unlike George Custer, he managed to skillfully extricate his
command and live to fight another day. He went on to serve in
the Union Army during the Civil War, but was court-martialed
and dismissed from the army on a charge of "disloyal conduct."
Following a court of inquiry convened in 1873, Haller was exon-
erated. Congress reinstated him to active service as a full colonel
in 1879, after which he took command of the newly reopened Fort
Townsend. He retired in 1882.

14 Haller, *San Juan and Secession*, pp. 7 and 11; and Thompson, *Historic Resource Study*,. p. 24, n.; *Roder Narrative*, Bancroft Library; BC, WWU; and Gordon, *Pickett*, pp. 62-63. Haller's argument is based on the way Casey was addressed by Harney in Special Orders 72—as "commander of Fort Steilacoom," a single military installation, rather than the entire "Upper Puget Sound." In Haller's opinion, the closure of Forts Bellingham and Townsend and Pickett's subsequent assignment to San Juan Island underscored the demotion. But lacking actual evidence of a conspiracy, Haller suggested that the officers "could read between the lines" in terms of interpreting orders. He prefaces the accusatory paragraph with "...I may be doing injustice, but my candid impression is..." His suspicions were aroused by the homes of record of the officers who gathered that evening at Fort Bellingham on Harney's inspection tour. Pickett and Edmund, Fitzhugh were from Virginia, while Harney was from Tennessee. Haller neglected to mention that also at Fort Bellingham that night were Harney's adjutant, Capt. Alfred Pleasonton, and department quartermaster Capt. Rufus Ingalls, who hailed from the District of Columbia and Maine respectively. Both rose to the rank of Major General of Volunteers in the Union Army during the Civil War. Roeder (actual spelling) was one of the founders of Whatcom, the precursor of today's Bellingham, Washington. He was in Whatcom the evening Harney and company stayed in Bellingham. The officers bunked with Roeder, Pickett and Fitzhugh in Whatcom. The quarters of each were somewhat more commodious than those of the fort. Fitzhugh was manager of the Bellingham Bay Coal Company and was one of the Americans who joined Cullen and Barnes in pinching Griffin's sheep four years before. The intrigue of a Southern cabal to start a war was given further impetus by a letter George Pickett wrote to one of his former officers after the Civil War. In the letter, Pickett mused that if the new President (and his prewar buddy) U.S. Grant should start a war with a foreign power it might reunite the nation. His wife, LaSalle, actually alleged in one of her

works that Pickett and Harney provoked the San Juan incident for that very purpose. Historian Lesley Gordon speculates that Pickett might have expressed that wish to LaSalle when they were living in poverty after the war.

15 *36ᵗʰ Congress*, p. 117. James W. Forsyth, a native of Maumee, Ohio, would go on to become a key officer on the staff of Union Maj. Gen. Philip H. Sheridan during the Civil War, eventually rising to the rank of brigadier general of volunteers. In one of the many ironies of the war, it would be Sheridan's corps that pierced the flank of Pickett's Division at Five Forks in the Spring of 1865, opening the door to Lee's surrender at Appomattox. Forsyth would continue in the service after the war mainly as a staff officer under Sheridan, who rose to Army chief of staff. Following Sheridan's retirement in 1885, Forsyth assumed command of the Seventh Cavalry in 1886, 10 years after the Little Big Horn disaster. He would lead the regiment at the so-called Battle of Wounded Knee in December 1890, in which 150 Sioux men, women and children and 25 soldiers were killed. Even though he was censured for bungling what was to have been a disarmament of Sioux warriors, he retired a major general in 1897.

16 Miller, *San Juan Archipelago*, p. 59 & 73; BC, Young to M. de Courcy, July 23, 1859; HBC, Ft. Victoria letters out, Dallas to Griffin, July 28, 1859. In the ensuing letter traffic, Harney insisted that the British had assumed wrongful jurisdiction in the disputed territory by dispatching a ship of war to arrest Cutlar and carry him off to Victoria. While Douglas vehemently refuted the charge, there is no denying official correspondence that includes a letter from the Governor's secretary, William Young, to senior naval officer Capt. Michael de Courcy, RN, dated July 23, 1859. The missive advised de Courcy that a commissioned stipendiary magistrate, Mr. John de Courcy, had been ordered to San Juan to treat with American squatters on the island. "If possible," the governor wanted John de Courcy conveyed to the island in a "ship of war."

The de Courcys shared a common ancestor in John de Courcy, the 18th Lord Kingsale. The Barony of Kingsale in County Cork, Ireland was established as part of the Norman Conquest in 1177 by Sir John de Courcy. Born March 30, 1821, John de Courcy was the grandson of the 19th Lord of Kingsale and would himself inherit the title on the death of a cousin in 1874. Before arriving in Victoria in 1858, de Courcy was a captain in the British Army, and fought in the Crimean War during which he was said to have commanded a company of Turkish irregulars who raided behind enemy lines. Before his commission from Douglas, he sat on the Police Court bench and was known to inflict heavy penalties for light offenses, which spurred the Victoria *Colonist* to refer to him as a "snob and a *Bashi-bazouk*," a slap at his Turkish adventures, no doubt. At the outbreak of the American Civil War, he applied directly to Secretary of State William Seward for a commission in the Union Army. Though Seward's daughter thought de Courcy's face looked like a "rocky beach" and was appalled by his one bad eye, Seward arranged for a commission as colonel of the 16th Regiment of Ohio Volunteer Infantry. De Courcy was in command of the 26th Brigade of the Army of the Ohio when he exceeded his orders and captured from the Rebels the saddle of Cumberland Gap on the Kentucky-Tennessee border. Utilizing a combination of skullduggery and hard spirits, he first fooled the Confederate commander into believing he had a larger force by switching cap badges and marching his troops hither and thither. He then sweetened the prospect of surrender by liberally distributing several barrels of whisky to the Southern officers. De Courcy's success did not save him from being immediately relieved of command by his superior, Maj. Gen. Ambrose Burnside, who unquestionably lacked the creative vision to understand a successful operation that did not involve monstrous loss of life and treasure. De Courcy was discharged several months later. He died in Italy in 1890.

Capt. Michael de Courcy was the grandson of Adm. Sir Michael de Courcy, an Admiral of the Blue, son of the 18th Lord Kingsale and brother of the 19th Lord, John de Courcy's grandfather. Capt. Michael de Courcy of San Juan fame would rise to the rank of admiral and would be invested as a companion of the Order of Bath (CB). He died in 1881 at age 70. D.W. Higgins, a Victoria pioneer, devoted an entire chapter of his memoir, *The Mystic Spring* (1904), to the de Courcys. According to Higgins, when John de Courcy introduced himself as a de Courcy to his cousin on the streets of Victoria, the naval officer looked down his nose and said "The hell you are."

17 John de Courcy to Douglas, as quoted in Miller, *San Juan Archipelago*, p. 73.

18 HBC, Dallas to Griffin, July 28, 1859. The full text of the first paragraph reads: "I am without any of your favors to reply to and only lament this morning that the *Satellite* had gone to San Juan with Major De Courcy as Stipendiary Magistrate to relieve you of all authority and responsibility. As to the course you are to pursue, I have now to instruct you that you are at once to lodge a complaint before Major De Courcy against the man Cutlar, who shot your boar, laying your damages at a reasonable amount. You will also lodge a complaint against him as a squatter, and trespasser on land claimed by the Company and in like manner against any other squatter interfering with your sheep runs. This course of proceeding is in accordance with the wishes of His Excellency the Governor."

19 *40th Congress*, pp. 183-184. How Constable G. T. Gordon ended up in the mix is a mystery, unless he was a de Courcy deputy. He may be the same Gordon who fought for the South during the Civil War and would be a lieutenant colonel in temporary command of a North Carolina brigade at the Battle of Gettysburg. In his classic *Pickett's Charge*, author George Stewart relates how Pickett introduced Gordon to one of his staff officers on the eve

of the famous charge: "This is Colonel Gordon, once opposed to me in the San Juan affair, but now on our side." The staff officer recalled that Gordon told Pickett "...my men are not going up today," as they had been heavily involved on the battle's first day.

20 Campbell to Haller, July 27, 1859, UWSC, *Haller* papers.

21 Pickett to Pleasonton, July 27, 1859, Letters Received, Adjutant General's Office, RG 94, NA; and Pickett to Pleasonton, July 27, 1859, Letters received, Department of Oregon, RG393, and NA. Pleasonton would rise to major general of volunteers in the Union Army during the Civil War, and be instrumental in reorganizing the cavalry of the Army Potomac into a single corps, which became a potent striking arm. At the Battle of Brandy Station in June 1863, the Union cavalry "arrived," matching for the first time the cavalry of Confederate Maj. Gen. J.E.B Stuart. They went on to win a smashing victory over Stuart at Gettysburg. An inability to keep his opinions to himself got him into trouble with Union Maj. Gen. George Meade, his commanding officer. He then became the odd man out when Ulysses S. Grant brought Maj. Gen. Philip Sheridan east to command the cavalry corps. He finished the war in the western theater and bitterly resigned from the army in 1868. He has earned lasting fame among Civil War buffs mainly for raising 23-year-old George Armstrong Custer from captain to brigadier general.

CHAPTER 9 - GEORGE PICKETT AND THE FRONTIER ARMY

1　Edson, *The Fourth Corner*, p. 35. Edson's book was first published in the early 1950s. Because she was raised in Whatcom County "before the coming of the railroad," she knew many of the people mentioned in her history.

2　Returns, Fort Bellingham, 1856. BC.

3　For more on George Pickett, see Gordon. Lesley J., *Pickett: General George E. Pickett in Life & Legend.* Chapel Hill, NC: University of North Carolina Press. 1998; Longacre, Edward G. *Pickett: Leader of the Charge.* Shippensburg, PA: White Mane Publishing Company, Inc. 1995; Selcer, Richard F. *Faithfully and Forever Your Soldier: General George E. Pickett, CSA.* Gettysburg, PA: Farnsworth House Military Impressions. 1995; Pickett, LaSalle Corbell. *Pickett and His Men*, Atlanta: Foote & Davis Company. 1889, and *The Heart of a Soldier as Revealed in the Intimate Letters of Genl. George E. Pickett, C.S.A.* New York: Seth Moyle. 1913; and Patterson, Gerard A., "George E. Pickett— A Personality Profile," Civil War Times Illustrated 5, May 1966.

4　Oregon Historical Society, Pickett to Alvord, Feb. 13, 1861. Selcer, Richard E. *How Did George Pickett Really get Into West Point? Or The Making of Major General George E. Pickett, C.S.A.,* Unpublished manuscript in possession of the author. Another uncle, Capt. John Symington, had gone to another, more distant relative, the army's Chief of Engineers, Col. Joseph G. Totten. If the U.S. representative from the Quincy district of Illinois submitted Pickett's name in nomination, Totten explained, he would be appointed. The Lincoln-Stuart partnership was dissolved after Stuart's election to a second term in Congress. Lincoln did know Pickett's uncle and had even published a few poems in Johnston's Whig newspaper, but did not visit Quincy while Pickett lived there from April 1840 to April

1842. Pickett did, however, visit Springfield on two occasions when he may have been introduced, but by then Lincoln and Stuart were not close and Lincoln would not become a U.S. Representative until 1847-1849, long after Pickett graduated from West Point. Sally Pickett miraculously produced what became known as the "Washington's Birthday Letter," in which Lincoln offered sage advice to the young Pickett on how he should conduct himself as a West Pointer. Extracts from the letter were published in *The Complete Works of Abraham Lincoln*, edited by John G. Nicolay and John Hay, Lincoln's White House secretaries. The letter was offered to Hay and Nicolay as a typed manuscript, but the original in Lincoln's hand has never surfaced. Moreover, the content of the letter changed over Sally's long publishing and lecture career.

5   Returns, Fort Bellingham, 1856-1857, BC.

6   Utley, *Frontiersmen in Blue*, p. 19. Former National Park Service Chief Historian Robert Utley has set the standard for historians of the army and Indian frontier. Most of the general information about the frontier army comes from this volume and the sequel *Frontier Regulars*.

7   Ibid., p. 29

8   BC.

9   1860 *U.S. Census*, Whatcom County, Washington Territory, SAJHA.

10 Report of Col. Joseph K.F. Mansfield on the U.S. Military Reservation at Bellingham Bay, Washington Territory, Dec. 7-8, 1858; and Port Townsend, Washington Territory, Dec. 3-4, 1858. RG 94, NARS.

11 Ibid.

The town of Pleasonton, California is named for him. Some correspondence in RG 94 and RG 393 is not included in either collection of Congressional documents and is more revealing of the personalities

CHAPTER 10 - GOVERNOR DOUGLAS RESPONDS

1   *Pioneer and Democrat*, July 29, 1859.

2   Pickett to Mackall, Sept. 10, 1857, BC.

3   Thompson, *Historical Resource Report*, p. 42; Edgerton p. 52; Norman, pp.222-229; Douglas' initial orders to Hornby no longer exist. William Symonds, a noted English marine architect, designed *Tribune* to be a 28-gun frigate (6th Rate), but in 1850 the plans were modified to make her a 31-gun auxiliary screw frigate, one of only 12 in the Royal Navy in 1859. Symonds' ships were usually swift and broad of beam, but also "wet," as Hornby wrote, meaning they rolled copiously, which not only admitted tons of seawater, but also made the guns almost useless in high seas. Steam propulsion had been practically applied to merchant shipping as a primary source of power since the 1840s. However, military steamers continued to rely primarily on sail on the open seas to ensure independence from coaling stations. Propeller-driven "combination" vessels such as *Tribune* were powered by low compression, side-lever engines that were challenged by heavy seas and headwinds. Therefore the term "auxiliary screw steamer." As with *Satellite*, the engines were mainly used to negotiate inland waters and transit harbors. For example, on her arrival at the mouth of the Strait of Juan de Fuca, the *Tribune* raised her collapsible smokestack, dropped her propeller into the water and steamed up the strait and into Victoria harbor.

4   Norman, pp.222-229; Edgerton p. 52; F&CO, U.K., *Biographical Sketch of Geoffrey Phipps Hornby*, SAJHA.

5   HMS *Ganges* was built in Mumbai (Bombay) 1819-1821, modeled after HMS *Canopus*, formerly the French warship *Franklin*. She was the Pacific Station flagship 1857-1861, after which she returned to England where she began a long life as a training ship that did not conclude until 1929. She was finally broken up the following year, however a Royal Navy training base operated under the name HMS *Ganges* until closure in 1976.

6   The punishments meted out by the U.S. Army in the wake of the Whitman Massacre in 1847 created an unsettling atmosphere among the tribes in what is now northeastern Washington State. The climate of mistrust was exacerbated by Isaac Stevens' round of whirlwind treaties completed in 1855, and continued to fester in a series of skirmishes into the spring of 1858. In August 1858, Ninth Infantry commander, Col. George Wright assembled a 600-man force from the Ninth, First Dragoons, and Third Artillery (fighting as infantry) and marched north from Fort Walla Walla. They faced an alliance of an estimated 700 Spokane, Coeur d'Alene, Palouse, and Pend d'Oreille warriors led by Kamiakin. Following several running fights, the opposing forces clashed on a plain north of the city of Spokane on Sept. 5, 1858. The Indians set fire to the prairie grasses, but Wright masterfully engaged the dragoons and infantry in a pincer movement that made optimum use of rifled muskets and howitzers. The fight covered nearly 25 miles and inflicted a crushing defeat on the Indians.

7   Hornby to de Courcy, July 30, 1859, as quoted in Miller, *San Juan Archipelago*, p. 71. A watercolor of *Satellite's* longboat heading for Pickett's camp on Griffin Bay, signed July 27, 1859, confirms Hornby's description. The painting, by a British midshipman, is contained in *Views of the Pacific Northwest*. Yale Collection of Western Americana, Bienecke Rare Book and Manuscript Library, WA MSS S-1817, Box 6, Folder 32; Campbell to Haller, July 27, 1859, UWSC, *Haller* papers.

8   Gough, *The Royal Navy and the Northwest Coast*, pp. 150-151.

9   Miller, *San Juan Archipelago*, pp. 76-78. Campbell claimed he met with Prevost at Griffin Bay on the 27th and 28th in an August 18 letter to Secretary of State Cass; Campbell to Haller, July 27, 1859, UWSC, *Haller* papers.

10 RG 153 Records of Offices of the JAG Court martial Case Files 1809-1894, Box 262, *John Howard Court Martial*, Sept., 23, 1859, Camp Pickett, W.T. During this trial, held at the height of the U.S. military occupation, Crosby testified that Pickett and Howard tussled so violently that they rolled around in the dirt before Pickett overcame his lieutenant. When asked by the court if Howard's pistol was "capped and loaded," Pickett replied, "I do not know, I did not examine the pistol." Pickett then ordered Howard's arrest, which Howard refused to acknowledge. During his testimony Pickett pointed out that Howard's stunt could not have come at a worse time as *Satellite* was anchored in the harbor and *Tribune* was on the way. Had he been killed, it would have resulted in "serious difficulties." Howard was convicted and cashiered from the service.

11 Hubbs, Jr., *Seattle Post Intelligencer*, June 4, 1892.

12 Pickett to Casey, *40th Congress*, p 152.

13 *Pioneer & Democrat*, July 29, 1859.

14 Hornby to his wife, July 31, 1859, Egerton, Hornby, p. 64. This same supposition would be offered by Prevost to explain the actions of Harney the Jacksonian. Perhaps both captains got it from Douglas. It has been cited in some works as "British intelligence." Hornby's correspondence is cited in the only biography of him published in 1896 by his daughter, Mary Augusta Hornby (Mrs. Fred) Egerton.

15 Ibid., pp. 65-66.

16 Pickett to Pleasonton, *40ᵗʰ Congress*, pp. 153-154.

17 Egerton, *Hornby*, pp. 65-66.

18 Casey to Pleasonton, Ibid., pp. 151-152. The British drill may have been conducting live firing demonstrations. In 2002, a park ranger caught two teen-age boys hauling a solid shot (cannonball) up from San Juan Island NHP's Old Town Lagoon. The boys found the 30-pound shot, of the variety employed by *Tribune*, half-surfaced in the bluff about 200 yards east of the lagoon. This would have been about a half mile from Pickett's first camp, close enough for Pickett and his men to feel the impact through the soles of their boots. No wonder he struck camp.

19 Haller, *San Juan and Secession*, p. 12.

20 Gough, *The Royal Navy and the Northwest Coast*, p. 161. The account by these officers underscores how time and distance spawned many of the apocryphal stories that characterize the Pig War.

21 Miller, *San Juan Archipelago*, pp. 75-77.

22 Ibid., p. 78. In a follow-up letter to Douglas, Finlayson also observed that the boundary dispute might have been settled but they had yet to receive word. There also was worry of events in Italy. Great Britain could hardly afford war with the United States.

23 Ibid., p. 75.

CHAPTER 11 - "TUT, TUT, NO, NO, THE DAMN FOOLS."

1 Douglas to Hornby, Aug. 2, 1859, as quoted in Miller, *San Juan Archipelago*, p. 79.

2   Hornby to M. de Courcy, Aug. 1, 1859, as quoted in Miller, *San Juan Archipelago*, pp.78-79.

3   Douglas to Hornby, Aug. 2, 1859 (second letter), San Juan Island NHP Archive (copy from BC Archive).

4   Hornby to Baynes, Aug. 5, 1859, as quoted in Thompson, *Historic Resource Study*, pp. 128-129.

5   Hornby to Douglas, Aug. 4, 1859, *40*[th] *Congress*, pp. 155-156. What we know of this conversation comes from letters that were exchanged, at Pickett's request, between Pickett and Hornby; and through correspondence between each officer and his superior. Pickett wanted a written record and Hornby was pleased to comply. Paul K. Hubbs, Jr., claimed to have been in the tent for the meeting in his 1892 Seattle *Post-Intelligencer* account. It is unlikely that a civilian would have been allowed in a meeting where martial law was the primary subject of discussion. Hornby's letter eventually ended up in the documents of the 36th Congress, to which Hubbs would have had access. He paints a belligerent Pickett, which would have been totally out of character at this point.

6   Selcer, *Faithfully & Forever*, p. 42.

7   Hornby to Pickett, Aug. 3, 1859; and Pickett to Hornby, Aug. 3, 1859, 11 p.m., *40*[th] *Congress*, pp. 155-157. A highlight of this exchange is Hornby's recollection that Pickett told him he "believed" Harney's orders came from Washington. In his reply to Hornby, Pickett corrected Hornby's version by stating that he was on San Juan "under orders from my government."

8   Pickett to Pleasonton, Aug. 3, 1859, *40*[th] *Congress*, pp. 153-154; Pickett to Pleasonton, Aug. 3, 1859, RG94, NA.; and Gordon, *Pickett*, p. 59. In an accompanying letter to Pleasonton, Pickett fumed over the "miserable subterfuge" of Douglas and how if it weren't for George Pickett and Company D Lyman Cutlar would

be in jail that moment and American settlers would have been run off the island. As biographer Lesley Gordon writes, "Perhaps to quell his anxiety and distrust, he asserted unquestioning belief in the mission." 'We are right,' he announced to Pleasonton,' tho' we all knew it before.'"

9 Douglas to Legislative Council, Aug. 3, 1859, ibid., p. 174.

10 Hornby to Douglas, Aug. 4, 1859, as quoted in Miller, *San Juan Archipelago*, p. 74-75.

11 Legislative Council to Douglas, *40th Congress*, p. 175-176.

12 *Pioneer and Democrat*, Aug. 5, 1859.

13 Campbell to Harney, Aug. 14, 1859, *40th Congress*, pp. 120-121; Campbell to Haller, July 27, 1859, UWSC, *Haller* papers.

14 Here's an excerpt from the letters exchanged, as per *40th Congress*, pp. 108-112. It is a good example of where these two men were taking matters: "...With a sincere desire to extract from your letter of the 27th of May the 'very explicit answer' to my communication of the 7th, which you 'submit when taken as a whole,' it conveys to me, I have again given it most careful perusal and consideration, and with due deference, candor compels me to say that, whether taken as a whole or in part, it only conveys to me a very circumlocutory and evasive answer..."

15 Prevost to Campbell, Aug. 4, 1859, *40th Congress*, p. 114.

16 Campbell to Prevost, ibid., p. 115.

17 Miller, *San Juan Archipelago*, n. 1, p. 72.

18 National Archives, RG23, MF642, Roll 208, p. 53, Alden to Bache, Aug. 8, 1859.

The official Coast Survey history notes: "The year 1858 was the only year from 1855 until the Civil War in which any significant hydrographic work was accomplished in Washington Territory and even that was a marginal year with only 7,742 soundings made and 847 miles of survey line run by the ship. By comparison, the year 1856 had 398 soundings and 16 survey miles, 1857 had only 1,485 soundings and 122 survey miles, and 1859 had only 967 soundings and 105 survey miles. In 1860 and 1861 the *Active* did not go north."

Coast Survey hydrographic vessels and commercial steam ships were usually commanded by naval officers such as Alden as command billets were scarce in the antebellum navy, where captains served until they nearly expired on deck. The Coast Survey experience would manifest itself a decade later in the American Civil War, when captains had to negotiate the maze of channels, shallows and estuaries along the Southeast coast and swift rivers during blockade duty. No officers were better prepared for these duties than those who created charts from Maine to the Gulf Coast. Alden would spend his entire Civil War service in command of the powerful steam sloops that intercepted blockade runners and penetrated Confederate defenses in bays riddled with hidden shoals and sewn with deadly mines.

19 McDonald, "A Few Items in the West," in *Washington Historical Quarterly*, No. 8, p. 196.

20 Baynes to Hornby, Aug. 13, 1859, as quoted in Miller, *San Juan Archipelago*, p. 87

21 Douglas to Baynes, Aug. 15, 1859, ibid., p. 88

22 Douglas to Lytton, Aug. 17, 1859, ibid., p. 88.

23 Hornby to his wife, Dec. 4, 1859, as quoted in Miller, *San Juan Archipelago*, p. 42

CHAPTER 12 - REINFORCEMENTS

1 *Victoria Gazette*, Aug. 11, 1859.

2 Harney to Scott, Aug. 18, 1859, *40th Congress*, pp.162-163.

3 As quoted in Thompson, *Historic Resource Study*, p. 63.

4 Pickett to Pleasonton, Aug. 3, 1859, *40th Congress*, pp. 153-154.

5 Harney to Assist Adjutant General, Aug. 6, 1859, ibid., pp. 147-148.

6 Harney to Assistant Adjutant General, ibid., pp. 180.

7 Pleasonton to Pickett, Aug. 6, 1859, ibid., p. 158.

8 Pleasonton to Casey, Aug. 6, 1859, as quoted in Miller, *San Juan Archipelago*, p. 97.

9 Harney to Pacific Squadron Commander, Aug. 7, 1859, *40th Congress*, pp. 158-159.

10 Harney to Cooper, Aug. 8, 1859, ibid., p. 160.. This time Harney claimed the warship was HMS *Plumper*, revealing his unfamiliarity with British shipping in the Pacific Northwest.

11 Faust, *Encyclopedia of the Civil War,* p. 5. Alden had a reputation for being a careful mariner and his record attests to it (he retired a rear admiral). He made a name for himself in the Civil War by playing key roles in naval actions that defined the start and conclusion to the war. In April 1861 he was tasked with going to Gosport Naval Yard in Norfolk, Virginia, reassembling the steam frigate USS *Merrimack's* engines and conning her out of the yard before the rebels took possession. With the assistance of the chief engineer of the U.S. Navy, Benjamin Isherwood, Alden accomplished the first part of his mission by making the ship seaworthy. But rather than taking initiative and steaming out of the yard as Isherwood urged, he chose instead to wait upon

the yard commander, an elderly man who was indecisive and ill-advised. Alden ended up returning to Washington where an exasperated Secretary of the Navy Gideon Welles scolded him for leaving the *Merrimack* behind. Alden was once more dispatched to Norfolk only this time in a subordinate role. The party arrived too late to save the ship so *Merrimack* was scuttled and burned to the waterline. The Rebels raised the ship and converted her into the CSS *Virginia*. Toward the end of the war, at Mobile Bay, Alden was in command of the USS *Brooklyn* and leading the line into the harbor. A monitor, the USS *Tecumseh*, struck a mine and sank to starboard, whereupon Alden backed off and started clearing the mines, which began to foul the Union line under the guns of the Confederate forts. That's when Admiral Farragut shouted, "Damn the torpedoes, four bells" or something to that effect. Incidentally, Alden was linked to Farragut during the war probably because they knew each other well from the West Coast days when Farragut was commandant of Mare Island Naval Yard, 1854-1858. In another sidelight, Alden and the *Active* retrieved William Tecumseh Sherman from the beach after the steamer SS *Lewis* ran aground near Bolinas Bay in April 1853.

12 Pickett's warnings reveal that despite several amicable meetings August 3-10, the Virginian still believed Hornby would attempt to stop the Americans from landing reinforcements. Hornby may have decided he was not going to press the issue, but he was not adverse to a good bluff.

13 Casey to Pleasonton, ibid., pp. 164-166. Most of what we know about Casey's landing comes from the colonel's report. This thorough document reflects Casey's "Old Army" reputation as a quietly competent and reliable officer, although even Casey could not resist drafting such passages as: "Seeing the danger of a collision at any moment, which would inevitably lead to war between two mighty nations connected by so many common bonds, and whichever way it might terminate would be eminently disastrous

to the cause of civilization and the interests of humanity, I resolved to make an attempt to prevent so great a calamity." A less
self-conscious Casey two weeks earlier wrote that he believed the
British were "bluffing a little." The native Rhode Islander also
graduated near the bottom of his West Point class, however his
grasp of infantry tactics was so formidable that he wrote a book
that was carried by officers on both sides during the Civil War.
His only fighting in that war came during the Peninsula campaign
when he opposed, of all people, Confederate Brig. Gen. George
Pickett. Pickett's men actually took a redoubt from Casey's forces
and held it for more than 12 hours during the battle of Fair Oaks
(Seven Pines). Casey was relegated to commanding a brigade (as
a major general of volunteers) in the Washington City defense
works for the remainder of the war. After the war, he reverted to
his regular army rank of colonel, retiring in 1868.

14 Hubbs, *Seattle Post Intelligencer*, June 4, 1892.

15 Casey to Pleasonton, Aug. 12, 1859, *40th Congress*, pp. 164-165.

16 Pleasonton to Casey, Aug. 16, 1859, ibid., p. 168.

17 Douglas to Lytton, Aug. 12, 1859, as quoted in Miller, *San Juan Archipelago*, p. 99.

Edward George Earle Lytton Bulwer-Lytton, 1st Baron Lytton
was not only a politician, but a distinguished poet, novelist and
playwright, who coined several other immortal phrases such as
"pursuit of the almighty dollar," and the opening line, "It was a
dark and stormy night." Douglas named the town of Lytton, BC
for him in 1858.

18 Douglas to Harney, Aug. 13, 1859, ibid., pp. 171-172. In Hunter
Miller's view, this allowed Harney to press his argument about British warships calling on the island. If a ship did not necessarily call
for Cutlar, it did not rule out that it could have brought Dallas.

19 Ibid., p. 172. The question remains: If Douglas was concerned with preserving the peace, why didn't he raise the issue with Harney?

20 Campbell to Harney, Aug. 14, 1859, ibid., p. 187.

21 Harney to Campbell, Aug. 16, 1859, ibid., p. 169. Miller believed this was little more than lip service in view of Harney's other reports and orders.

22 Campbell to Harney, Aug. 30, 1859, ibid., p. 188; and Campbell to Cass, Sept. 3, 1859, ibid., pp. 119-120. The incident caught Campbell by surprise, but he clearly viewed it as Prevost's fault. In Campbell's mind, if the British commissioner had not been so prejudiced against the agreement in the first place, it would have been resolved long before Harney arrived on the scene.

23 Victoria *Colonist*, Aug. 15, 1859; and Casey to Pleasonton, Aug. 14, 1859, *40th Congress*, pp. 167-168. Along with the naval guns came Granville O. Haller and Company I, finally released from three weeks aboard the ship. Wheezing about the islands aboard the old tub must have made the men feel like the *Massachusetts* was Wagner's *Flying Dutchman*; that they were doomed never to see land again. However, their cruise was broken on August 10 by an excursion up the Nooksack River to apprehend raiders from the tribe of the same name. The Indians had slipped into the town of Whatcom the night before in an attempt to break one of their number out of jail. Guns were drawn at the corner of today's E and West Holly streets in Bellingham, and three Indians and a white man were killed. Haller quickly rounded up the "war party" and dispatched them to Fort Steilacoom where they were held on the good behavior of the tribe as a whole. Ironically, Haller achieved what George Pickett never did in Whatcom County: fight Indians.

24 Hornby to Baynes, Aug. 15, 1859, as quoted in Miller, *San Juan Archipelago*, p. 90.

25 Baynes to Hornby, Aug. 16, 1859, ibid., p. 91.

26 Hubbs, *Seattle Post Intelligencer*, June 4, 1892.

27 Dallas to Douglas, Aug. 5, 1859, San Juan Island NHP Archive.

28 Casey to Pleasonton, Aug. 14, 1859, *40th Congress*, p. 167.

29 Casey to Pleasonton, Aug. 22, 1859, ibid., p. 180. The new site actually was Casey's second choice. He had preferred an open area about three and half miles north, near False Bay, but it was too far from the HBC dock, which he believed he needed to control. Griffin left Belle Vue Sheep Farm and the island in 1862 and was replaced by Robert Firth, Sr. The HBC leased the site to Firth a year later and backed out altogether by 1864.

Three of the box-frame structures from Fort Bellingham still stand at American Camp. The officers' quarters, HS-11 as per the National Park Service inventory, was converted into a farmhouse and remained on the site. The exterior was restored by the NPS in the 1970s. A laundress quarters, HS-6, was returned to the site from Friday Harbor in 1972 and also underwent exterior restoration. In December 2010, another officers' quarters, HS-10, was also moved to American Camp from Friday Harbor.

30 Peck, *The Pig War*, pp. 98-101. Henry Martyn Robert, described as "sickly" by William Peck, enjoyed a long career in the Corps of Engineers, retiring as a brigadier general in command of the Corps in 1903. However, he is most renowned for writing *Robert's Rules of Order*, a primer on parliamentary procedure still in use throughout the world. Largely because of this book, he is the only individual to be honored with a plaque in the national park.

31 Pleasonton to Casey, Aug. 16, 1859, *40ᵗʰ Congress*, p. 168.

32 Prevost to "Dear Sir," Aug. 22, 1859, as quoted in Thompson, *Historic Resource Report*, p. 132. Many of the British naval and military men present on and in the vicinity of San Juan Island were Crimean War veterans who probably remember the exchanges at the Greater and Lesser Redoubts emplaced above the Alma River.

33 Victoria *Gazette*, Aug. 24, 1859. Stevens landed and had a look around within days of Pickett's landing. While calling out the army was not something he had been prepared to do as governor—therefore it is doubtful that he counseled Harney to do it—he was nevertheless full of support for his old Mexican War comrades.

34 Macfie, *Vancouver Island and British Columbia*, pp.____

35 Victoria *Colonist*, Aug. 17, 1859, 40ᵗʰ Congress, 176-177.

36 Douglas to Baynes, Aug. 17, 1859, as quoted in Miller, *San Juan Archipelago*, p. 89.

37 Baynes to Admiralty, Aug. 19, 1859, San Juan Island NHP Archive (copy from BC Archives). Here again lies the disparity between Capt. Michael de Courcy's and Douglas's versions of when and for what purpose Magistrate John de Courcy received his commission. True, rumors of the landing were circulating throughout the Puget Sound and Strait of Juan de Fuca, as evidenced by the newspaper articles. But Douglas was genuinely floored by the information that came to him from John de Courcy via *Satellite* on July 28.

38 Ibid. In the 19ᵗʰ century filibusters were armed adventurers attempting to foment revolution in foreign countries, mainly Latin America. The most famous was William Walker, another Tennessean, who in 1856 took over the government of Nicaragua, introduced slavery and was formerly recognized by U.S. President Franklin Pierce. He was deposed and deported back to the United

States but twice returned. His career came to an end in 1860 when the Royal Navy captured him in Honduras, and handed him over to Honduran officials, who executed him by firing squad.

39 Newcastle to Douglas, Sept. 20, 1859, as quoted in Miller, *San Juan Archipelago*, p. 95.

Henry Pelham-Clinton (1811-1864), was the 5th Duke of Newcastle under Lyme. In addition to serving as Secretary of State for he Colonies, 1859-1864, he was also was Secretary of State for War. He resigned that office in 1855 in protest over the Crimean War.

40 Harney to Douglas, Aug. 24, 1859, *40th Congress*, pp. 171-172.

41 Harney to Cooper, Aug. 29, 1859, ibid, pp, 177-178; and Miller, *San Juan Archipelago*, p. 101. Harney mistakenly referred to the body of water around the San Juan Islands as Puget Sound. Actually several bodies of water surround the island, including the Haro, Rosario, Georgia and Juan de Fuca straits, collectively known as the "Salish Sea" by anthropologists. Puget Sound begins at Admiralty Inlet near Port Townsend, about 20 miles southeast of San Juan Island. Harney's comments about the HBC's treatment of native populations seem hypocritical, especially when one considers that his central strategy in the Brule Sioux War was attacking winter encampments occupied by women and children.

42 Harney to Cooper, Aug. 30, 1859, ibid., p. 179. This reference may have been to Cronstadt, or Kronstadt, was a Russian fortress city near St. Petersburg that the British unsuccessfully shelled during the Crimean War in 1855.

43 For more on William Moore, see Chapter 14, n. 25. Mistrust of the federal government remains a constant to this day among some San Juan Islanders as attested by 2010-2011 controversies over non-native species management and federal law enforcement.

44 McDonald, "A Few Items from the West," *Washington Historical Quarterly*, July 1917.

CHAPTER 13 - WASHINGTON AND LONDON

1   Kendall, *The Panama Route*, pp. 179-199

2   Drinkard to Harney, Sept. 3, 1859, 40th *Congress*, pp. 148-149.

The 1850s U.S. steam frigates were notoriously underpowered. The most famous of these was the USS *Merrimack*. The U.S. Navy also added several new classes of steam sloops of war in the 1850s armed with heavy Dahlgren guns, but the Royal Navy outclassed the U.S. Navy in almost every department.

3   Lyons to Cass, Sept. 3, 1859, FO *Abstract*, pp. 159-160.

4   Ibid., p. 160.

5   Lyons to Cass, Sept. 7, 1859, *40th Congress*, pp. 225-226.

6   Cass to Lyons, Sept. 9, 1859, ibid., pp. 226-227.

7   Russell to Lyons, Aug. 24, 1859, FO *Abstract*, p. 153.

8   Russell to Lyons, Sept. 22, 1859, ibid., p.161.

9   Lyons to Russell, Sept. 12, 1858 and Sept. 13, 1859, ibid., pp. 169-174. According to Hunter Miller, this passage appears in the original letters, but was omitted in the version sent to the U.S. Government Printing Office for inclusion in the Congressional Record. Hawkins left Victoria again on the 8th, catching a mail packet from San Francisco on the 20th. He arrived in New York on Sept.12 and Washington D.C., the next day where he reported to Lyons and also met with Cass. He left for London on the 14th and arrived there on the 23rd.

10 Lyons to Russell, Sept. 13, 1859, ibid., pp. 172-174.

11 Russell to Lyons, Sept. 26, 1859, ibid., p. 174

12 Drinkard to Scott, Sept. 16, 1859, 40th Congress, pp. 160-161.

13 Lay was an asset to Scott during the San Juan crisis, as the smooth Virginian established amicable relations with Douglas. He resigned his commission and joined the Confederacy in 1861, serving obscurely in an administrative capacity. Thomas had been Scott's chief of staff since 1853. During the Civil War he served for a time as adjutant general for the Army of the Potomac, but ran afoul of Secretary of War Edwin Stanton and was banished to the West to organize Negro regiments. After the war President Andrew Johnson, who also had good reason to despise Stanton, made Thomas Acting Secretary of War. Thomas testified in the president's behalf during Johnson's impeachment proceedings.

This is the same *Star of the West* that in January 1861 was fired upon while attempting to re-provision Fort Sumter.

14 Lyons to Russell, Sept. 15, 1859, FO *Abstract*, p. 175. In regards to Cass's secrecy, Lyons wrote: "The Secretary of State told me, both yesterday and to-day and he had received no further intelligence respecting the occurrences at San Juan. Despatches as late a date as the 12th instant must, however, in all probability have reached the war department from General Harney; and it is possible that alarming information contained in them respecting the intentions or disposition of the writer may have led to General Scott's being sent to supersede him."

15 Lyons to Cass, Oct. 1, 1859, *40th Congress*, pp. 228-229.

16 Cass to Lyons, Oct. 22, 1859, ibid., pp. 230-231.

CHAPTER 14 - STAND DOWN

1   As quoted in Eisenhower, *Agent of Destiny*, p. 198. John S.D. Eisenhower's 1997 work is a good source of information on Scott. Edward Mansfield's *Life and Services of General Winfield Scott*, written to coincide with Scott's presidential candidacy in 1852, is another good secondary source. Most of the background on Scott in this work is drawn from both books.

In the Buffalo-Niagara Falls incident in late 1837, Canadian reformers who called themselves "Patriots" decided on armed revolt to throw the British out of Canada. Americans south of the line—led by "General" Rensselaer Van Rensselaer, son of the War of 1812 general—provided money and weapons. When British authorities exerted pressure, the Patriots and their American allies steamed over to Navy Island, north of the line, and issued their own declaration of "independence" of Canada from Britain. Loyal Canadians responded by assaulting the island, capturing the steamer, setting it afire and sending it over Niagara Falls. Unfortunately, an American was killed in the fracas, which prompted an eruption of war fever, never mind the Canadian protest that the steamer was little more than a "pirate ship." With the country mired in a financial crisis, the last thing Pres. Martin Van Buren needed was war with Great Britain. Scott quickly restored calm and disbanded Van Rensselaer's tin-pot military force, but his efforts were nearly unhinged when the British mistakenly set fire to a ship that had recently been placed in the service of the United States.

The Aroostook War was another loose end in the Treaty of Ghent. The area of contention was a forest in which locals from both nations claimed harvest rights. The crisis erupted when respective local posses sent to apprehend "timber poachers" collided, each side capturing a man, with the Americans bagging the Royal Warden of the Canadian province. Reinforcements were called in and Van Buren once again ordered Scott to do all he could to avoid an "untoward mistake." Scott replied: "Mr. President, if you want war I need only look on in silence. The Maine people will make it for you fast and hot enough. But if peace be your wish, I can give no assurance of success. The difficulties in the way will be formidable." The people of Maine assumed Scott came to fight, but were soon disappointed. Scott convinced both governments to return their prisoners and revert to the status quo, but no Maine politician would go along with the agreement for fear of alienating his constituency. That's when Scott waded in, stroking and cajoling, convincing all parties to let him handle it and offering to take the blame if any were to be assigned. He then took advantage of his friendship with the British Maj. Gen. Sir John Harvey, the British lieutenant general who had opposed him during the War of 1812. The two came to an amicable settlement and the crisis and war had been averted.

2   Thomas to Cooper, Oct. 22, 1859, *40th Congress*, pp. 188-189.

3   Harney to Scott, Sept. 14, 1859, ibid, pp. 181-182. All of these observations were partially true, but they actually applied to the early years of white settlement when the Royal Navy called intermittently and Douglas was enforcing his "forest diplomacy" against Indian villages harboring raiders. The *Beaver* and *Otter* were not effective during Sheriff Barnes's sheep raid, or against the onslaught of American miners during the Fraser River gold rush. Those days were gone. The Royal Navy's Pacific Station squadron protected British interests and Harney knew it. Harney could have refuted Douglas' remarks by pointing to the recently expired HBC charter to colonize Vancouver Island; to Douglas' long executive tenure with the company, which only ended that spring when he became governor of British Columbia as well as Vancouver Island; and to the fact that A.G Dallas, his son-in-law, was a governor and major power with the company.

4   Harney to Floyd, Oct. 10, 1859; and Campbell to Harney, Aug. 14, 1859, ibid, pp. 184-188.

5   Gholson to Cass, as quoted in Miller, *San Juan Archipelago*, p. 112. Gholson wrote, "...thus declining to give me an opportunity to comply with my instructions 'to cooperate with' him, and also the benefit of whatever information my official position, and residence in the Territory had enabled me to acquire."

6   *Daily Alta California*, Nov. 23, 1859, typewritten copy, San Juan Island NHP Archive.

7   Ibid.

8   Peck, *The Pig War*, p. 103-11, 138.

9   *Daily Alta California*, Nov. 23, 1859.

10 Ibid.

11 Ibid, p. On October 31, Peck reported that the command was drilled in preparation for the ceremony, under the direction of "... his Royal Highness Major Haller, who takes much pride and pleasure in the pomp and circumstance of war, albeit, he has been court martialed for cruelty to enlisted men within the last twelve months."

12 The photographs are in the collections of San Juan Island NHP, the Provincial Archives in Victoria, B.C., and the Whatcom Museum of History and Art in Bellingham, WA. Photos of the camp, including a photomural of the artillery men, were on view in the American Camp visitor center in 2012.

13 *Daily Alta California*, Nov. 23, 1859.

14 Douglas to Scott, Oct. 29, 1859, *40ᵗʰ Congress*, pp. 193-194.

15 Harney to Scott, Oct. 29, 1859 with enclosure, ibid, pp. 190-191.

16 Scott to Douglas, Nov. 2, 1859, ibid, pp. 194-195.

17 Ibid, p. 196.

18 Miller, *San Juan Archipelago*, p. 114.

19 Douglas to Scott, Nov. 3, 1859, *40th Congress*, pp. 196-197. This conformed to the old HBC charter that discouraged expansion that would require the company to pay for the maintenance of troops (See Chapter 5). On the other hand, Douglas also had insisted heretofore that San Juan Island was a sovereign dependency of the Vancouver Island colony.

20 Scott to Douglas, Nov. 5, 1859, ibid, pp. 197-198.

21 Peck, *The Pig War*, p. 138.

22 Lay to Douglas, Nov. 7, 1859, as quoted in Miller, *San Juan Archipelago*, pp. 115-116.

23 Young to Scott, Nov. 7, 1959, ibid, pp. 116-117. This letter and Lay's (above) are not included in the official correspondence relating to the matter in the 40th Congress. Moreover, a postscript concerning Pickett's removal was added to Scott's letter of the 5th for official purposes and Thomas's order removing all reinforcements from the island also was backdated to the 5th.

24 Hunt to McBlair, date unknown, ibid, p. 20.

25 Casey to Young, Nov. 21, 1859, p. 205; Crosbie to Gholson, Nov. 30, 1859, p. 205-206; and Douglas to Scott, Nov. 7, 1859, with enclosures, pp. 199-200, 40th Congress. Moore, who claimed to be a British subject, contended he was unjustly punished for selling liquor. Magistrate Crosbie arrested him on September 16 for selling a bottle of rum to a soldier named "Crow." Moore claimed he never sold liquor to any soldier, but was judged guilty, deprived of his purse, which contained $160 in cash, and thrown into a tent jail with seven miscreant soldiers. He was ordered to work the next morning with the others on the redoubt, which in-

volved "rolling stones and shoveling earth." Late in the afternoon the constable, none other than Lyman Cutlar, took him from his duties and brought him before Crosbie again. Cutlar removed $75 from Moore's purse, which Crosbie pronounced as Moore's fine. Moore was then released. According to Crosbie, Moore had been "sick and destitute" in Whatcom and cared for at the public expense of $300 not 16 months before. At that time he claimed American citizenship. Back on his feet again Moore had, in fact, sold large quantities of liquor to all persons on the island, Crosbie wrote. The matter was dropped.

26 Thomas to Harney, Nov. 9, 1859, ibid, pp. 202-203. Thomas's letter arrived with enclosures including Scott's November 5 and 9 letters to Scott establishing that no U.S. territorial official would interfere with British subjects nor claim exclusive jurisdiction over the island until the boundary dispute was settled. Miscreant British subjects were to be turned over to British authorities and vice versa. The other enclosure was the order sending Casey's reinforcements back to Forts Bellingham, Townsend and Steilacoom and replacing Pickett with Hunt.

27 *Pioneer and Democrat*, Dec. 2, 1859.

28 Tacoma Public Library, *Northwest Ships & Shipping Database*. Scott was lucky to make it. The *Northerner*, a twelve-year-old side-wheeler, was wrecked two months later in a similar storm off northern California. Forty people were killed. Considered old and worn for her day, the *Northerner* had been on the San Francisco-Columbia River-Puget Sound route at irregular intervals for several years, most of the time in command of either William or Chris Dall. She left San Francisco on her last trip January 4 at 4:30 p.m., bound for the Columbia River and Puget Sound ports. At 4 p.m. the next day, when about two miles off shore, she struck Blunt's Reef near Cape Mendocino. The captain ran for shore and grounded the vessel on the reef, about 20 miles south of Hum-

boldt Bay. Passengers and crew died when lifeboats overturned in the heavy seas.

29 Scott to Harney, Nov. 15, 1859, *40ᵗʰ Congress*, p. 203.

30 Harney to Scott, Nov. 17, 1859, ibid, p. 204.

31 Peck, *The Pig War*, p. 140.

32 Throughout his army career, U.S. and Confederate, George Pickett could somehow find a reason to be absent from his post. Army leaves in those days could extend to six months or more. He also developed a talent for being appointed to court martial boards, which, because of the low quality of antebellum enlisted men, were assembled often. Court martials could only be called on the regimental level so that meant board members had to travel to the headquarters post. For the Ninth it was Fort Vancouver, even though, as with most frontier regiments, the companies were scattered throughout the territory. Pickett was a popular officer in the old army with lots of connections, which in the case of Fort Vancouver, included Rufus Ingalls, the regimental quartermaster, Alfred Pleasonton, the acting adjutant general, and, of course, William Harney himself. James Forsyth was usually in charge as in the case of the *Harney* wreck and the inspection visit in 1858 of Col. Joseph K. F. Mansfield. Forsyth was an extremely capable officer and this did not hurt his career.

33 Camp San Juan Island, Fort Bellingham letter books, RG 393, NA, San Juan Island NHP Archive.

34 Ibid.

CHAPTER 15 - PICKETT LANDS AGAIN

1   George E. Pickett to George E. Cullum, Feb. 19, 1860, as quoted in Longacre, *Pickett: Leader of the Charge*, pp. 48-49; Gordon, *Pickett*, p.p. 61-62; and RG94, NA, SAJHA. Pickett requested a court
of inquiry in September 1860 "to investigate his conduct while in
command at S.J.I., W.T." The request was forwarded by Department of Oregon commander Col. George Wright, but was never
acted upon. That Pickett should wonder why he was being censured
seems to further demonstrate his ignorance of issues of the day.

2   Resolution, Council of Washington Territory, Jan. 7, 1860,
40th *Congress*, pp. 207-208; and Gordon, *Pickett*, pp. 61-62.

3   LC Hunt to Mrs. McBlair, Nov. 24, 1859, as quoted in Murray, "Pig War Letters," *Columbia* 1:3, p. 17.

4   Hunt to McBlair, date unknown, ibid., p. 20.

5   As quoted in Miller, San Juan Archipelago, pp. 119-121.

6   Ibid., pp. 121-122.

7   Ibid., pp. 127-128.

8   Russell to Lyons, Oct. 6, 1859, FO *Abstract*, pp. 176-178.

9   FO14/414, Baynes to Douglas, March 2, 1860, Moody to
Douglas March 13, 1860.

10 Ibid., Baynes to Douglas, March 2, 1860; Thompson, pp 199-
200. During the Pig War crisis, Hubbs, as deputy collector of
customs, had insisted that British officials pay customs duties on
personal baggage brought ashore. As they were to do time and
again during the joint occupation, U.S. military officials intervened on the British behalf.

11 NA Canada, FO5/815, Baynes to Douglas March 17 & 19, as

quoted in Thompson, p. 200; and Wood, pp. 114-115, RG76, NA, *Geographical Memoir*, pp.115-116. Roche was probably more familiar with the San Juan Islands than any other British officer. He was a midshipman aboard HMS *Herald* in 1846 47 during surveys of the Strait of Juan de Fuca by Capt. Henry Kellett. He also served with Kellett in 1852 during the search for Admiral Sir John Franklin's lost arctic expedition. William J. Warren, secretary of the U.S. Northwest Boundary Commission camped at the site fitting this description on Feb. 7, 1860. His journal describes ruins of an "old lodge House" that had been about 500 to 600 feet long and 50 to 60 feet wide. He reports "immense quantities of clam shells on the shore." Archaeologist Dr. Julie Stein of the University of Washington has suggested that the structure may not have been a ruin as such, but a winter dwelling belonging to Coast Salish Indian clans. It was common for the villagers to remove the planks and take them along to spring and summer food gathering areas. Dimension lumber even then was at a premium. If Dr. Stein's assumptions are correct, imagine the surprise of the original inhabitants when they returned to find red-coated infantry raking the shell midden and throwing up barracks. However, there is no known record of such an encounter. Warren's site could also be the immediately adjacent Mitchell Bay to the south, which also lies below the slope of Young Hill, according to Dr. Stein.

12 BC Archives, Richard Charles Mayne, *Journal kept in HMS Plumper, Feb. 17, 1857 — Dec. 31, 1860*, MS handwritten in bound volume, 1 inch thick, as quoted in Thompson, p. 98.

13 BC Archives Victoria *Gazette*, March 22, 1860, Parsons to Moody, March 23, 1860; and Young to Parsons, March 20, 1860. It is believed that Parsons later visited the campsite in mufti to complete the drawings that bear his signature.

14 FO14/414, Baynes to Admiralty, March 21, 1860.

15 Joy, W. Journals. Portsmouth City Museum, England, U. K., typed copy, SAJHA. Joy did not mention the lodge house ruin described by Warren.

16 FO14/414 Baynes to Admiralty March 28, 1860, Inc. #3 Instructions to Bazalgette.

17 Hunt to Pleasonton, with attachments, March 27, 1860, *40th Congress*, pp. 208-209.

18 Petition to Harney, March 7, 1860; Pleasonton to Hunt, March 21, 1860, *40th Congress*, p. 214-215.

19 Hunt to Pleasonton, with attachments, March 30, 1860, *40th Congress*, pp. 215-217; and Hunt to McBlair, date unknown, Murray, "Pig war Letters," *Columbia* 1:3, p. 20.

20 Pleasonton to Pickett, April 10, 1860, *40th Congress*, pp. 210-211,

21 Ironically, when Harney chose to become a peacemaker rather than a fighter in Missouri at the outset of the Civil War in 1861, he was fired and recalled to Washington City by the Lincoln administration. En route he endured the ignominy of being the first Union general officer captured by Confederate forces. While in Southern custody he was urged to follow his native Tennessee into secession. A staunch Unionist, Harney declined and was honorably released. But the encounter cast doubt on his loyalties and he sat out the war. He was recalled to duty in 1868 to help negotiate the end of the Red Cloud War.

22 Hunt to Scott, April 24, 1860, *40th Congress*, pp. 213-214.

23 Baynes to Admiralty, May 5, 1860, as quoted in Miller, San Juan Archipelago, p. 136.

24 Pickett to Pleasonton, May 21 and June 1, 1860, RG393, NA, SAJHA.

25 Ibid. Pickett's soldiers were Christopher Rosler, a native of

Germany and Patrick Beigen from Ireland. Rosler married Anna Pike, a Tsimshian (*Ts'msyan*) from Alaska with whom he had eight children. Beigen married Lucy Morris, a Haida, also from Alaska. Both soldiers claimed land under the Homestead Act when the boundary dispute was resolved. Some of their descendents still live on San Juan Island

26 Scott to Floyd, May 14, 1860, *40th Congress*, pp. 212-213.

27 As quoted in Miller, San Juan Archipelago, p. 122.

28 Lyons to Cass, June 6, 1860, *40th Congress*, pp.. 256-257.

29 NAGB, 30/22/34 ff. 130-33, Lyons to Russell, April 10, 1860; Miller, *San Juan Archipelago*, n. p 139; and Cooper to Harney, June 8, 1860, *40th Congress*, p. 213.

30 Wright would capably hold the post until he and his wife drowned in a shipwreck off the Pacific Coast in 1863.

31 Mariners of the period went "down Sound" from Olympia to Port Townsend...."up Sound" from Port Townsend to Olympia (or Shelton).

32 As quoted in Miller, *San Juan Archipelago*, p.140.

33 Pickett to Bazalgette, Sept. 8, 1860, SAJHA (copy from BC Archives).

CHAPTER 16 - JOINT OCCUPATION AND SETTLEMENT

1 Miller, *San Juan Archipelago*, pp. 142-144.

2 Russell to Lyons, Aug. 24, 1859, FO *Abstract*, pp. 147-156. Before offering arbitration in 1858, the British, however reluctantly, decided to wait for a report from Captain Richards aboard the *Plumper*. Many in the government still believed that San Juan

Island was vital to British interests. Richards reported to Prevost in November 1858 that both channels presented problems for sailing vessels, although Rosario tended to be best. Either channel was acceptable for steamers. Ships transiting for Nanaimo—a source for coal and spars—and the Fraser River would find the Haro easier going, he reported, while those going from Port Townsend north would find the Rosario preferable (as they do today). The San Juan Channel, while considerably narrower, offered safe passage for steamers. Next, in an intriguing opinion—at least for an Englishman—Edmund (later Lord) Hammond, the Permanent Undersecretary for Foreign Affairs in February 1858, opted for the Haro Strait as the "best navigable channel." Hammond was probably influenced by General Sir John Fox Burgoyne, who in 1856 wrote that the British should not insist on Rosario "if a decidedly more important one in width and depth be found." The Admiralty once again in March 1859 stated that giving up the islands was hardly critical so long as British shipping had free access to the channel selected. That's when Russell, as earlier noted, proposed the "Middle Channel." This was the compromise Russell proposed in August 1859 when, unbeknownst to him, the crisis was in full swing. And it was this proposal that was rejected by Secretary of State Lewis Cass in October. By then the issue was in such turmoil, so many toes had been trod upon, that the British considered it a point of honor to hold onto the islands.

Edward Henry Stanley was the 15th Earl of Derby

3   Lyons to Cass, Dec. 10, 1860, *40th Congress*, pp. 264-265.

4   Lyons to Russell, Feb. 18, 1861, as quoted in Miller, *San Juan Archipelago*, pp. 151-153.

5   Marryatt, Frederick. *A diary in America: with remarks on its institutions.* Part 2, Volume I, 1839.

6   NA RG567, Pickett to Mackall, Dec. 3, 1860; Bazalgette to

Pickett; Petition of S. Meyerbach to Commanders of U.S. and British forces; Colonist, Sept. 25, 28, 1860. Meyerbach, in his deposition taken in Whatcom, contended that Hoffmeister at first meeting had claimed the quarry for himself under U.S. pre-emption laws. It was only later that Bazalgette maintained that the land and mineral rights belonged to the Crown.

Lime was mined at several locations on the island during the joint occupation. The "San Juan Lime Company" was founded on the current site of Lime Kiln State Park (on the west side of the island) in 1860 by the firm of Cutlar, Newsome, and Gillette. Gillette sold his share to Augustus Hibbard in 1861, after which Hibbard bought out Cutlar and Newsome in 1864. Hibbard sold the company in 1865, then bought it back in 1868. A receipt for $10 for 20 barrels of lime appears in the camp letter book, signed by Lyman Cutlar (now an employee) and dated June 18, 1869. When a disgruntled employee shot Hibbard in 1870, the current American Camp commander, Captain J.T. Haskell, posted guards at the kiln until ordered to leave the kiln and their ownership to the civil courts.

Possibly the above enterprise spurred Meyerbach and Hubbs to do a little claim jumping.

7   RG393, NA, San Island letter books, SAJHA; NA RG393, San Island letter books, Pickett to Casey.

8   Johannsen, Robert, W. "The Secession Crisis and the Frontier: Washington Territory, 1860-1861," *Mississippi Valley Historical Review*, Vol. 39, No. 3, (Dec., 1952), p. 427-429.

9   OR, 455-456, 464.

10   OR, 509-523.

11   Johannsen, *Mississippi*, p.430-435.

12 Oregon Historical Society, Pickett to Alvord, Feb. 13, 1861.

13 Bagstraw, Robert L., editor. *No Better Land: The 1860 Diaries of the Anglican Bishop George Hills.* Victoria, British Columbia: Sono Nis Press, 1996. Feb 1-3, 1861. pp. 52-53. Hills characterized the U.S. officers' quarrel as a "feud."

14 OR, pp., 519-523. Archibald Campbell, the Northwest Boundary Survey commissioner for the United States, in an October 1861 letter to William Seward wrote that he was in Washington at the time of the announced closure of San Juan and immediately protested action to Winfield Scott. Scott, he claimed, on June 21 ordered Sumner to reverse the decision. They must have used the Pony Express. NA, RG 76, NW Boundary Survey, Campbell to Seward, Oct. 3, 1861.

15 NA Canada RG8 Series IIIB Vol 36

16 *Official Records, War of the Rebellion,* Vol. L., Pt. I. , BC. Pickett is not listed on the passenger manifest of the *Sonora,* which sailed from San Francisco to Panama on August 10, 1861. But the manifest does list Sam Barron, a young naval officer and Pickett associate, whom LaSalle wrote traveled east with George. The manifest also lists Edward Eldridge, a close friend from Pickett's Whatcom years who in photographs bears a strong resemblance to the Virginian. Eldridge later would look after the Whatcom County interests of Pickett's son, James, and rise to Pickett's defense after his death in 1875. The author gratefully acknowledges the work of Mr. George Stammerjohan, a historian for the State of California, who found the *Sonora's* manifest while researching ship movements in San Francisco.

17 Arriving in Virginia in September 1861, Pickett was behind his peers in acquiring a general officer's billet. But he was well connected and by January 1862 he was brigadier general. He fought his brigade in three actions before taking a bullet in the

shoulder during the Battle of Gaines Mill in 1862. He was promoted to major general and given a division in September 1862.
His first real fight with his division was at Gettysburg, where
it was destroyed through no fault of his own. There were some
Pig War connections during the Battle of Gettysburg. Brig. Gen.
Henry J. Hunt, brother of Lewis Cass Hunt, whom Pickett replaced on San Juan only three years before, directed the cannon-
ade directed by the Union artillery on the battle's third day. The
Union cavalry that thwarted Maj. Gen. Jeb Stuart's attempt to fall
on the Union rear was under the command of Maj. Gen. Alfred
Pleasonton, the acting adjutant of the Department of Oregon who
drafted all of Harney's Pig War correspondence. Meanwhile, the
quartermaster of the Army of the Potomac was Brig. Gen. Rufus
Ingalls, Pickett's best friend and the former acting quartermaster
of the Department of Oregon. Brig. Gen. James J. Archer, CSA,
his fellow 9th Infantry company commander, was captured on the
battle's first day.

Pickett next appears in 1864, when he ordered 22 North Carolinians in Union uniform hanged as deserters following a failed
assault at New Berne. U. S. Army Brigadier General John Peck
sent Pickett a note claiming the men were Union soldiers and as
such should be treated as prisoners of war. Pickett thanked Peck
for the men's names, adding that he now knew precisely who to
hang. Pickett's Civil War career came to an inglorious end when
his division was overwhelmed and again destroyed at Five Forks.
After the war, he had to flee to Canada for several months when
Secretary of War Edwin Stanton wanted him tried for war crimes
for the North Carolina hangings. General Ulysses S. Grant, an
old army friend, interceded on his behalf and Pickett was allowed to return home. However, he could never return to the
army so he tried farming for awhile and eventually became an
insurance agent in the greater Richmond area. He worked dili-
gently to compile a division history until his death in July 1875

from an "abscess of the liver." He was only 50. He left LaSalle and their surviving son behind. His first son, James Tilton Pickett, remained in the Pacific Northwest where he worked as a newspaper illustrator. LaSalle deeded George's Bellingham property to James, but in the process stated that she and her son, George Junior, were the only legal heirs, essentially declaring James a bastard. This impression was quickly set right by Whatcom founders Henry Roeder and Edward Eldridge in a testimony filed a few days later. James died, childless, at 30 of typhoid fever. George E. Pickett, Jr., had two sons, George E. Pickett III and Christiancy Pickett, whose offspring live throughout the United States. Several Pickett descendents have visited San Juan Island over the years, with George E. Pickett III being the first in 1938.

18 Dougas to Newcastle, Dec. 28, 1861, CO, NAGB, 305/17. Newcastle replied to Douglas by confidential dispatch on March 14, 1862. While the Trent affair had been resolved amicably he thought "...the despatch may not be without interest as affecting the question of defence of that part of British North America."; Winks, Robin, *The Civil War Years: Canada and the United States.* Baltimore: Johns Hopkins Press, 1960, pp 157-161. The Colonial and Foreign offices at different times asked the British War Office for troops for Vancouver Island to guard British interests from an American squatter population estimated to be as high as 12,000. But both requests were denied.

19 Bagstraw, pp. 242-244

20 Port Townsend *Register,* June 27, 1860 and July 17, 1861; *Colonist,* May 26, 1866, as quoted in Thompson, p 104-106; Bazalgette and his "Jerry" took two out of three races the following July 4, a day in which "...the betting was lively, but for small amounts." As the San Juan Lime Company, on the north end of the island, was entertaining its employees, "several familiar faces were missing."

21 McDowell to Alvord, Sept. 18, 1864, as quoted in Miller, *San Juan Archipelago*, pp., 169-171. Former Army of Potomac commander McDowell stumbled from one disaster to another in northern Virginia and was finally sent West to replace George Wright who drowned in July 1865 when his ship sank off Cape Mendocino. A job without field duties was to McDowell's liking and complimented his abilities. He continued to serve on the Pacific Coast until his death in 1882 .

22 *40th Congress*, pp. 266-268, NA Canada RG8 Series IIIB Vol 36, Official Records; BC Archives, Bazalgette to Spencer, May 12, 1863.

23 NA, RG567, Bazalgette to Grey, Jan. 4, 1867, Grey to Bazalgette, Jan. 5, 1867

24 NA Canada, RG8, Series III B, Buckingham to Admiralty, March 22,1867; Halleck to Oldfield, Jan. 21, 1867, Pacific Station Records 1859-1872/; NA, RG567, Grey to Bazalgette, Dec. 29, 1866; NA RG617, Reel 1112/Post Returns for Camp Steele, March 1867. Throughout the American Civil War, British shipyards and brokers had been providing commerce raiders to the Confederate Navy, which decimated the U.S. merchant and whaling fleets. The most famous and successful of these was the CSS *Alabama*. The United States wanted restitution and Britain had thus far refused to pay. The issue became known as the "*Alabama* Claims" and was not settled until the Treaty of Washington of 1871.

The transcontinental telegraph to Washington Territory was completed in 1864, with first message sent by Governor William Pickering to President Abraham Lincoln on September 7,

25 ADM201/38, Deputy Adjutant to Admiralty, April 1, 1867; Admiralty to Deputy Adjutant April 8, 1867. Delacombe was permitted to bring his wife, nurse and four children. The fares for

the latter five were to be deducted from Delacombe's wages.

Globe and Laurel, 1898 edition. William Addis Delacombe was born 1833 in Devonshire, the son of General H. Ivatt Delacombe, R.M., and C.B. Delacombe was commissioned a second lieutenant in July 1850 at age 17. He served with the Baltic expedition during the Crimean War in 1854, as well as in North America and the West Indies. In 1864, he won national acclaim after being dispatched aboard the HMS *Bombay* to assist in protecting British interests in Montevideo while that city was under siege by insurgents. While on station the *Bombay* was attacked and blew up at sea, with 97 officers and men perishing, 34 of them Royal Marines who died at their posts. The ship's survivors were celebrated by Parliament on their return. After the ceremony, Delacombe astounded Londoners by marching his men through the streets on their way to the barracks at Woolwich, the detachment clad in a mixture of Spanish, French, and Italian uniforms given them by ships from those nations also stationed off Montevideo. Delacombe was rewarded in 1875 when, on being promoted to major, his commission was backdated to 1864 by order of the Horse Guards (Army command). Superiors also recognized his service at San Juan from 1867 to 1872 with numerous public plaudits, but a recommendation for promotion and a nomination for the order of St. Michael and St. George were not confirmed. He retired a lieutenant colonel in May 1876 and was shortly thereafter appointed chief constable of Derby from 27 applicants. He retired from the force in 1898 and died in August 1902 at his home in West Kensington 64.

26 NAC, April 21, 1870 Haskell to Delacombe; April 28, 1870, Delacombe to Haskell; May 11, 1870, McKenzie to Farquhar; May 15, 1870, Delacombe to Farquhar; May 19, 1870, Farquhar to McKenzie, copy Delacombe; June 20, 1870, Delacombe to Farquhar; June 24, 1870, Delacombe to Farquhar; November 7, 1870, Testimonial to Admiral Farquhar. McKenzie had friends among

U.S. citizens, as well as British subjects, on the island, as a petition was circulated attesting to his good citizenship. About a third of these also sign a petition that lauded the character of Delacombe and requested that he remain to protect their interests immediately following the boundary settlement. See Addenda.

27 James, *The Rise and Fall of the British Empire*, pp. 172-173. James writes that dividends on British foreign investments rose from £5 million in 1830 to £50 million in 1870.

28 McCabe, *San Juan Water Boundary Question*, p. 10. Bancroft was the U.S. ambassador to Great Britain during the Polk Administration and was a key player in the Treaty of Oregon negotiations. McCabe writes that Bancroft had opposed the proposal of the Swiss Federation as arbiter in 1869, and was adamant that the "Middle Channel" not be considered as a compromise.

29 Miller, *Northwest Water Boundary*, pp. 31-67.

30 Ibid., pp. 31-67.

31 ADM 201/38 159796 *San Juan Papers*. Documents connected with evacuation of San Juan Island by and return to England of the Detachment recently stationed at that island.

ADDENDUM I

MILITARY POST, SAN JUAN ISLAND

Washington Territory,

July 27, 1859, San Juan Island

I. In compliance with orders and instructions from the general commanding, a military post will be established on this island, on whatever site the commanding officer may select.

II. All the inhabitants of the island are requested to report at once to the commanding officer in case of any incursion of the northern Indians, so that he may take such steps are necessary to prevent any further occurrence of the same.

III. This being United States territory, no laws other than those of the United States, nor courts, except such as they are held by virtue of said laws, will be recognized or allowed on this island.

By order of Captain Pickett:

JAMES W. FORSYTH

Second Lieut., 9th Infantry,
Post Adjutant

ADDENDUM II

U.S.C.S. Steamer Active

Victoria, V.I., Aug. 8, 1859

Dear Sir:

We arrived here on Friday last somewhat sooner than I intended having been driven out of Port Orford (I.) and hurried up the coat by a strong southerly gale.

Our anchor was hardly down before information reaches us that general Harney had landed troops on San Juan island, which is a portion of the disputed territory, causing thereby the most intense excitement among English officials, as well as the residents generally.

After a short interview with the Governor (2.), who informed me that he should most certainly land troops on San Juan Island, I repaired thither and had a conference with Captain Pickett at his camp. It appears that since his landing the British officials have done everything in their power, without proceeding to positive force, to get him off the island, or to get a footing there themselves. He has resisted every attempt thus far, and assures me that if they land any force he will open fire upon them.

Feeling satisfied that that was his fixed determination, and knowing the overwhelming force that the British could, and I had every reason to suppose would, bring against him, I returned at once to this place and in an interview with the Governor explained to him how inevitable a collision would follow his landing of troops on the island under existing circumstances. The Governor in reply said that it was his duty, that he had orders to extend British rule over the islands and that he should do it, that captain Hornby of H.B.M. Frigate Tribune, then lying at San Juan, had his orders and would execute them. But as we were expecting dispatches from General Harney and to gain time, I asked what captain Hornby's orders were and if he was ordered to land why he didn't? In reply to this the Governor said that if the Magistrate called upon Captain Hornby for assistance in the proper execution of the laws he would land.

"Then," said I, "there must be a collision, for Captain Pickett will not permit it."

"What," said his Excellency," Captain Pickett has only about fifty men? Would he fire upon six hundred?"

"Yes," said I, "six thousand."

"Oh!" said Captain Richards, R.N. (3.), who was present, "that would be madness."

"Call it anything you like," I replied, "madness or anything else. Captain Pickett has made up his mind to do it and I pledge you upon my honor he will, if he should be (to use a rather inelegant expression, but one very much to the purpose) 'wiped out' the next moment."

After many more expressions of incredulity on their part, upon that head, and as often repeated asseverations on mine, I left, not however without intimation from the Governor that nothing would be done before we could hear from General Harney.

The opportune arrival of the British admiral a day or two since will I trust avert so great a calamity as a collision between us.

I ought to mention that the Governor remarked in the interview referred to above, that while the white men were at peace it was just as much as they could do to keep back the savages, but if war should ensue between us, their depredations would be most frightful.

In reply to which I remarked that our army of volunteers would take care of them, a specimen of which (volunteers I mean), he the Governor, had seen poured into this town, to the amount of some twenty-five thousand, during the few months of the Frazer River (4.) gold excitement last season, a circumstance that he will not soon forget, for if I am informed rightly, the authorities here had serious apprehensions that they should be overrun by Yankees and that their sway would be incontinently swallowed up.

I shall return immediately to San Juan Island and without stopping to discuss the merits of the case, I shall afford all aid and comfort in my power to our troops and cooperate with them till quiet is in some measure restored. That done, I shall resume the hydrographic duties of the survey of the Strait of Georgia.

Please communicate the contents of this letter to the Navy Department, and believe me, with

Great Respect

Your Obt. Servt /s/

James Alden (5.)
Com., U.S.N. Assist, U.S.C.S.

Prof. A.D. Bache (5.)
Supt. Dt. U.S. Coast Survey

Washington DC

ADDENDUM III

Dear Pleasonton,

I have but one moment to say to you I am here with my command.

It was very well that I was so quick. The Satellite got in the day after (we arrived after dark in the Massachusetts). She brought a British stipendiary magistrate who came over this morning an (sic) officially informed me that he wished to know by what authority I was here? I informed him that I did not recognize his authority to make any such demand, that I was on American soil – if he had authority from any higher power to show it and to make his communication in writing – but at the same time I had no hesitation in proclaiming to him as to any other individual. I was here to protect the right of American citizens and that the only laws which would be acknowledged here would be those of the United States. I then called up Crosbie, justice of the peace of Whatcom County and pitted them. They had a terrible time. Crosbie put it to him beautifully. Dog eat dog. This Mr. (he calls himself Major) De Courcy is I think a man of some education but a little of the snobbishness inevitable with Englishmen. Now, my dear old fellow I must say there has been a very great want of courtesy exhibited towards us by these Bulls. You know that I am a peaceable man but we cannot stand everything.

I am perfectly willing to meet them half way, but do not feel inclined to yield one jot nor do I intend to. The Victoria papers this morning are pretty severe. The *Julia* is just in from that Port. There is a rumor that they will send a force to reoccupy the island as a matter of course. I will prevent anything of the kind if they attempt it. Some twenty more American citizens have come over to locate on the island. Mr. Campbell happened to be here on the *Shubrick* the evening we arrived and he and Mr. West, in command, have been most kind in assisting us in every way – our boat having been stove in transporting our freight.

Please my dear amigo mio tell me anything – entre nous – that you think ought to be done. But rest assured that everything will be conducted properly – or I will go under. Will you be kind enough to suggest to the General the necessity of a Post Office here, we must have regular communication with you, and the *Julia* which takes the mails to Bellingham Bay, will of course be our best chance. Scranton(???) will be all right I think and it may be of some importance to communicate *vitement*.

By the way, is it not proper for officers commanding a foreign ship of war when he enters a port where there is a military post to communicate with the commanding officer of said post and then, if necessary, the required salute, gun for gun, be fired? The *Satellite* came in and took no notice of my camp. I met Capt. Prevost on the *Shubrick*. Mr. Campbell had told him previously that he had not acted courteously toward me – he was surprised and I rather think we will not have any difficulty unless it comes to the hard knocks.

There is a tremendous excitement at Victoria among the English, you will see by the papers they call us "Filibusters."

Excuse this write with some troln(???) by people about me, and constantly calling on me for information.

Yours truly,
George
(noted on cover sheet)

This communication was received from Capt. Geo. E. Pickett of the 9th Infantry in an official enclosure with another communication, dated July 27, 1859.

A Pleasonton
Capt., 2nd Dragoons
Acting Adjutant

Dear Alfred:

What a miserable subterfuge of Gov. Douglas—when he says no <u>British ship of war</u> came to San Juan?

The intention was to <u>intimidate</u> and they afterwards clearly carried out that intention by sending a British official viz. A stipendiary magistrate who summoned a posse and made three or more attempts to take up an American citizen, Cutler (sic). Had I not been on the Island the probability is they would have tried him (if he would have submitted and if not there would have been bloodshed by or a row) and sent him *in durance vile* to Victoria as there is no jail here.

Doubtless such would have been the upshot of the business – so the Gov.'s reasoning is most falicious (sic). I tell you this old fellow merely to show you that we are right, tho' we all knew it before. It only makes our case stronger.

(noted on cover)

(Geo. Pickett author)

An official enclosure with another publication Aug. 31, 1859.

A Pleasonton

ADDENDUM IV

VICTORIA V.I. BRITISH COLUMBIA

11TH NOVEMBER 1867

William G. Smith, Esquire
Secretary

Sir

1.   We have now the honor of addressing you on the subject of the losses sustained by the Company at the Island of San Juan since its occupation by use, through damage by State or Federal Acts.

2.   Until the occupation of San Juan Island by the Military Forces of the United States in 1859, the whole island was in the possession of the Hudson's Bay Company and was pastured by their flocks of sheep and herds of cattle, horses, and pigs. The Company also carried on farming operations there, having had in different localities farm buildings, inclosed fields, sheep stations a wharf and fisheries, particulars of several of which as they existed in 1859 is given below.

3.   The arrival of the Military, and of numerous American settlers following in their train, made it impracticable for the Company to continue in

the operation for their live stock was dispossessed
and deprived of their usual range. The Military
and those who supplied them, imported Beef
Cattle which were herded on the open lands, and
the settlers squatted upon the lands inclosed and
unenclosed, taking possession thereof and of the
buildings. These aggressions may be considered as
consequent on the act of the Federal Government
in placing troops on the Island etc and testimony
in proof of the same can, if needed, we believe
obtained.

4.   Thus, interfered with the Company operations
had to be gradually discontinued, and their livestock
reduced and ultimately withdrawn.

5.   In 1858 & 59 the Company owned, and
occupied the following amongst other buildings and
improvements in the localities now known as

1st   Stubbs Point viz.
> A Fishing Station having thereupon a
> large log building, and strong Cattle
> Pens for shipping stock.

2nd   Main Station or "Bellevue Farm"
> Consisting of several squared log
> dwelling houses, a Granary, large Barn,
> and enclosed fields, etc. The United
> States Military Post is built on part of
> this Station. A portion of it is leased to
> an old employee of the Company, named
> Robert Firth, for a minimal rent, in
> order to retain possession.

3rd "Frasers Farm" viz.
          Sheep Station, Pens, etc.

4th "Droyen   do."   "
          Log dwelling House, Garden and Pens,
          enclosed fields.

5th "Blakes   do."   "
          Log House and Pens

6th "Longacres do."   "
          Two Log Houses   "   do.

7th "Chandlers Prairie" "
          Dwelling house   "   do.

8th "New Station"   "
          Do.   "   do.

9th "Limestone Station" "
          Sheep pens

10th "John Bull do."
          Dwelling house and sheep pen also a
          cultivated field.

On the Main Station, Dwyon Farms, and Bulls
Station land was cultivated by the Company, and the
Stations as a whole gave complete command of all
the pastures on the Island.

6. In paragraph 4 of Mr Dallas's letter of 20th
February 1860 to Mr Secretary Fraser to which we
would beg to draw particular attention, the balance
of Account against the San Juan Establishment as on
31st May 1859, say for Outfits 1854 to 1858 inclusive—
is stated at £6633.15/5 besides the least of many

services of steamers etc., rendered to the Island, but for which no charge has ever been made. We now beg to inclose an abstract Statement of the Account thus referred to, exhibiting apart from the Steamboat – and other service rendered as above mentioned, the Company's Outlay in Establishing and stocking the Farms etc., on the Island, after crediting proceeds or Returns there from each year, and to be regarded as expenses incurred by the Company, with the other uncharged items aforementioned up to that time, in retaining possession of San Juan Island, as a dependency of Vancouver Island. It amounts to £6633 " 15 " 5 exclusive of interest, which at 5% per annum come to £3920 " 1 " 20 making all a sum of £10553 " 16 " 7 as shown in the statements.

7.   The above includes a sum of £1450 13/" transferred in Outfit 1855 to the debit of the United States Government for that Outfit on account of loss sustained, as shown by the Accounts that year transmitted to London – with £870 " 7 " 10 Interest thereon at 5% per annum for the (12) twelve years from 1855 to 1867, being together £2321 " 0 " 10 and which we presume is still unpaid in London. In this connexion we beg to refer to Chief Trader Douglas' letter of 28ᵗʰ September 1855 to the Secretary, on the subject of the losses inflicted on the Company by the unlawful proceedings on San Juan Island of certain American citizens, residing in Washington Territory, and pretending to act under authority of its laws. The damages in consequences as claimed against the United States amounted to £2990 " 13/ " and were by Mr. Douglas represented as a moderate

estimated of the losses sustained. The details of the same were set forth in a Report and Statement from Mr Griffin the Company's Officer in 1855 and till 1859 and subsequently in charge at San Juan.

We trust that the documents are to be found in the London Office, as we have not been able to find them here. Copy of Mr Douglas' letter therein referred to is enclosed.

8. This aggression which is clearly chargeable against the Territorial Government of Washington Territory is the first on record, although for some time prior to the year 1855, the Legislative Assembly of that Territory pretended to include the Aro Islands in the County of Whatcom, and San Juan is the principle of these. The next aggression recorded is the killing in June or July 1859 of a Boar Pig belonging to the Company at San Juan by a recently arrived Squatter there named Cutler, and this is also to be regarded as a consequence of the Territorial Act of claiming these Islands as United States Territory, although it was ostensibly the immediate cause of the Establishing of troops there by the U. S. General Harney.

9. We also enclose an abstract Statement of Account for Outfit 1859 to 1864 inclusive, showing by amount realized from the Sale of Stock etc. after deducting Wages and Interest as shown in the Statement:

$$£4247.8.2$$

@ 5% per annum   1147.5.6

$$£5394.13.8$$

The Company have now no stock on any part of the
Island. We have given the above mentioned Accounts
in separate Statements, and have calculated the
Interest in the particular manner, shown on the
documents, as being the most desirable course in
our ignorance of the present position of the case,
as well as of the manner in which the Governor and
Committee purpose dealing with it.

10. The particulars of the Accounts in the two
Statements will be found in the detailed Accounts
for the several Outfits in London.

I have the honor to be etc., etc., etc.

W. F. Tolmie

Note: The British government consistently rebuffed
all Hudson's Bay Company entreaties to be recom-
pensed for their efforts to entrench the Empire's
claim to the San Juan Islands.

*The abbreviation "do." is an archaic form of "ditto."

BIBLIOGRAPHY

STUDIES

Boswell, Sharon A. and Hudson, Lorelea. *Heritage Resources Investigations at the Limekiln Preserve*. San Juan County Land Bank, Friday Harbor, Washington, 2001.

Boxberger, Daniel L.. *San Juan Island Cultural Affiliation Study*. MMS, San Juan Island National Historical Park, Friday Harbor, Washington, 1993.

Floyd, Dale. *Comparative Analysis, American Camp Fortifications, San Juan Island National Historical Park*. Washington City: CEHP Incorporated, 1996

Lentz, Florence K. *Historic Furnishings Report: British Camp Hospital San Juan Island National Historical Park*. Seattle: Cultural Resource Division, Pacific Northwest Region, National park Service, Department of the Interior, 1990.

Pratt, Boyd. *Belle Vue Sheep Farm*. MMS. San Juan Island National Historical Park, Friday Harbor, Washington. 2003.

_____. *The Disputed Islands: Ordinary Life in Extraordinary Times, The San Juan Archipelago, 1850-1874*. MMS. Friday Harbor, Washington, 2008.

Sprague, Roderick, Ed. *San Juan Archaeology*. Bound MMS, two volumes. Moscow, ID: University of Idaho, 1983.

Thompson, Erwin N. *Historic Resource Study: San Juan Island National Historical Park, Washington*. Denver, CO: Denver Service Center, National Park Service, 1972.

Vouri, Michael P. *George Pickett and the Frontier Army Experience, Washington Territory 1854-1859*. MMS. San Juan Island National Historical Park, Friday Harbor, Washington. 1994.

_____.*Safe Passage: The Coast Survey Steamer Active and the Defense of Puget Sound*. MMS. San Juan Island National Historical Park, Friday Harbor, Washington. 2006.

_____. *Pig War Connections: George Pickett, James Alden, Jr., and the Officer Corps in Washington Territory on the Eve of the Civil War*. MMS. San Juan Island National Historical Park, 2009.

Wray, Jacilee. *The Salmon Bank: An Ethnohisoric Compilation*. San Juan Island National Historical Park, Friday Harbor, Washington. 2003.

MANUSCRIPTS

Haller, Granville O. *The San Juan Imbroglio*. Typewritten MMS, Bancroft Library, University of California, Berkeley. 1889.

Roder (Roeder), Henry. Dictation by Hubert H. Bancroft. Handwritten MMS, Bancroft Library, University of California, Berkeley. 1878.

Selcer, Richard E. *How Did George Pickett Really get Into West Point? Or The Making of Major General George E. Pickett, C.S.A.*, Unpublished manuscript in possession of the author.

Vouri, Michael P. *George Pickett and the Frontier Army Experience, Washington Territory 1854-1859*. MMS. San Juan Island National Historical Park Archives (SAJHA), Friday Harbor, Washington. 1994.

NEWSPAPERS

Friday Harbor, (Washington), *San Juan Islander*, 1909

London, (England), *Illustrated News*, 1859.

Olympia, (Washington), *Pioneer and Democrat*, 1855-59.

Seattle, (Washington), *Post-Intelligencer*, 1892

Victoria, (B.C.), *Colonist*, 1859-72.

Victoria (B.C.), *Gazette*, 1859.

DOCUMENTS

U.S. GOVERNMENT DOCUMENTS

NATIONAL ARCHIVES, WASHINGTON D. C. 20048.

RG23, MF642, Roll 208, p. 53, Alden to Bache, Aug. 8, 1859.

RG 92, Records of the Office of the Quartermaster General

RG 94, Records of the Office of the Adjutant General

E225, Consolidated Correspondence Files, San Juan Island, Box 985

RG 393, Records of the United States Army Continental Commands, 1821-1920

Post Records, San Juan Island, eight volumes.

Vol. 1: Letters Sent (Camp Pickett Only, August 1859–July 1861)

Vol. 2: Letters Sent (August 1863–July 1867)

Vol. 3: Letters Sent (October 1868–January1872)

Vol. 4: Letters Sent (August 1867–September 1868)

Vol. 5: Orders and Special Orders (August 1859–December 1861)

Vol. 6: General Orders, Special Orders (January 1861–September 1868)

Vol. 7A: Orders and Special Orders (1868-1874)

Records and Reclaims, Vol. 7 (History and Description of Post)

RG76, E198, Journals of Exploring Surveys. *Geographical Memoir of the Islands between the Continent and Vancouver Island in the Vicinity of the 49th Parallel of North Latitude*, SAJHA. Archibald Campbell with appendices by Dr. C.B.R. Kennerly, George Gibbs, Henry Custer and W.J. Warren. [The memoir, without the appendices, was published as part of the record of the 40th Congress. The appendices were hand-copied by Mr. Greg Lange and kindly provided to the author by Dr. Wayne Suttles].

Microfilm, M617, Returns from U.S. Military Posts, 1800-1916, Roll 1112, San Juan Island, Washington Territory.

Report of Col. Joseph K.F. Mansfield on the U.S. Military Reservation at Bellingham Bay, Washington Territory, Dec. 7-8, 1858.

NATIONAL ARCHIVES OF CANADA, OTTAWA, ONTARIO

RG8, Series II B, Microfilm, C-12616, Admiralty, Pacific Station Records 1859- 1872

MG12, 5-1475 -- ADM 1/6151, Records pertaining to San Juan Island

BRITISH COLUMBIA ARCHIVES

K/RS/Sa5 San Juan Island papers

WASHINGTON STATE ARCHIVES, NW REGION

3rd District Court, 1854-1873

NATIONAL ARCHIVES OF THE UNITED KINGDOM OF
GREAT BRITAIN

FO14/414 Correspondence Pertaining to San Juan Island

ADM38/3532 Mustering records from Her Majesty's Ships

ADM38/3532

ADM38/5647

ADM38/5649

ADM38/7120

ADM38/7211

ADM38/7428

ADM 157/271 Personnel files

ADM 157/475

ADM 157/ 483

ADM 201/38 Settlements: papers from nine overseas posts
1809-1878

ADM201/380

ADM 201/38 159796, San Juan papers

ADM12 Digests, 1855 – 1862, Vancouver's/San Juan island

ADM12/670

ADM12/686

ADM12/702

ADM 101/281

Journal of Her Majesty's Hospital Esquimalt,
Pacific Station, Edward L. Moss Surgeon, Between 1 January and
31 December, 1873

GOVERNMENT PUBLICATIONS

British Foreign Office. *San Juan Boundary: Abstract of Correspondence Relative to the Disputed Right of Territory Watered by the Oregon, or Columbia River. 1842 to 1869.* December 1871. (Marked "Confidential.") This document is essentially a narrative of correspondence and documents related to the issue compiled by the British Foreign Office.

National Park Service, Pacific West region. *Cultural Landscape Inventory, 2004, English and American Camps, San Juan Island National Historical Park.*

Official records of the Union and Confederate Navies in the War of the Rebellion. Series I - Volume 4: *Operations on the Atlantic Coast* (January 1, 1861– May 13, 1861).

The war of the rebellion: a compilation of the official records of the Union and Confederate armies. / Series 1 - Volume 50 (Part I), Series I, Vol 50, Part 1

U.S. Congress. Senate. Executive Document No. 10. 36th Cong., 1st. Sess. *The Northwest Boundary Discussion of the Water Boundary Question: Geographical Memoir of the Islands in Dispute: and History of the Military Occupation of San Juan Island.* Washington City: 1868.

U.S. Congress. Senate. Executive Document No. 29. 40th Cong., 2nd Sess. *Report of the Secretary of State.* Washington City: 1867-1868.

U.S. Navy Department, Office of the Chief of Naval Operations, Naval History Division. *Dictionary of American Naval Fighting Ships.* Washington City: GPO, 1969.

Fields, Virgil, F., ed., The National Guard, State of Washington, Collection of Official Documents on the San Juan Imbroglio, 1859-1872. (N.D., N.P.)

OTHER DOCUMENTS

The Globe and Laurel, 1898 edition (Journal of the Royal Marines)

Howard E. Buswell Collections, Center for Pacific Northwest Studies, Western Washington University, Bellingham, WA 98225. Buswell was a Bellingham historian, who compiled an extensive collection of pamphlets, photographs, maps, journals, historical reference works, newspapers, microfilms and audio-tapes. His primary interest was lower Nooksack Valley history.

Hudson's Bay Company Records, microfilm, *Post Journals, Belle Vue Sheep Farm, 1854-1855 and 1858-1862*. Hudson's Bay Company Archives, Winnipeg, Manitoba, Canada.

Joy, W., *Journals*. Portsmouth City Museum, England, United Kingdom. Copies housed in San Juan Island NHP Archive.

Robertson ,A. MacGregor, Captain, Royal Marines, Historian,. Royal Marines Barracks, Eastney, Southsea, Hants, England, letter to Terry Pettus, Seattle, WA, 9 January 1962. San Juan Island NHP Archive.

Roder, Henry, Capt. *Narrative*, dictation by Hubert Howe Bancroft, Port Townsend, Washington, June 22, 1878. H.H. Bancroft Collection, Bancroft Library, University of California, Berkeley, CA.

Views of the Pacific Northwest. Yale Collection of Western Americana, Bienecke rare Book and Manuscript Library, WA MSS S-1817, Box 6, Folder 32.

Whitlock, Charles. Correspondence 1859-1869, excerpts, RM Museum, Eastney Barracks, Southsea, Hampshire, England

San Juan island NHP Archive.

INTERNET

Northwest Ships & Shipping Database. Tacoma, WA: Tacoma Public Library. This database is available over the Internet.

BOOKS

Bagstraw, Roberta L., editor. *No Better Land: The 1860 Diaries of the Anglican Colonial Bishop George Hills*. Victoria, B.C.: Sono Nis Press, 1996.

Bancroft, Hubert Howe. *The Works of Hubert Howe Bancroft: History of the Pacific States of America* Volume XXVI, *History of Washington, Idaho, and Montana, 1845-1889*. San Francisco: The History Company, Publishers, 1890.

Bancroft, Hubert Howe. *The Works of Hubert Howe Bancroft: History of the Pacific States of North America*. Volume XXVII, *History of British Columbia, 1792-1887*. San Francisco: The History Company, Publishers. 1887.

Barkan, Francis B., ed. *The Wilkes Expedition Puget Sound and the Oregon Country*. Olympia, WA: Washington State Capital Museum, 1987.

Bemis, Samuel Flagg. *A Diplomatic History of the United States*. New York: Henry Holt and Company (3rd ed.), 1950.

Bennett, Robert A., ed. *A Small World of Our Own: Authentic pioneer stories of the Pacific Northwest from the Old Settlers' Contest of 1892*. Walla Walla, WA: Pioneer Press Books, 1985.

Billings, John David. *Hardtack and Coffee: Or the Unwritten Story of Army Life*. Williamstown, MA: Corner House Publishers, 1973.

Billington, Ray Allen. *Westward Expansion: A History of the American Frontier*. 3rd edition. New York: The Macmillan Company, 1967. Billington's thesis of the westward expansion remains the seminal work on the subject in the historiography of the American West. His view that the passage of Walker Tariff and the repeal of the Corn Laws sped the signing of the Oregon Treaty of 1846 is further underscored by fiscal realities. The British then, as now, were the largest foreign investors in the fledgling United States.

Blumberg, General Sir H.E., KOB. *History of the Royal Marines, 1837-1914*, Royal Marines Historical Society Archives Series, Vol. 3.

Clow, Richmond L. "William S. Harney." In Soldier's *West: Biographies from the Military Frontier*, edited by Paul Andrew Hutton. Lincoln, NE: University of Nebraska Press, 1987.

Coffman, Edward M. *The Old Army: A Portrait of the American Army in Peacetime, 1884-1898*. New York: Oxford University Press, 1986.

Cutter, Donald. "The Malaspina Expedition and Its Place in the History of the Pacific Northwest." Inglis, Robin, ed. *Spain and the North Pacific Coast: Essays in Recognition of the Bicentennial of the Malaspina Expedition, 1791-1792*. Vancouver, BC: Vancouver Maritime Museum, 1992.

Deutsch, Herman J., ed. *Surveying the 49th Parallel, 1858-61*. Tacoma, WA: Washington State Historical Society, 1962.

DeVoto, Bernard. *The Year of Decision 1846*. Boston: Houghton Mifflin Company, 1943.

Duncan, Janice K. *Minority without a Champion: Kanakas on the Pacific Coast, 1788-1850*, Portland, OR: Oregon Historical Society, 1972.

Eardly-Wilmot S., Lieutenant, ed., *Our Journal of the Pacific by the Officers of HMS Zealous*. London: Longmans, Green and Co. 1873.

Edgerton, Mrs. Fred, *Admiral of the Fleet, Sir Geoffrey Phipps Hornby*, Edinburgh, 1896.

Edson, Lelah Jackson. *The Fourth Corner*. Bellingham, WA: The Whatcom Museum of History and Art, 1968.

Eisenhower, John S.D. *Agent of Destiny: The Life and Times of General Winfield Scott*. New York: The Free Press, 1997.

_____. *So Far From God: The U.S. War with Mexico 1846-1848*. New York: Doubleday, 1989.

Elliot, Charles Winslow. *Winfield Scott: The Soldier and the Man.* New York: The MacMillan Company, 1937.

Faust, Patricia L., ed. *Historical Times Illustrated Encyclopedia of the Civil War.* New York: Harper & Row, 1986.

Fernandez-Armesto, Felipe. *Pathfinders: A Global History of Exploration.* New York: W.W. Norton & Company, 2006.

Foreman, Amanda. *A World In Fire: Britain's Crucuial Role in the American Civil War.* New York: Random House, 2010.

Frost, Alan. "Nootka Sound and the Beginnings of Britain's Imperialism of Free Trade." Fisher, Robin and Johnston, Hugh, Eds. *From Maps to Metaphors: The Pacific World of George Vancouver.* Vancouver, BC: UBC Press, 1993.

Gardiner, Robert, ed. *Steam, Steel & Shellfire: The Steam Warship 1815–1905.* London: Conway Marine Press, 1992.

Gardner, Alison F. *James Douglas.* Don Mills, Ontario: Fitzhenry & Whiteside, Ltd., 1976.

Gates, Charles Marvin, ed. "Report of Col. Joseph J.K. Mansfield on the U.S. military reservation at Port Townsend, Washington Territory, Dec. 3-4, 1858." *Readings in Pacific Northwest History, Washington 1790–1895,* Seattle, WA: University Bookstore, 1941.

Gibson, James R. *Otter Skins, Boston Ships and China Goods: The Maritime Fur Trade of the Northwest Coast, 1785–1841.* Seattle: University of Washington Press, 1992.

Goetzmann, William H., and Glyndwr Williams. *The Atlas of North American Exploration From the Norse Voyages to the Race to the Pole.* New York: Prentice Hall General Reference, 1992.

Goetzman, William H. *Army Exploration in the American West, 1803–1863.*

_____, *New Lands, New Men America and the Second Great Age of Discovery.* New York: Viking Penguin Inc., 1986.

Green, Frank L. *Captains, Curates and Cockneys: The English in the Pacific Northwest.* Tacoma, WA: Washington State Historical Society, 1981.

Austin: Texas State Historical Association, 1991.

Gordon, Leslie J., *Pickett: General George Pickett in Life & Legend.* Chapel Hill: University of North Carolina Press, 1998.

Gough, Barry M. *The Royal Navy and the Northwest Coast of North America, 1810-1914.* Vancouver: University of British Columbia Press, 1971.

_____. *Fortune's A River: The Collision of Empires in Northwest America.* Madeira Park, BC: Harbour Publishing, 2007.

Green, Frank L. *Captains, Curates and Cockneys: The English in the Pacific Northwest.* Tacoma, WA: Washington State Historical Society, 1981.

Haller, Granville, O. *San Juan and Secession.* Seattle: The Shorey Book Store, 1967.

Hart, Herbert M. *Pioneer Forts of the West.* Seattle: Superior Publishing Company, 1967.

Haycox, Stephen; Barnett, James K.; and Liburd, Caedmon A.., eds. *Enlightenment and Exploration in the North Pacific 1741-1805.* Seattle: University of Washington Press, 1997.

Heidler, David S., and Jeanne T. Heidler. *Old Hickory's War Andrew Jackson and the Quest for Empire.* Mechanicsburg, Pennsylvania: Stackpole Books, 1996

Higgins, D.W. *The Mystic Spring and Other Tales of Western Life.* Toronto: William Briggs, 1904.

Hill, J.R., ed. Oxford *Illustrated History of the Royal Navy.* Oxford: Oxford University Press, 1995.

Howay, Frederick, W. *British Columbia from the Earliest Times to the Present.* Vancouver: The S.J. Clarke Publishing Company, 1914.

Holmes, Richard. *Redcoat: The British Soldier in the Age of Horse and Musket.* New York: W.W. Norton & Company, 2001.

Hutchinson, Bruce. *The Struggle for the Border*. New York: Longmans, Green and Co., 1955.

James, Lawrence. *The Rise and Fall of the British Empire*. New York: St. Martin's Griffin, 1997.

Johansen, Dorothy O., and Charles M. Gates. *Empire of the Columbia: a History of the Pacific Northwest*. New York: Harper & Brothers, Publishers, 1957.

Josephy, Alvin M., Jr. *The Civil War in the American West*. New York: Vintage Books, 1991.

Johnson, Timothy D. *Winfield Scott: The Quest for Military Glory*. Lawrence, Kansas: University Press of Kansas, 1998.

Kaufman, Scott. *The Pig War: The United States, Britain, and the Balance of Power in the Pacific Northwest, 1846-1872*. New York: Lexington Books, 2004.

Kemble, John Haskell. *The Panama Route, 1848-1869*. Columbia, S.C.: University of South Carolina Press, 1990.

Lavender, David. *Land of Giants: The Drive to the Pacific Northwest, 1750-1950*. Garden City, New York: Doubleday & Company, Inc., 1958.

James, Lawrence. *The Rise and Fall of the British Empire*. New York: St. Martin's Griffin, 1994.

Longacre, Edward G. *Pickett: Leader of the Charge*. Shippensburg, PA: White Mane Publishing Company, Inc., 1995.

Macfie, Matthew. *Vancouver Island and British Columbia, their History, Resources and Prospects*. London: Longman, Green, 1865.

Mackie, Richard Somerset. *Trading Beyond the Mountains: The British Fur Trade on the Pacific 1793-1843*. Vancouver, B.C., Canada: University of British Columbia Press, 1997

McCabe, James O. *The San Juan Water Boundary Question*. Toronto: University of Toronto Press, 1965.

McDougall, Walter A. *Let The Sea Make A Noise: A History of the North Pacific from Magellan to MacArthur.* New York: Basic Books, A Division of Harper Collins Publishers, Inc., 1993.

Miller, David Hunter. *San Juan Archipelago: Study of the Joint Occupation of San Juan Island.* Belows Falls, VT: Wyndam Press, 1943.

_____. *Northwest Water Boundary, Report of the Experts Summoned by the German Emperor as Arbitrator Under Articles 34-42 of the Treaty of Washington of May 8, 1871, Preliminary to His Award dated October 21, 1872,* Seattle: University of Washington, 1942.

Milton, Viscount W. Fitzwilliam, M.P. *A History of the San Juan Water Boundary Question as affecting the Division of Territory Between Great Britain and the United States.* London: Cassell, Peter and Galpin, 1869.

Morgan, Murray. *Puget's Sound: A Narrative of Early Tacoma and the Southern Sound.* Seattle and London: University of Washington Press, 1979.

Morison, Samuel Eliot. *The European Discovery of America: The Southern Voyages, A.D. 1492-1616.* New York: Oxford University Press, 1974.

Mozino, Jose Mariano. *Noticias de Nutka: An Account of Nootka Sound in 1792.* Seattle and London: University of Washington Press, 1970.

Murray, Keith. *The Pig War.* Tacoma: Washington State Historical Society, 1968.

Nokes, J., Richard. *Columbia's River The Voyages of Robert Gray, 1787-1793.* Tacoma: Washington State Historical Society, 1991.

_____. *Almost a Hero: The Voyages of John Meares, R.N., to China, Hawaii and the Northwest Coast.* Pullman, WA: Washington State University Press, 1998.

Norman, Francis Martin. *"Martello Tower" in China and the Pacific in HMS Tribune 1856-60.* London: George Allen, 156, Charing Cross Road, 1902.

Peck, William A., Jr. (Coulter, C. Brewster and Webber, Bert, eds.). *The Pig War and other Experiences of William Peck, Soldier, 1858-1862,* edited by C. Brewster Coulter and Bert Webb. Medford, OR: Webb Research Group, 1993.

Pethick, Derek. *James Douglas: Servant of Two Empires*. Vancouver: Mitchell Press Limited, 1969.

Philbrick, Nathaniel. *Sea of Glory: America's Voyage of Discovery, The U.S. Exploring Expedition, 1838-1842*. New York: Viking, 2003.

Pickett, LaSalle Corbell. *Pickett and His Men*. Atlanta: Foote & Davis Company, 1889.

_____, ed. *The Heart of a Soldier as Revealed in the Intimate Letters of Genl. George E. Pickett, C.S.A.* New York: Seth Moyle, 1913.

Polk, James Knox. *Polk: Diary of a President, 1845-1849*, edited by Allan Nevins. New York: Longman's, Green and Co., 1929.

Richards, Kent D. *Isaac I. Stevens: Young Man in a Hurry*. Pullman, WA: Washington State University Press, 1993.

Richardson, David. *Pig War Islands*. Eastsound, WA: Orcas Publishing Company, 1971.

Roth, Lottie Roder, ed. *History of Whatcom County*. Vol. I. Seattle: Pioneer Historical Publishing Co., 1926.

Scott, James W., and Roland L. DeLorme. *Historical Atlas of Washington*. Norman, OK: University of Oklahoma Press, 1988.

Selcer, Richard F. *Faithfully and Forever Your Soldier: General George E. Pickett, CSA*. Gettysburg, PA: Farnsworth House Military Impressions, 1995.

Stanley, George, F.G., ed. *Mapping the Frontier: Charles Wilson's Diary of the Survey of the 49ᵗʰ Parallel, 1858-1862, While Secretary of the British Boundary Commission*. Toronto: Macmillan of Canada, 1970.

Stein, Julie K., *Exploring Coast Salish Prehistory: The Archaeology of San Juan Island*. Seattle: University of Washington Press, 2000.

Sterne, Netta. *Fraser Gold 1858!: The Founding of British Columbia*. Pullman, Washington: Washington State University Press, 1998.

Stewart, George R. *Pickett's Charge: A Microhistory of the final attack at Gettysburg, July 3, 1863*. Boston: Houghton Mifflin Company, 1987.

Swan, James G. *The Northwest Coast: Or Three Year's Residence in Washington Territory*. Seattle: University of Washington Press, 1992.

Utley, Robert M. *Frontiersmen in Blue: The United States Army and the Indian, 1848-1865*. Lincoln and London: University of Nebraska Press, 1967.

_____. *Frontier Regulars: The United States Army and the Indian, 1866-1891*. Bloomington and London: University of Indiana Press, 1973.

Stein, Julie K., *Exploring Coast Salish Prehistory: The Archaeology of San Juan Island*. Seattle: University of Washington Press, 2000.

Vouri, Michael (Mike). *Outpost of Empire: The Royal Marines and the Joint Occupation of San Juan Island*. Seattle and London: 2004.

_____. *The Pig War*. San Francisco: Arcadia Publishing, 2008.

_____and Julia Vouri and the San Juan Historical Society. *Friday Harbor*. San Francisco: Arcadia Publishing, 2009.

_____and Julia Vouri and the San Juan Historical Society. *San Juan Island*. San Francisco: Arcadia Publishing, 2010.

Wilkes, Charles. *Narrative of the United States Exploring Expedition: During the Years 1838, 1839, 1840, 1842*. Philadelphia: Lea and Blanchard, 1845.

Wood, Bryce. *San Juan Island Coastal Place Names and Cartographic Nomenclature*, University Microfilms International, Ann Arbor, Michigan, 1980.

Wright, E.W., ed. *Lewis & Dryden's Marine History of the Pacific Northwest*. New York: Antiquarian Press, Ltd., 1961.

JOURNAL AND MAGAZINE ARTICLES

Barry, J. Nielson. "San Juan Island and the Civil War." *Washington Historical Quarterly*, 20:2. April 1929.

Clark, Robert Carlton. "The Diplomatic Mission of Sir John Rose, 1871." *Pacific Northwest Quarterly*, 27:3, (July 1936).

Fish, Andrew. "The Last Phase of the Oregon Boundary Question: The Struggle for San Juan Island." *Oregon Historical Quarterly*, XXII: 3, (September 1921).

Hamblett, E.T. "Sovereign Americans on San Juan island." *Washington Historical Quarterly*, 1:1, (October 1906).

Howard, Joseph Kinsey. "Manifest Destiny and the British Empire's Pig." *Montana, The Magazine of History*, 5:4, (Autumn 1955).

Howay, F.W., Lewis, William S., and Meyers, Jacob A., "Angus McDonald: A Few Items from the West." Washington Historical Quarterly, 8:3, (July 1917).

Johannsen, Robert, W. "The Secession Crisis and the Frontier: Washington Territory, 1860-1861," *Mississippi Valley Historical Review*, Vol. 39, No. 3, (Dec., 1952), p. 427-429.

Jordan, Mabel E., "The British on San Juan Island." *Canadian Geographical Journal*, LIX:1, (July 1959).

Long, John W., "The Origin and development of the San Juan Island Water Boundary Controversy." *The Pacific Northwest Quarterly*, 43:3, (July 1952).

McKay, Charles. "History of San Juan Island." *Washington Historical Quarterly*, 23:1,2,3,4 (January-October 1932): 290-293.

Murray, Keith. "Pig War Letters: A Romantic Account of the San Juan Crisis." *Columbia, The Magazine of Northwest History*, 1:3, (Fall 1987).

Magnuson, Warren G. "One-shot War with England." *American Heritage*, XI:3, (April 1960).

Patterson, Gerard A. "George E. Pickett—A Personality Profile." *Civil War Times Illustrated* , (May 1966).

Selcer, Richard F. "George Pickett: Another Look." *Civil War Times Illustrated*, (July/August 1994).

Smith, Albert Goldwin. "Notes on the problem of San Juan." *Pacific Northwest Quarterly*, 31:2, (April 1940).

Vouri, Michael P. "Raiders from the North: Northern Indians in Washington Territory in the 1850s." *Columbia The Magazine of Northwest History*. (Fall 1997).

_____. "The San Juan Sheep War." Columbia Magazine, 14:4 (Winter 2000-2001).

PAMPHLETS

Vouri, Michael, P. "Royal Stand-off in Griffin Bay." San Juan Island National Historical Park, April 1996.

_____. " San Juan Island Civil War Connections." San Juan Island National Historical Park. November 1995.

_____. "American Camp: in war's dark shadow." San Juan Island National Historical Park. May 1996.

_____. "English Camp: half a world from home." San Juan Island National Historical Park.

_____. "American Camp: A Historic Guided Walk." Northwest Interpretive Association, San Juan Island NHP. 1997.

_____. "English Camp: A Historic Guided Walk." Northwest Interpretive Association, San Juan Island NHP. 1998.

INDEX

(Subtopics listed in chronological order.)